A HOUSEHOLDER'S VINAYA

A HOUSEHOLDER'S VINAYA

With Home and Saṅgha Retreat Guides

namo tassa bhagavato arahato
samma sambuddhassa

Homage to the Blessed One, the Perfected One,
the Fully Self-Enlightened One

Allan Cooper

KUSINARA PRESS
Silver City, New Mexico

Publisher's Cataloging-in-Publication Data

Names: Cooper, Allan Lee, author.

Title: A householder's vinaya with home and saṅgha retreat guides / by Allan Cooper.

Description: "namo tassa bhagavato arahato samma sambuddhassa Homage to the Blessed One, the Perfected One, the Fully Self-Enlightened One"--from title page. I Silver City, NM: Kusinara Press, 2020.

Identifiers: ISBN: 978-0-578-67289-2

Subjects: LCSH Theravāda Buddhism. I Vipaśyanā (Buddhism) I Meditation--Buddhism. I Spiritual life--Buddhism. I Spiritual retreats. I BISAC RELIGION / Buddhism / Rituals & Practice. I BODY, MIND & SPIRIT / Meditation. I RELIGION / Buddhism / Theravada.

Classification: LCC BQ4262 .C66 2020 I DDC 294.3/422--dc23

ISBN (paperback): 978-0-578-67289-2

ISBN (ebook): 978-0-578-67445-2

Edited by Rudy Grad

Cover and interior design and layout by Ann Lowe

Rouse yourself! Sit up!
Resolutely train yourself to attain peace.
Do not let the king of death, seeing you are careless,
lead you astray and dominate you.

– *Utthana Sutta*: On Vigilance (Sn 2.10)

TABLE OF CONTENTS

Part III: The Home Retreat Guide

Part IV: The Saṅgha Nonresidential Retreat Guide

Part V: Appendices

ACKNOWLEDGEMENTS

WITH RESPECT AND GRATITUDE I thank my three main teachers. Without their wisdom and presence of character the Path of this practice may not have been available to me. Joseph Goldstein, Sayadaw U Pandita, and Sayadaw U Vivekananda each in their unique ways have met me where I needed to be met and offered inspiration through their teachings and modeling.

> *The greatest gift is the act of giving itself. Traditionally, three kinds of giving are spoken of. There is beggarly giving, which is when we give with only one hand, still holding onto what we give. In this kind of giving we give the least of what we have and afterward wonder whether we should have given at all.*
>
> *Another kind of giving is called "friendly" giving, in which we give open handedly. We take what we have and share it, because it seems appropriate. It's a clear giving.*
>
> *Then there's the type of giving that's called "kingly" giving. That's when we give the best of what we have, even if none remains for ourself. We give the best we have instinctively with graciousness. We think of ourselves only as temporary caretakers of whatever has been provided, as owning nothing. There is no giving; there is just the spaciousness which allows objects to remain in the flow.*
>
> – Levine, A Gradual Awakening

A number of people have given to this project with time, money and encouragement; two stand out. Ruby Grad, the wise and skilled editor, and Steve Katona, friend, financial supporter and *kalyāṇamitta*. Without each of them, and without everyone else who has contributed in their own way, this project would not, could not have come this far. Thank you.

May what we've offered serve the *Dhamma* and provide a basis for wholesome intention and direction for wise practice to arise for many in the years to come.

BIOGRAPHY OF THE AUTHOR

IN 1973, WHEN I WAS 23 YEARS OLD and a dedicated hippie, I was exposed to Burmese-style Buddhist meditation while hitchhiking throughout the world. My first teacher, S.N. Goenka, stripped the notions of suffering away from any cultural context and offered a clear and practiced method to explore and ultimately change how the mind works, and investigate how suffering arises and passes . . . *without drugs*.

I have practiced *vipassanā* and *samatha* meditation since then. My primary teachers have been the Burmese meditation master Sayadaw U Pandita; his student, Sayadaw U Vivekananda, Abbott of Panditarama Lumbini International Vipassana Meditation Center; and Joseph Goldstein, co-founder of the Insight Meditation Society (IMS).

Mahasi Sayadaw is considered the 'father' of the style of meditation I practice. U Pandita was the chief student of Mahasi Sayadaw; Joseph was a student of U Pandita. Joseph was among the first lay teachers in this tradition to offer long residential retreats in the United States. Thus, the road of practice led me to IMS in 1976, where I sat many three-month retreats. I later served as the mental health night contact twice in the 1990's.

U Vivekananda was U Pandita's protege and translator for many years. U Vivekananda continues to teach in the Mahasi tradition with his own personalized style, which is especially suited to *yogis* willing to accept that: meditation is a gradual path; it is not just about bliss and what we like and don't like; and wisdom arises when we train our minds to being open to all sense experience without reactivity. U Vivekananda is German-born, African-raised, polylingual and a worldly monastic. His near perfect command of English, his ability to understand lay Westerners without the filter of Southeast Asian cultural context and his profound understanding of *The Path of Purification* [Pāli: *Visuddhimagga*] established our connection and made him another natural fit as a teacher for me. For most of the last 20 years, I have traveled to Lumbini in Nepal

to sit with U Vivekananda for 3 to 4-month retreats, served as his attendant [Pāli: *kapiya*] on retreat, and traveled with him through the Western
United States.

I am a retired hospice and mental health RN.

I am a householding *yogi* who teaches how to make lay life one's
practice instead of trying to fit practice into lay life. I have been teaching
meditation and leading retreats for over 15 years. Currently I live just
outside Silver City, New Mexico.

You can contact me at: nama2rupa@gmail.com.

DĀNA/DONATIONS

A Householder's Vinaya, *The Home Retreat Guide*, and *The Saṅgha Nonresidential Retreat Guide* are offered freely, without a price tag. They are for the use of anyone who wishes to use them. "The *Dhamma* is priceless," and therefore no one can be charged for its transmission.

Should these offerings serve you or inspire you to practice generosity, you can send a donation to:

Allan Cooper
510 Broken Arrow Dr.
Silver City, NM, 88061
USA

To offer a donation online via PayPal, please go to: householdersvinaya.com and click on Donate.

Any donation or royalty earned from the publishing and distribution of this book, after expenses, will be donated to Buddhist Global Relief.

HOW TO READ THIS BOOK

Meditate, bhikkhus [meditators], do not delay or else you will
regret it later. This is our instruction to you.
    – Dvedhavitakka Sutta: Two Sorts of Thinking (MN 19:27)

A HOUSEHOLDER'S VINAYA WITH HOME AND SANGHA RETREAT GUIDES offers
practical instructions and tools to any householding meditator who is
inspired to make one's life a navigable sea of exploration and change.

Much of this book offers the reader many spiritual, social and
psychological reasons to follow the practice advice. For some, this
more theoretical material will not be as valuable as the instructions
themselves. For those of you who think you already have the foundation in theory and the gumption to just jump in, I still suggest you read
The Heart of Buddhist Meditation by Nyanaponika Thera (with special
emphasis on the section on clear comprehension [Pāli: *sampajañña*],
and *Ambalaṭṭhikārāhulovāda Sutta*: Advice to Rāhula at Ambalaṭṭhikā
(MN 61), and then skip to the chart in Chapter 4.)

Please be advised that it is critical to understanding the practices
described in this book and vital to the success of applying them, that the
reader understands both in theory and practice what *sati* and *sampajañña* are.

References to 'formal meditation' in this book include walking
meditation as well as sitting meditation. The method of walking meditation I recommend teaches you how to observe what appear to be
continuous movements in ever increasingly small segments, which
highlights and makes real the intuitive learning of impermanence. It
also acts as a physical conditioning that helps you to slow down all
physical movements. When your entire life is slowed down, both your
intention towards the continuity of attention and your unconscious
attention embracing impermanence are increased and supported. Those
unfamiliar with walking meditation as a practice, or this style of

walking meditation, can listen to the following instructions on walking meditation:

> https://www.dharmaseed.org/talks/audio_player/96/1293.html
> (instructions by Joseph Goldstein, begin at 28:34)

For more complete residential retreat instructions that include sitting, walking and daily practices listen to:
> https://www.dharmaseed.org/talks/audio_player/186/23326.html
> (instructions by U Vivekananda, begin at 29:04)

After reviewing the chart, read the rest of *A Householder's Vinaya* and start practicing. After reading and experimenting with the *Vinaya*, I suggest you return to the text and read the entire book. To create the best route of discovery in practice, we need to meditate *and* study. Both.

Once the combined *A Householder's Vinaya with Home and Saṅgha Retreat Guides* is available from Amazon as a Kindle electronic book and an on-demand paperback, it will also be available for free download in PDF at householdersvinaya.com. An advantage to reading it on the website or in the Kindle edition is instant access to the Glossary for definitions. Also, on the website you will be able to download or print each section separately with the full Appendices.

Introduction

The Foundation of the Practice: *Dāna, Sīla, Bhāvanā*

SINCE BUDDHIST PHILOSOPHY AND MEDITATION began to be introduced to an audience in America and the West in general in the late 19th Century, many thousands of books, articles, and PhD dissertations have been written to explain *annica* [impermanence], *dukkha* [suffering, dissatisfaction], *anattā* [non-self], *kamma* [Skt: *karma*; actions and results or cause and effect], and dependent origination [Pāli: *paṭiccasamuppāda*], to mention just a few of the more subtle intellectually challenging concepts that underpin the Buddha's teachings. But those of us who just want to relieve ourselves from the chronic nature of the reactive mind need only to practice with sincere continuity, and the rest will take care of itself, which is much simpler and makes it unnecessary to completely understand all the subtleties of the dogma. This is true for the monastic, the intellectual, and the ordinary householder.

The principles of *dāna, sīla, bhāvanā* point us to the Path, and in a much valued shorthand, they say it all. They are really all one needs to know and practice to learn first hand and intuitively the promise and the gift of the liberated mind. What are these principles, why is understanding and practicing them so simple, and why do they speak in a way that can bypass and make unnecessary our self-important intellectual dalliances and preferences?

In English, *dāna* simply means generosity, *sīla* means virtue, and *bhāvanā* means mental development. These three concepts point to and encompass the entirety of the Buddha's teaching. They are both notions and practices that one can train in and test. Because these notions are simple and the practices are simple, they present a very low bar for beginning these spiritual practices. A lot of thinking is unnecessary at the beginning of practice. All that is needed is to accept with 'blind faith' that generosity is good and wholesome [Pāli: *kusala*], that virtue serves oneself and others in simple and profound ways, and that with focus and continuity one can retrain the mind towards and into more continuous states of wholesomeness.

And yet . . . if we examine almost anything, the action is simple, but it also relies on a sequence or a process in order for the activity to be done normally and with skill. Take the example of walking. Pretty simple, yes? All able-bodied people do it without thinking or examining the complexity of it. But to walk, first we need the intention to walk, secondly the legs, thirdly sufficient strength in the legs, and lastly we need balance.

Practicing *dāna*, *sīla*, and *bhāvanā* works in just the same way. A person wanting to study and develop wholesomeness in life using meditation needs the intention, the basis, the strength, and the balance. Intention is discussed *below* as the 'about to' moment. *Dāna* is the first intentional step towards compassion, which is a wholesome reason to practice. *Sīla* is the strength that permits locomotion towards the perfection of the teachings by creating a field of wholesomeness. *Bhāvanā* is the teachings and the practices themselves.

Dāna

Giving is good, dear sir!
Even when one has little, giving is good.
An offering given from what little one has
Is worth a thousand times its value.

                                   – Saddhu Sutta: Good (SN 1:33)

We discuss *dāna* in Chapter 5 in more detail, but here, in the introduction, let's say *dāna* is that state of mind, speech and action that
explores and establishes the mind and heart towards a native state of
wise and compassionate generosity. Not unusual. Almost any tradition,
any religion will have this as part of the basic tenets of their teachings.
The unique quality in this case is that this quality of mind and action is
tied directly to the other two and is known to be a critical plank in the
development of a pure mind.

Sīla

*Do no evil. Engage in what is skillful, And purify your mind. This
is the teaching of the Buddhas.*
> — *Buddhavagga*: The Buddha (Dhp XIV, 183)

Generosity alone does not guarantee that an action of body, speech
or mind will be wholesome. Without wise and virtuous reflection,
generosity can be self-serving and even morally unwholesome [Pāli:
akusala]. Take the very mild examples of giving something in order
to get something in return or in order to create an indebtedness for the
recipient. You can think of other examples in your own experience.

But when *dāna* is linked to *sīla*, which is linked to five types of
non-harming—the Five Precepts—actions toward self and others, the
dāna is guaranteed to be of value to both the giver and the receiver.
Practicing both *dāna* and *sīla* establishes a quality of mind that allows
the third leg of this triad to be explored.

Bhāvanā

*Mind precedes all mental states. Mind is their chief; they are all
mind-wrought. If with an impure mind a person speaks or acts,
suffering follows him like the wheel that follows the foot of the ox.
Mind precedes all mental states. Mind is their chief; they are all*

*mind-wrought. If with a pure mind a person speaks or acts, happiness
follows him like his never-departing shadow.*

– Yamakavagga: Pairs (Dhp I 1-2)

Because of the unusual flavor of the words 'mental development,'
one may not necessarily have an ah-ha experience and understand that a
mind that is virtuous and generous is a mind that is also ripe for training
in meditation. *Bhāvanā* is about the development of the mind through
the practice and training of meditation known throughout this guide as
sati-sampajañña. As householders we live in zones of experience in
which we are constantly bombarded by conflicting choices with frequent
moral ambiguity. *A Householder's Vinaya* directly addresses these experiences and offers the practitioner context and practices that incline the
mind towards a continuous practice of *dāna, sīla, bhāvanā*.

The Five Hindrances to Happiness

It's always the case. It's always true: we want something, and we have
to do something in order to do it or to get it. It's the way of the world.
Two aphorisms come to mind when examining the effort it takes to get
something worthwhile:

There ain't no free lunch.

– Anonymous

If it's easy, it's cheap.

– U Pandita

What both aphorisms point towards is that it takes effort and determination to realize both our most modest and our most lofty goals. They
imply that the more precious and sublime the goal, the more effort it
usually takes to achieve its promise. This understanding that there are

barriers and tests that guard the precious is a time worn and very familiar path in almost every tradition the world over.

So it is with formal meditation and *vinaya* practice in everyday life. The Buddha frequently spoke how we all must come to terms with these barriers and hurdles before we can realize the promise of the practice. He listed the most common and most debilitating in a list he called the Five Hindrances [Pāli: *pañca nīvaraṇāni*]:

- Sensual desire [Pāli: *kāmacchanda*]
- Ill will [Pāli: *vyāpāda*]
- Sloth and torpor [Pāli: *thīna-middha*]
- Restlessness and worry [Pāli: *uddhacca-kukkucca*]
- Subjective (skeptical) doubt [Pāli: *vicikicchā*]

Each of these mental states will in varying degree be our companions for most of our journey on the Path. They will entice, depress, confuse, agitate, and distract us from our intended purpose. It is their nature, and it is the nature of the untrained mind to entertain them. So, whether we are on formal retreat or practicing in everyday life, it is important to know these unwholesome mental states and to be able to disidentify with them, in degrees or for stretches of time. The consequence will be that our practices will feel so much more pleasant and productive.

But the hindrances will remain with you. So please always stay aware that just because we are feeling good and the practice seems to be pleasant and going along fine, it doesn't mean that they will not reappear.

It is also helpful to learn and to accept that being in the throes of what can be called a hindrance attack is often a manifestation of advancing practice. As a matter of fact, the closer we get to equanimity and a liberated mind, the more subtle the hindrances become. We need increased acceptance of the hindrances and continuity of *sati-sampajañña*.

Practice, Practice, Practice

I'm reminded of a humorous parable told on a residential meditation retreat I attended many years ago. A tourist in New York City once asked a taxi driver, "How do you get to Carnegie Hall?" The taxi driver, over the traffic noise, shouted back to the tourist, "Practice, practice, practice." The taxi driver was parroting what most saints and wisdom teachers over the millennia have said. Patient diligence, combined with the proper physical and mental tools, increases success in almost any endeavor. This is true in our everyday lives and is especially true in our spiritual lives.

A Householder's Vinaya set out in this guide might be likened to practicing the scales should one want to develop the fundamental skills necessary to play Bach or Mozart or Joplin all the way to Carnegie Hall. As in developing music skills, the everyday life of a meditator is how the scales are developed and honed, the field on which one trains the mind and heart [Pāli: *citta*] towards and into liberation from suffering. Think of going from scales to the crescendo of Beethoven's 9th Symphony.

The Categories of *A Householder's Vinaya*

The keys to how we practice in our everyday meditative lives are grouped into the following categories:

1. Cooperation, Patience, Generosity
2. Harmlessness
3. Materiality
4. Sexuality
5. Speech
6. Intoxication
7. Food, Meals, Eating
8. Livelihood
9. Family, Friends, Community
10. Activities of Daily Life

11. Style, Preferences
12. Entertainment
13. Creativity
14. Choosing a Spiritual Practice
15. Practice, Study, Ceremony

Each category highlights various aspects of lay life in which *sati* and *sampajañña* are often not utilized and, in consequence, our practices suffer the inevitable reconditioning of old habits and patterns that lead the mind into delusion, which inevitably morphs into various levels of suffering. The discussion of each category instructs the reader on how to apply our lay *vinaya* to the type of situation being explored and explains some of the nuances that detail why and how we can apply more attention and more care. In these discussions you will find the 'how to' aspect of this offering.

The discussions in each of 15 categories are intended to teach methods for us as lay *yogis* in order to bring practice to where we live. This includes while doing daily chores, going to work, loving our friends and family, etc. Applying these teachings will allow a natural momentum towards a more wholesome and a more organized relationship with both our outer and inner worlds.

The Enlightenment Project

A friend of mine has labeled his spiritual journey his 'enlightenment project.' He uses every wholesome tool and skill available to increase the likelihood of his stumbling with intention into *nibbāna* [enlightenment; Skst: *nirvāṇa*]. The way he chooses to live his life reminds me of a couple of aphorisms:

Meditation doesn't guarantee enlightenment, it just increases its probability.

– Anonymous

Enlightenment is always an accident. Meditation just makes those who practice accident prone.

— Anonymous

My friend deeply understands that he cannot make *nibbāna* arise with will and determination alone. So with patient focus and with kindly attention throughout his life, he builds his continuity of meditative focus. The greater the continuity of his practice, the greater his likelihood of stumbling onto his goal. Whenever I ask how his enlightenment project is going, he smiles and comments something like, "Between here and wherever *there* is, things are so much better." When he gets specific, he reports that he's discovered that the path to *nibbāna* is a process of incremental purifications that has led him to greater peace and deeper happiness. I guess he happily considers himself an accident waiting to happen.

Home practice occupies the lion's share of his and any similarly-inclined householder's time. He understands that home practice is not just formal meditation, which is unfortunately what most of us think home practice is. For him, home practice happens as much as possible and as often as possible throughout his day while doing his everyday activities. Again and again he reminds himself when his mind is not otherwise focused to bring a meditative focus into the mix. In order to become 'accident prone,' he understands that activities of every waking moment, whether doing formal practice or buying tomatoes, are just parts of what we will call home practice. Home practice is the mortar holding the structure of any enlightenment project together.

May your enlightenment project be swift, filled with adventure, and fun.

A Gradual Path

When, bhikkhus, a carpenter or a carpenter's apprentice sees the impressions of his fingers and his thumb on the handle of his adze, he does not know: "I have worn away so much of the adze

handle today, so much yesterday, so much earlier;" but when it
has worn away, he knows that it has worn away. So too, when
a bhikkhu [meditator] is intent on development, even though he
does not know: "I have worn away so much of the taints today, so
much yesterday, so much earlier," yet when they are worn away, he
knows that they are worn away.

– Bhāvanānuyutta: Committed to Development

(AN 7.71)

The development and the harvest of the practice of *sati-sampajañña*
is likened to a gradual path throughout the Pāli Canon. The notion of a
gradual training leading to any type of success is also our everyday lesson
throughout our lives. One must practice with all the highs and lows of
one's learning curve. Comes with the territory both in everyday life and
in our meditative lives.

Questions for the *yogi*:
- Do you want to learn to play the guitar? Practice with all the
  highs and lows of your learning curve.
- Want to be a good parent? Practice with all the highs and lows
  of your learning curve.
- Want to grow up? Practice with all the highs and lows of your
  learning curve.
- So why would it be different with meditation and spiritual
  practice?

I remember an anecdote attributed to Pablo Casals, the world's most
renowned cellist of his time. In celebration of his 90-something birthday
he was being feted with international acclaim and attention. A journalist
interviewing him knew that Casals had a reputation of practicing four to
eight hours a day even into his nineties, so he asked the maestro, "Why
do you practice so much at your age? Haven't you done enough? Aren't
you accomplished already?" Casals answered, "I do it because I think
I'm seeing some improvement."

Casals' approach to his study was much like the Buddha's. After the Buddha's enlightenment under the Bodhi tree at 35 years old until his death at 80 years old, the Buddha practiced what he preached. He meditated and taught, maintained his body, and took care to serve both the monastic and lay *sanghas* up until his last breath.

Both in the temporal world and the spiritual world, in order to serve and honor our gifts, skills, and community we must give our lives the focus and determination they deserve. Focus and determination don't mean pleasant and easy, and they certainly don't mean this can wait until tomorrow. We don't know when we'll die; tomorrow may not be available. This also means that wisdom does not necessarily equal bliss, nor does bliss necessarily equal wisdom. Wisdom and skillful service mean maintaining focus and determination whether in the face of unpleasant or pleasant. Only then, with patience [Pāli: *khanti*] and an open-hearted interest, does one become a Casals or an *arahant* [fully enlightened being].

If, on the other hand, one habitually yields to all whims, or allows oneself too easily to be deflected from one's purpose, then such qualities as energy, endurance, concentration, loyalty, etc., will gradually be undermined and weakened to such an extent that they become insufficient for achieving that original purpose, or even for truly appreciating it any longer. In that way, it often happens that, unheeded by the person concerned, his ideals, religious convictions, and even his ordinary purposes and ambitions, are turned into empty shells which he still carries along with him, solely through habit.
– Nyanaponika Thera, The Heart of Buddhist Meditation, p. 48.

A Householder's Vinaya will help us to cultivate both worldly and spiritual growth by constantly honing our skills and training our inclinations towards being present with meditative wisdom and compassion in every waking moment. *A Householder's Vinaya* and its practice teach us in real time that in the end, everyday life and a spiritual life cannot be separated. So, if you choose to practice this method for either worldly happiness and success or for spiritual wisdom and freedom you'll not be disappointed; both are strengthened simultaneously.

What a *Vinaya* Is

Here is the definition for *vinaya* that I like best and the one used in this guide:

> *Vinaya is thus, in its essence, the Buddhist lifestyle [meditation coupled with sīla]: the way serious Buddhist practitioners arrange, organize, and structure their lives in order to support Dhamma study, practice, realization, and service. This covers all physical and verbal actions. It involves all forms of relationships: interpersonal, social, economic, political, ecological, as well as with one's own body.*
>
> – Badiner & Hill, p. 303

This working definition for *vinaya* is used in this guide because it embraces us all, not just the ordained, and, in its embrace of us all, it delineates the spectrum of normal lay activities and responsibilities.

Building a *Vinaya*

The building and making of a *vinaya* by monastics and laypeople must always remain a process. The Buddha created the monastic rules (known as the *Pātimokkha*) contained in the *Vinaya Piṭaka* as he went along. The creation of the rules ended with the Buddha's death. And because the process of building and adjusting the *Pātimokkha* ended with the Teacher's death, it may be argued that it has grown stiff within the context of history.

A particularly important way to approach what appears stiff and out of context to our modern sensibilities and yet, if understood, remains basic to our spiritual development, is to examine our lay life through the filter of the intentions of the original *Vinaya Piṭaka*. *A Householder's Vinaya* attempts to address precisely this enterprise.

In creating *A Householder's Vinaya*, I learned many valuable lessons from the monastic model. The first and most important is that a *vinaya* is created to funnel one's intentions into practical skills for the cultivation of ever more continuous and subtle understanding that comes from practicing *sati-sampajañña*. At the roots of *sati-sampajañña* are practices that steer the *yogi* towards the development of wisdom and compassion. *Sati* points us towards ultimate wisdom, *sampajañña* towards generosity, virtue and compassion. Without virtue and compassion *sati* is just a mental exercise. Without *sampajañña, sati* is easily fooled.

Building a personal practice rooted in a template shared with others gives those that follow it the benefit of mutual experience with intrinsic ways of sharing and supporting one another. However you choose to use *A Householder's Vinaya* and however the lay *saṅgha* chooses to amend it in the future, the *vinaya* must always root itself in the balance between the reality of a householder's everyday life and ways to use that life as the field of practice.

Sati

Throughout this guide *sati* is variously described as *sati*, *vipassanā*, mindfulness or bare attention, and occasionally alluded to with terms such as 'focus,' 'attention,' 'focused attention.' All of these terms point in one direction. They all point to the training of the mind in a specific way. Each is describing the quality of mind that meets whatever object arises in consciousness as directly and in as rendered and primary a way as is possible, as quickly as possible, with as much frequency and continuity as the mind permits. The intention is to train the mind to know an object of consciousness in its most elemental characteristics as quickly as possible in order to have consciousness and the object intuitively known without self-identification, and therefore, from a non-manipulative perspective and non-habituated reactivity. Simply to be present.

When *sati* matures and becomes second nature, it allows the mind to be present intuitively as the mind-body process unfolds. If we continually observe consciousness and its objects with this quality of attention, the mind will automatically begin to be present and freed of blind habit and preference. Being free of blind habit and preference opens the mind to spontaneous avenues of never before experienced realities of wholesomeness and happiness. Happiness in this context means to be spontaneously manifesting a *citta* that arises from universal wisdom and compassion rather than from self referencing. This training can become the software program that our mind and body begin to run.

Sampajañña

Vipassanā meditation uses the Three Characteristics of Existence [Pāli: *ti-lakkhaṇa*], primarily impermanence, as a perspective filter. This has become one of the standards of practice in many spiritual traditions. Nowadays there are plenty of approaches on how to apply, practice and harvest the fruits of mindfulness in any setting. However, there is little emphasis on or commentarial support for how to study, cultivate and practice *sampajañña* in either the formal retreat setting or in everyday life. This is especially true if we look at the current resources available for those of us who have studied directly with monastics and have mimicked their trainings by doing long silent meditation retreats.

Sampajañña provides the framework for a meditator to examine what they think, say and do through filters that are imbued with *sīla* and the realities of *annica*, *dukkha*, and *anattā*. Until sufficient levels of universal wisdom and compassion, like software, are operating on the hardware of the mind, context plays a significant role in how the practice can be applied. When *sampajañña* is operating, the meditator will have the filters that allow them to take reflective care in speech and action.

Whereas *sati* trains the mind to observe its own process on an almost neurochemical level, *sampajañña* contextualizes what we do on a more relative level. *Sati* and *sampajañña* work together throughout a meditative life.

Why a Householder's *Vinaya*?

We live a very short time, which makes it all the more urgent for us to acknowledge that the people we love, the communities in which we live, and the planet itself are in need of wise and compassionate people. The full understanding of spiritual urgency [Pāli: *saṃvega*] is a powerful motivator to practice in service to self and others. Wisdom and compassion, unfortunately, don't often happen on their own. They take practice, patience, kindness and gumption to arise and develop.

Making life a spiritual practice is what each and every human does. The differences between us are how we understand what a 'spiritual practice' is and how to act to best support and achieve what we speculate are its promises.

For almost all of us, it's not a good idea to leave the development of our spiritual and meditative life exclusively to our own judgment. Only a few of us have the natural ability to transcend our own ignorance and distinguish clearly between what is useful and wise from what is easy and pleasant. On the other hand, without guidance we tend to get confused and disheartened when the inevitable and necessary periods of darkness and difficulties arise with thoughts like, "I must be doing something wrong or this must be bad practice," or "I can't do this."

To solve the conundrum of being motivated to discover spiritual freedom and being blinded by our own ignorance, and to avoid the self-serving and self-reinforcing habits of clinging to pleasant and rejecting the unpleasant, many spiritual traditions rely on ancient texts, provide wise mentors, and have developed monastic orders. A wise impartial mentor helps us cut through our ignorance and tendencies of confusing pleasantness with good practice or difficult practice with something bad, and then steers us towards a quicker, more stable, and lasting understanding in spiritual wisdom.

Without quality mentorship, the tendency of the meditator or spiritual seeker is to get lost in the unconscious pursuit of what is pleasant, fun, and easy, and reject what is unpleasant—and therefore not fun—and hard. Falling prey to this type of practice, rather than remaining true to intuitively learning how to understand reality with an unattached open hand—which is the bedrock basis for the development of wisdom and compassion—is unworthy of our time and effort. To keep our meditation practice from getting trapped in this potentially constant type of confusion, we must train the mind to be present in an equal and accepting fashion to both the pleasant and unpleasant.

This book, *A Householder's Vinaya With Home and Saṅgha Retreat Guides*, is especially suited for those who yearn to make their everyday lives their practice, but see a need for a better approach and new tools in order to help build their own enlightenment project. This guide is about *doing*, about helping householders elevate their practice in ways that will support them on the path to freedom.

A Householder's Vinaya is built on the foundation of important but too often overlooked principles of Buddhist practice: *dāna, sīla, bhāvanā*, discussed *above*. In the following chapters we further discuss generosity and the behavior that flows from undertaking to practice virtue in the form of the Five and Eight Precepts [Pāli: *pañca sīla and attha sīla*, respectively], mixed with a discussion of mental development with the influence of the monastic *Vinaya Piṭaka* on how to apply a new approach to willful preference in everyday life. The intentions to train in *sīla* and *sati-sampajañña* are the same for both *vinayas*. The conditions are different for lay people and monastics, and therefore there is a need for somewhat different tools.

Mentors, spiritual friends [Pāli: *kalyāṇamitta*], and the instructions found in the texts are fine and dandy, and especially profound when one is on retreat. But logic and personal experience tell us that householders, as much as monastics, can and do benefit from having a *vinaya* to support them. The reality for those of us who live a householder's life is that our mentors and the community of like-minded people are usually not available to inspire us when picking up cranky children at school or having to work with unskillful co-workers, to name just two normal everyday realities in most householders' lives. Going to work, doing domestic errands and chores, living a householder's life is where meditative wisdom and meditative practice must be applied for wisdom to develop and deepen and be shared. It is here, where we spend most of the time, where learning and practicing *A Householder's Vinaya* has the most impact for ourselves and others.

Along with *The Home Retreat Guide*, *A Householder's Vinaya* is a 24/7 template that actively supports our moment to moment potential to make wise attention the focus of our lives. Those who have already chosen to experiment with the *The Home Retreat Guide* report how the intensity of turning up the focus and continuity of practice has helped them while practicing, and that one of the lingering benefits includes the self-realized permission to practice both *sati* and *sampajañña* with what feels like an increased gravitational pull after the home retreat is over. *The Home Retreat Guide* is *A Householder's Vinaya* on steroids, similar to monastics on retreat or living their everyday lives.

Similar to the *Vinaya Piṭaka*, *A Householder's Vinaya* is not a 'thou shall' or 'thou shall not' template. Its training principle rests in offering a constant reminder for potential practice. Because all training is a practice, when we 'fail' or get lost, we simply begin again as fresh as our courage and wisdom permit.

Who Can Use This Guide

Many who are called to read and use this guide will have glimpsed profound and life-altering wisdom while on retreat, while others will be more or less just starting out. This guide is written primarily for those who already have some significant meditation practice. However, this guide can be used as a template for anyone's spiritual practice. The only requirement for using it is that you want to explore your life by refocusing the lens on how and why you do what you do, and that you are willing to move from fitting a spiritual life into everyday life to making the entirety of your life a spiritual practice. This guide is helpful in both cases.

This guide is useful for three types of readers:

1. Those who have a skilled meditation practice already.
2. Those not trained in meditation and not necessarily interested in training themselves in that way.
3. Beginners.

I do not presume any skill or expertise in any meditative tradition or technique other than the one in which I've been trained. So here I speak simultaneously from two sides of my mouth. I say that this type of practice will serve the many, but I have only this technique to offer. And yet, having some understanding of the universal nature of both the untrained and the trained mind, I know for certain that this is a practice that will train the mind and heart towards wholesomeness when anyone practices with an open and patient heart, diligently and with a touch of humor.

For those who do not yet have a meditation practice and want to start, this is a good place to make sure you have a few useful pointers. The type of practice this guide points the reader towards is not about 'finding one's bliss' or residing in long pleasant states of mental happiness. Practicing this style of meditation is about the development of spiritual wisdom and universal compassion and, as a consequence, only as a secondary gain does one experience the sweetness of those types of *citta* that result from advancing mental development.

How to Use *A Householder's Vinaya*

It's helpful to make friends with *A Householder's Vinaya*. For most of us, it is better to be friends with your spouse than to try to join at the hip. So it is with meditation, spiritual practice, and using *A Householder's Vinaya*. First make friends, explore, and save your more mature vows of marriage or long-term commitment to when you have sufficient wisdom to really say "I do." Committing to being a wise and faithful spouse comes with the initial vows, but it is time, failures, and determination that allow the realization that "Yes, in fact, I'm really doing it!"

Use this *vinaya* with patience, kindness, courage, and the understanding that being able to do it all is not something that happens just because you want it to. There is no magic. It takes time, and like a marriage, it takes sufficient constancy to make it work. I suggest you work on your intention first and then couple it with some segment of the practice and see if you can bring wholesomeness to the process, and then the next step, and the next. Play with it like a child plays, a child's work.

Like the Noble Eightfold Path [Pāli: *ariyo aṭṭhaṅgiko maggo*], all parts of *A Householder's Vinaya* make up the whole, while each part —or category—can be separated and actively investigated with focus and precision; it's the balancing of the whole that ensures best results. Many of the sections will have echoes in others, and may occasionally reinforce the same points helping to cement it all together. The practice and the training of the mind is a constant and repeating process. It is precisely this character of the training that calls for perspective, focus and repetition. As with any spiritual practice, patience is required, and similar to the Noble Eightfold Path, *A Householder's Vinaya* always meets us where we are on our spiritual journeys. So, no need to worry or compare yourself to yourself or others. To make *A Householder's Vinaya* work for you is to just develop your own intention and skill and incline them towards greater wisdom and greater compassion. This is true on the first day of practice, the day of our full enlightenment, and with our final breath in this life. The categories are just a template; the investigation and effort is a personal and lifelong affair.

Use of Pāli Words and Phrases

Pāli words and phrases are used regularly in this text. When Pāli words and phrases are used, they have been chosen because there are no adequate English words or phrases to capture the precise meaning or nuance. When taking a journey, it is useful to have a map with a legend; in this case, the map is a technical language that speaks directly to the meditative experience. Having a common and agreed on understanding of the legend helps to point anyone using the map in the right direction. Good maps forewarn and prepare one for the many ups and downs that come along the way, thus helping to avoid injury or the necessity of taking extra effort and time due to taking a wrong turn or choosing to camp in the wrong place. In this sense, a clear language permits us to explain to ourselves what we are doing, and allows us to communicate with our teachers and our friends in clear and precise language rather than having to rely on subjective metaphor or simile. I liken the gift of a clear language to being a traveler in a foreign land and being able to speak the language. Having adequate language skills can make the difference between being a tourist on a tour bus or being an adventurer living with the locals.

A scholar's understanding of written and spoken Pāli is not required to practice or study *vipassanā* meditation or to build a home practice. However, being familiar with Pāli terms that pertain directly to the Buddha's teaching does allow those who practice in this particular way to share an idiomatic language and to be more able to read the map and prepare oneself for the travel. It will be especially useful when reading and using this guide to have a working understanding of these basic terms: *sati, sati-sampajañña, sampajañña, yogi, vipassanā* and *vinaya*. The definition of these terms can be found in the Glossary.

Familiarity with these Pāli terms has wide-ranging benefits:

- It can serve to reduce confusion when applying one's own understanding to one's practice.
- It assists when speaking with others regarding meditation practice.
- It creates community.

Resources for Practice

READING MATERIAL

Material treated in this guide is explained in more detail in Nyanaponika Thera's *The Heart of Buddhist Meditation*, especially the section on *sampajañña*. Also helpful is Bhikkhu Bodhi's short book *The Noble Eightfold Path: The Way to the End of Suffering*. These two texts will help any householding *yogi* better appreciate what clarity of language can do to assist us in the process of learning skillful means in meditation practice both at home and on formal retreat. Though not absolutely necessary, reading these two suggested texts will give you a significant head start in establishing an intellectual understanding of the Buddha's teachings, the constancy of clear process in applying them, and the idiomatic language. When combined, these are helpful to anyone truly wishing to crack the nut of the already very hard shell of our enlightenment projects.

AUDIO INSTRUCTIONS

Below are links to three recordings by Joseph Goldstein giving *vipassanā* instructions at Insight Meditation Society. Readers will be assisted in the practice of *A Householder's Vinaya* if they have some intellectual understanding of the basics of the Buddha's teachings. But to truly practice and learn how to apply the techniques to everyday life, one needs to learn how to do these meditations. I suggest that anyone who is relatively new to meditation listen and practice as instructed. For those of you who have practiced *vipassanā* before, even for those who have practiced for some time, I suggest you listen again to the instructions and try, with as much of a beginner's mind as possible, to see if you don't hear something new. My experience practicing meditation has reminded me over and over again that if I listen with an open mind, even to an instruction or a *Dhamma* talk I've heard many times, I will hear things that appear new or have a slant that previously I missed or didn't understand.

https://www.dharmaseed.org/talks/audio_player/96/36191.html
https://www.dharmaseed.org/talks/audio_player/96/36192.html
https://www.dharmaseed.org/talks/audio_player/96/36190.html

I highly encourage anyone who wants to use all the handholds and footholds this guide provides to listen carefully and more than once to these suggested instructions by Joseph Goldstein, and to read the supporting materials suggested *above*. These instructions will help you do a self-analysis of whether or not your meditation is helping you or hindering you towards your well-intentioned goal.

FIND A TEACHER

If you don't already have one, find a qualified teacher! Chapter 18 addresses in some detail how to proactively address this hugely important aspect on a spiritual path.

The difference between the Buddha and an *arahant* isn't the depth of the wisdom that one has over the other. In fact, they are the same. What is different is that the Buddha rediscovered the *Dhamma* without a teacher to guide him. He needed to explore and experiment before he realized these teachings. In the cosmology of Buddhism, the teachings of the Buddha—the *Dhamma*—come and go just like anything else. What we study today may be gone tomorrow without anyone being able to teach or practice in this particular fashion. In this way, a Buddha comes to be now and then, and re-discovers the *Dhamma* and chooses to teach in order that the many can realize the fruits of this universal wisdom.

So, unless you are a Buddha to be, a teacher is almost a necessity if one is to realize the promise of these teachings. A teacher helps a *yogi* from getting caught in their ignorant tendencies towards believing that what is pleasant is good practice and what is unpleasant is bad practice, thus steering with a compassionate hand to not identify with the highs and lows that come and go. A teacher is able to inspire and to direct. A teacher speeds the process. A teacher is a wonderful asset in practice.

RETREAT

I also highly encourage all of you, when circumstances allow, not to miss the opportunity of doing a formal residential retreat of some length. Many *yogis* who have practiced for some time have come to realize that retreats should be no less than 9 days long. Almost no matter who you are, the first three to five days of retreat for a beginning meditator are hard and often miserable. It takes three to five days to begin to see the fruits of what continuous practice can do for the retraining of the mind.

If a residential retreat is not in the cards for you, I suggest you do a home retreat. If that is not possible, practice *A Householder's Vinaya* with as much continuity and integrity as possible. All these options with any and all permutations will have benefits.

Meditation Principles

This guide relies heavily on the Mahasi Sayadaw school of *Theravāda* Buddhist practice as its foundation. However, because spiritual practice is not exclusive to any one tradition, this guide can be of service to anyone who is sincere in cultivating an integrated and effective meditative life at home. Anyone unfamiliar with Mahasi practice or Buddhist meditation techniques may use their own spiritual tradition's language and apply these instructions to their practice where it appears to be a useful fit.

This guide instructs the *yogi* to develop a meditative eye towards what the Buddha identified as the Three Characteristics of Existence [Pāli: *ti-lakkhaṇa*]:

1. *Anicca* [impermanence].
2. *Dukkha* [dissatisfaction or suffering].
3. *Anattā* [non-self].

It isn't important that you agree with this assessment of what meditation is or is not about, or whether you believe doing the meditation and
the activities at home is turning the eye towards the *ti-lakkhaṇa*. What
is important is that these practices train the mind to intuitively observe
the transient nature of phenomena over and over again. The rest takes
care of itself regardless of one's philosophical or religious perspective.

The language or the poetry one chooses to describe the fruits of
the intuitively realized understanding of *anicca, dukkha, anattā* or the
consequences of how this understanding affects the ways we walk in
the world doesn't matter. It all comes down to the same thing no matter what labels we put on it. What does matter is whether a meditator
is training the *citta* to intuitively understand the reality that whatever
starts will end, whatever takes birth will die, and being at peace with
this process can free us from the clinging of habits and patterns that
reinforce the suffering that brought us to investigate meditation in the
first place.

This guide understands and addresses the fact that it isn't easy
to intuitively know impermanence or the other two characteristics.
This training is also about not fooling ourselves by doing practices and
embracing notions that slow or distract us from our highest and noblest
intentions. It matters what we do. It matters what we do 24/7, and it matters whether or not when we are meditating, we are, in fact, . . . meditating!

As a practitioner and as a teacher, I have seen in myself, my friends,
and in many students the confused notions of what is and what is not
meditation practice. All too often I've seen the tendency to just sit there
when doing what they think is good meditation, and they are really just
lost in pleasant or unpleasant thought or doing one-pointed practice
[Pāli: *samatha*] while convinced they are doing *vipassanā* practice.

This guide offers all of us the choice to check in and refocus and
retrain and make our time as valuable as it deserves.

Use of the Appendices

The appendices include:

- Glossary: English/Pāli-Pāli/English dictionary and phrase guide. In order to understand the material in this guide these words and phrases need to be understood. The Glossary is intended to be more than a quick resource for the meaning of a word or the context of a phrase. Along with definitions of Pāli and English words and phrases utilized in the text, the Glossary includes a number of definitions of words or phrases not used in the text. Mixed in the definitions is a rich vein of information with links to commentaries and original texts that if otherwise inserted into the text would make reading and applying the instructions unwieldy. These veins and threads offer the reader the opportunity to study a wide-ranging body of work of ancient and current texts and commentaries. Using the Glossary as a field of additional study provides a *yogi* a way to best utilize this guide.
- Table of Quotations and Aphorisms: A collection of useful and inspiring quotes from the *Suttas*, quotations in common usage, quotations from notable people, and aphorisms.
- Table of Abbreviations: Throughout the text there are a number of quotations from sources in the Pāli Canon. The abbreviated citations in the text are explained.
- Table of Lists, Chants and Reflections: The chants are offered for those who may not be familiar with them and want to add this element of practice to their meditation routines, or for those familiar but yet to experiment with this type of practice. The lists are concise ways that, for some, can serve to help organize one's thinking about the structure of the teachings; and, along with the reflections, open more doors to perhaps untested ways to support the practices of *sampajañña* and balancing of the five controlling or spiritual faculties [Pāli: *indriya-samatta*].

- Bibliography and Suggested Reading and Listening List: The listing of sources cited in the text and other useful resources.
- Table of Retreat Centers and Monasteries: A listing of retreat centers and monasteries where you can go for an introduction to formal meditation and possible long-term development, with a short description of each center. Either the author or someone he trusts has practiced in each center. For future editions of this book, we will gladly accept verified suggestions for other practice centers.

Good luck! Better skill!

PART ONE

Basic Principles for the Vinaya

CHAPTER 1

Practicing Every Day in the World

It is very important to keep trying to maintain the intention to remain aware all the time, whether awareness is actually continuous or not. This points to the essential quality of Right Effort: persistence. It's not a forceful effort but rather an inner determination to sustain the tiny bit of energy you need in each moment to know you are aware and to keep that going.

— U Tejaniya

Our Intention to Practice

THOSE WHO HAVE EXPERIENCED some type of life-altering event through meditation on a residential retreat in all likelihood came away from that event with strong wholesome intentions coupled with great energy to deepen everything that was learned and make it useful in lasting ways. Those who are new to meditation yearn for relief or to find a practice that points to a tested method to change and improve the quality of their life. Both circumstances are fertile fields for intention--one experiential, the other from a clear sense of dissatisfaction with the ways things are.

It is common at the end of a powerful retreat at which significant mind changing events occurred to leave the retreat with plans to structure our daily lives so that we will 'sit more,' 'practice more,' and use the entire scope of our lives to learn more wholesome and skillful ways to live. At the end of such retreats, we clearly understand the value of the practice and want to integrate our newly realized meditative skills and wisdom to have them more accessible and relevant to our everyday lives.

We think, and we are taught frequently by our teachers at the end of a formal retreat, that all we need to deepen our practice at home is to maintain as much mindfulness as we can and sit as much as our routines will allow. It is common that these instructions are offered to both the lay meditator and the monastic in the same way without nuance or sensitivity to what can and can't be done skillfully for lay people. And, as laypeople, we try to maintain as much mindfulness as we can and sit as much as our routines will allow. We make resolutions to formally sit once, twice, thrice daily; study the texts; go to sitting groups; share what we've learned; make time for short residential or nonresidential retreats as frequently as possible. We do this for as long as our intentions and our support buoy us against the tide of our lives, till the ruts of our old routines and habits of mind once again take over.

Due to our everyday commitments, we often find it beyond our capacities to meaningfully sustain, build, or integrate those insights at home. All of us know that as modern-day householders, we live busy lives with almost countless responsibilities and distractions making a life of perfected virtue or a retreat-like environment difficult if not impossible to create or sustain. It is almost impossible to formally meditate two or four or six hours a day on any kind of routine basis while meeting the requirements of our livelihoods, families, social pleasures and responsibilities. Quickly we also learn that trying to maintain the type of mindfulness we had on retreat either is not accessible or simply doesn't work in most everyday situations. And yet for many of us, there remains a tidal-like pull to practice, and so we yearn without specific instruction to find skillful ways to support and deepen our meditative wisdom.

So I ask: What can contemporary house-holding meditators, both experienced and new to practice, do to support the wholesome intentions and the wisdom gleaned on retreat during our workaday lives?

Using Our Lives as Practice

We can begin home practice by following the teachers' instructions at the end of retreats and do more formal meditation every day. But we can also expand the notion of what it means to meditate more broadly than is commonly envisioned after a retreat.

We can teach the *citta* how to integrate our retreat wisdom in a variety of ways during everyday activities. The instructions are right under our noses: we simply have to practice the core teachings and apply them. To find instructions that will decondition us, if practiced with diligence and continuity, from the habituated notions that deep wisdom only arises on retreat and that home life is, at best, relegated to a status of trying as best we can to hold ourselves together till the next retreat, we don't need to go any further than:

- *Satipaṭṭhāna Sutta*: The Four Foundations of Mindfulness (MN 10).
- The *Ambalaṭṭhikārāhulovāda Sutta*: Advice to Rāhula at Ambalaṭṭhikā (MN 61).
- This guide, *A Householder's Vinaya*.

If you are like me and virtually every committed meditator I know, this type of commitment gets eroded by one's habits of mind and one's routines unless adequately supported by intuitive wisdom and daily practices. The type of support needed to bolster these types of strong wholesome intentions on anything resembling an ongoing moment-to-moment basis must start with what we do most: living our lives. Without a baseline of intuitive wisdom and as much moment-to-moment support as possible, as lay practitioners we quickly find ourselves either doing our daily meditation as a ritual and a chore or we let the formal sitting fall away altogether. Many of us learn our practices have eroded when we discover ourselves during our meditations lost in the planning mind trying to figure out when and how to get to the next retreat. Instead of watching our practices erode in these predictable ways, we can support and build on what we've learned on retreat using our everyday life as the basis for the practice. By applying simple techniques throughout our days, we can instead move our practice not only deeper but further on a track that formal practice alone can't and doesn't allow.

We can use precisely both the ancient orthodox teachings of *sati* and *sampajañña* to build a contemporary householding practice. For an everyday practice to work, it has to fit our temperament and our situation. If we try to build a general practice that isn't suited to the societal and historical realities of our lives in modern times, or doesn't suit us individually, the potential of a sustainable everyday practice taking root is very small. Like an immigrant who does not learn the language of their new home, one might make do, but without access to the local language, it won't be possible to fully integrate or understand the offerings of the new home.

There are two sensible reasons for the imbalance of instruction for the lay person's practice at home after retreat that we've been discussing:

1. *Sampajañña* is integral to how we live while on retreat and therefore doesn't need to be emphasized. On retreat, lay *yogis* take the Five or Eight Precepts and meditate most of the day. *Yogis* are encouraged to restrain the senses [Pāli: *indriya-saṃvara*] and, in subtle and direct ways, to pay attention to the Three Characteristics while doing formal practice. These qualities, virtue and wisdom, are the main emphasis of what *sampajañña* teaches us; and retreatants are in a controlled environment that has as its basis the practice of *sampajañña*. This is the unique gift of retreat. We are not challenged by many of the usual causes of interruption and choice that come with everyday routine and responsibility. Therefore, on retreat we give emphasis to *sati* because the retreat is designed to support out-of-the-ordinary focus and development of *sati*. *Sampajañña* plays a support role on retreat when practicing *sati*, because our *sīla* and our environment are taken care of, and as a consequence, the *sati* practice can often leap forward in ways that are difficult to replicate at home. In the reverse, during everyday life, householders must give *sampajañña* the greater degree of focus and let *sati* become the support.

2. Buddhist practice and theory, for the most part, comes to us from monastics or lay people who learned their practices from monastics in retreat environments. It is therefore logical that

lay people receive their home practice instructions through the filters of retreats and monastics who live practicing the *Vinaya Piṭaka*, a practice guide which is not available to or developed for the lay meditator.

Basis for Using Our Lives as Everyday Practice

Everyone who consciously inclines the mind towards *sīla* and *samādhi* [concentration] has an everyday practice. All of our individual practices will, of course, vary in tone, commitment, intensity, and school and may therefore look somewhat different from one another. It is, however, a given that if one is aware of one's own spiritual life and has a desire to harvest the benefits of such a life, regardless of the differences, we must be seen as having a spiritual practice.

Each person's practice will vary because everyone's character, commitment, and level of wisdom will be unique to their station and circumstance. As an example, monastics not on retreat and not focusing with strong and sincere continuity on their vows have an everyday practice similar to that of the householder. Both in degree are inclining toward wholesomeness; both will actively say they have a spiritual practice. One difference is the conscious integrity and the intensity of commitment of each. Another is that the monastic is more likely to know what that practice is and how to do it, apply it more frequently, and reap quicker and deeper benefits. We all do our best with the circumstances and station in which we find ourselves. What is critical to our happiness and what differentiates monastics from most householders is how active each is in support of their intended spiritual goal.

It is equally true that whoever we are, whatever the rootedness of our wisdom, in order to fulfill the Buddha's promise of freedom from dissatisfaction or suffering in this very life, we must incline the mind and then practice with the tools offered towards that end as often as possible in order to fulfill its potential.

Micro-Moments Make a Whole

All too often during our everyday lives, the momentum of doing and getting things done creates an illusion of constancy, a forest rather than many individual trees. Home retreat and home practice support us to look at the trees in order to better appreciate and understand the forest.

Another tool that supports our study of the forest is noticing micro-moments of direct and clear *sati* when they arise. For many of us these moments happen spontaneously and frequently. Every day, there will be moments when we experience a sight, sound, smell, taste, sensation or even a thought as simply a sight, sound, smell, taste, sensation, or thought without the automatic identification that this is MY sight, sound, etc. or that these objects of consciousness are happening to ME. If we don't notice the thoughts of ME or MY, they will arise with a story or concept. Directly, impersonally, at the moment of our awareness these micro-moments inform us and show us that undertaking the training will lead us to attaining the promise of the practice. We see, or taste, or feel something, or simply notice a thought as a thought and nothing more; or we sense a touch or see only color or form with little or no attachment in the moment. Just the experience without the normal cascade of self-referencing or concept or story. Fortunately and unfortunately, these moments are brief, which both allows us to have the moment of awakening and to move on in rather seamless ways with our task and day.

Ignoring these moments, instead of supporting them with a few added moments of reflection, can cause them to lose some of their power and value. The more often we string moments of *sati-sampajañña* together or simply add these types of moments to our day, the more we are effectively de-conditioning our patterns as well as the blindness to our patterns. I often look at this type of practice like a string of pearls. Our lives are the string and the moments of wisdom are the pearls. The more moments of wisdom, the more valuable and beautiful the necklace becomes.

SUGGESTIONS FOR PRACTICE:

I suggest two exercises to help notice these moments:
- When a micro-moment of pure *sati* arises, bring your focus to the totality of the mind-body moment. Notice what happens with this added focus. See if you can notice the quality of the *sati* and then watch carefully for what happens next. Is it simply watching or observing, or does it quickly become "I am watching or observing?" If it is the latter, notice the posture of "I'm watching" and try not to evaluate or judge. Just carry on, yet try to remember what 'just observing' was like.
- Cultivate these types of micro-moments of *sati* on a fairly regular basis throughout your day. The more frequently we support the arising and noticing of micro-moments of *sati*, the more we strengthen a variety of wholesome mental factors [[Pāli: *cetasika*] and also give rise to a greater probability for *sampajañña* to come forth. The increased frequency of exercising and inclining the mind in turn enables us to access *sati* more readily both spontaneously in everyday life and when doing formal practice.

Two quick tips:
1. Take an activity you do mindlessly over and over again throughout the day. Give a moment's quick *sati* or reflective *sampajañña* to that activity as it occurs. For instance, reaching, then touching, then holding your keys. Are they cold, sharp, heavy, light? Also notice the intention to pick up the keys and ask yourself, "Am I going someplace for wholesome reasons? Is this trip necessary?" Observe reaching, then touching, then using pressure to open, pass through, and close the door. For another situation in which to cultivate your practice, focus on the urge to urinate or defecate, the intention to do so, the process of getting you to the bathroom, the process of evacuating or urinating. Notice also what the mind is doing. Pay attention to cleaning and the transition to the next activity.

2. The second tip may be the most challenging as well as the most rewarding: Wake up to the automatic behaviors that surround your use of screen time. This is especially true regarding your smartphone. Bring attention to every urge to touch your phone, the reaching, the activity, the value of the activity, the putting it away, or simply notice the urge and observe the urge until it changes.

Diligence

In my experience, the monks [Pāli: *bhikkhu*] and nuns [Pāli: *bhikkhunī*] we meet in the West and in Asia, who are quite sincere and diligent in their practices, are not the norm for monastic Buddhist practice in general. In Asia, one is much more likely to meet monastics who are coasting or not embracing their livelihood or their practice with sincere diligence. So too with householders. Each of us brings to our meditation practices certain sets of *karmic* conditions. Whether a monastic or a householder, we have a choice of whether or not we take our practices seriously enough to apply focus and effort.

> *Continuous effort—not strength or intelligence—is the key to unlocking our potential.*
>
> – Winston S. Churchill

Or said with a slightly more colloquial emphasis:

> *Milarepa and his student came to a bridge. . . . When the student had crossed the bridge, Milarepa called him back. "Come back once more, I have a very special teaching to give you. If I do not give you this advice, to whom shall I give it?"*
>
> *He cautioned him not to waste the advice, but to put it in the deepest recesses of his heart. Then Milarepa turned his back on the student, lifted up his robe, and showed him his bare bottom. The student saw that Milarepa's bottom was all calloused, just like hardened leather.*

*Milarepa said, "For practice there is nothing greater than medita-
tion – provided you know what to meditate on and how to meditate
on it. I, who have gained knowledge and understanding of many
different meditation methods, meditated until my bottom became as
hard as leather. You need to do the same. This is your last teaching."*

— Geshe Ngawang Dhargyey

Significant rewards come to those who work diligently to develop
continuity in their practices. Maintaining continuity takes intention,
energy, effort, and investigation, coupled with mindfulness. What
Winston Churchill and Milarepa are saying about diligence applies both
to formal meditation and to the practice of *A Householder's Vinaya*. *A
Householder's Vinaya* provides concrete ways to live our lives that parallel many of the advantageous conditions a monastic has compared to
a layperson.

The material in *A Householder's Vinaya* is offered to everyone,
and especially to those who have discovered how difficult it can be to
sustain and deepen formal practice and to realize meditative wisdom
while navigating through our everyday lives. Most of the instructions
are specifically tailored to those who seek wholesome tools that can
be used to skillfully cut through any confusion arising from conflict
between personal inclination and the demands of wholesome practice.
A Householder's Vinaya offers practical tools and techniques that can
provide courageous householders a meditative life that embraces all that
we are and all that we do to become all that we want for ourselves and
all beings everywhere.

A Householder's Vinaya presents an invitation and a question. The
invitation is to acknowledge and accept the gift of the privilege of affluence and relative security we have, if that is true for us. The question is:
How much energy, effort, and investigation do we have for this type of
spiritual path? We have to do the practice to discover both the gift of the
invitation and the responsibility of having been invited.

One Against 23

A student once asked her teacher at the end of a retreat if one hour of formal meditation practice every day would be enough to sustain and deepen the insights and meditative skills learned on retreat. The teacher replied, "Imagine 24 people representing 24 hours. Now imagine them in a tug-of-war, 23 against 1."

Clearly one hour of formal practice is not enough for most of us to sustain and gradually deepen our meditative wisdom when faced with the multiplicity of everyday choices. If we truly honor the notion that we can take responsibility for training the *citta* towards its release from habit and reaction, it seems a simple conclusion that one hour of practice a day, or a 10-day or even 3-month retreat every so often will be of benefit, but will be insufficient to retrain a mind that has spent a lifetime, perhaps many lifetimes, conditioning itself to view reality in just one way.

How can lay *yogis* help support the *citta* with all its thoughts and subsequent speech and actions in ways that will provide the opportunity to gradually train itself towards greater wisdom, greater loving-kindness, greater equanimity?

Most folks who have done a formal retreat will probably say to themselves in response to the 23 hour against one hour parable, "But I have a job, a child; I go to school; there are others dependent on me; there are other things to do. How can I possibly find the time to practice?" This is true, and these issues and responsibilities are important and fundamental in a householder's everyday scheme of things; at the same time, the consequences of acquiescing again and again and giving up the continuity of our intention to practice are that we inevitably lose a bit of our resolve each and every time. We lose our momentum. We lose a context to nurture in active ways our highest spiritual aspirations.

What's a householder to do in the face of the complex and frequent avalanche of everyday requirements and chronic wants and preferences? How can we support the insights we've realized during formal practice, deepen them, make them relevant to our everyday lives and still meet our everyday responsibilities? Is there a way we can do this without adding 'shoulds' and more burden to an already busy and often overextended life?

> *When we meditate at home and in daily life, the challenges and benefits of practice become much more real than when we are on a meditation retreat. It takes a real practice to deal with real situations and real unwholesome reactions.*
>
> – U Tejaniya

In the *Satipaṭṭhāna Sutta*, the Buddha speaks about *sati and sampajañña*. Throughout the *suttas* the Buddha emphasizes the importance of both *sati* and *sampajañña* but remains somewhat vague on the particulars on how to cultivate *sampajañña*, providing only a sketchy framework. It has taken the later commentaries to offer clear *sampajañña* teachings. These commentaries teach us that the practice of *sampajañña* is the tool we need to tie our meditative intentions into a whole.

CHAPTER 2

Monastics and Householders

The Monastic *Vinaya*

WHILE ON RETREAT, a *Theravāda* monastic and a layperson receive the same meditation instructions and are given the same opportunities to practice. However, the reality of everyday life for each of them becomes radically different at the end of retreat. The monastic transitions back into a lifestyle that is conceived to automatically reinforce and encourage *sampajañña* through the practice of the *Vinaya Piṭaka* and the social environment. The lay person is often jettisoned into an environment that offers little or no opportunity to maintain a meditative life or a strong *saṅgha* to support wholesome intentions.

The *Vinaya Piṭaka* is a complex set of practice rules that are linked to a tradition-laden social network that encourages and supports continuity of practice by emphasizing *sampajañña*. In addition, the vows a *Theravāda* monastic takes when ordaining—227 for monks or 311 for nuns—allows the monastic to segue into daily life, often in a seamless manner, when coming out of retreat.

The Buddha did not provide either a *vinaya* or vows for lay people aside from the Five or Eight Precepts. Thus the transition into everyday life from the rarified protection of retreat is not the same for householders as it is for monastics. Lay people who do long residential retreats will often have the same transformative spiritual insights as a monastic, but after retreat they have little or no cultural or societal framework to support meditative wisdom. *A Householder's Vinaya* can speak to whoever you are, whatever your life's context, and wherever you think you may be on your path to liberation. It is also written so that, in stages, anyone who trains in this way can apply in direct ways techniques that will affect the quality of one's continuity of consciousness.

You can liken it to the potential of a gym. Whether you are weak or a buffed-up body builder, the tools in the gym are the same; the exercises are the same. The differences between us will be in how we choose to utilize our skills and strengths, what focus we give our practices, and how much continuity we will be able to build and then sustain within the context of an everyday tableau. A gym offers choice. The practice offers choice. Both are individual and universal at the same time. Both at the gym and in meditative practice we use the machines and weights and stretch room with the appropriate frequency, with the proper posture; depending on our effort and continuity, we will see results congruent to what we offer in effort, continuity, and skill.

Enlightenment as a Monastic Versus as a Layperson

Frequently the *suttas* describe individual monastics, small groups, and even large groups of five hundred or more who came to enlightenment by merely listening to a discourse, by an event, or as a result of personal study and meditative effort. By contrast, there are only a few examples of lay people achieving the full promise of the Buddha's teaching. The importance of being a monastic in order to become enlightened is further underscored by many stories of those who were not monastic when their practice first began, but who either became monastics while on the path or who died after their full enlightenment if they didn't take robes within a short period of time.

The latent message monastics believed then, and for the most part— along with some lay people—continue to believe today, is that the best way to achieve significant progress towards full enlightenment is the result of meditation and study as an ordained monk or nun. The obvious imbalance between the number of *suttas* offered to monastics versus lay practitioners, the different subjects covered, and the disparity in the number of stories of monastics compared to lay people achieving enlightenment has morphed over the centuries into what can be described as a spiritual caste system separating monastics and the laity. Within this system, the monastic's role has morphed into one that assumes authority, wisdom, and moral superiority, and gives the laity the job of supporting the *saṅgha* with proper veneration and financial support.

This separation has traditionally relegated the laity to a different style of practice with a different orientation, and, as a consequence, a great difference in the potential outcomes. The emphasis of lay practice over the centuries has been in large part to cultivate conventional moral purity and generosity, and to support the *saṅgha* by providing them with their basic requisites. There has been little emphasis to teach or support the laity to train the *citta* with meditation except in the context of ceremony rather than as a life of meditation practice. The natural outcome has been that most of the laity have chosen to practice in ways that they think will help to ensure a more fortunate rebirth, a birth that will allow them the opportunity to practice as a monastic or gain a heavenly rebirth. This has directly affected the types of practice to which the householder is exposed and given opportunities to practice, and has imposed the self-limiting notions this caste system creates.

While this caste-like separation has protected and sustained the teaching and produced many enlightened beings, it has also created conditions that self-limit the laity from their full potential of realizing the depths of practice. Therefore, to this day throughout the world, some who embrace a strong motivation to study Buddhist texts or meditation with the belief that study and practice will lead to the cultivation of wisdom and compassion, make the decision to leave the householder's life behind and ordain into a monastic order. Monasteries still exist because they provide excellent teachings and facilities to study and meditate, and because they have a good track record of delivering on their promise.

Some monasteries are like Ivy League schools, and some are like junior colleges, while others can be likened to schools without proper certification. The best monasteries provide the optimal conditions and teachings from top teachers; and some of these invite lay *yogis* to practice with and alongside monastics. These types of monasteries are few and are the best environments in which to practice and study meditation. Just as an undergraduate looking to be a world-affecting lawyer might seek to attend Harvard or Yale Law School in order to get the best teachings and meet future colleagues and teachers, so might a lay *yogi* seeking the most direct path to enlightenment choose the best place to practice.

The Draw and Benefits of *Theravāda* Monastic Life

In *Theravāda* Buddhist practice, the monastic order has played the pivotal role in sustaining and sharing the 2,500-year-old teachings of the Buddha. This monastic order is the oldest in the world. It has survived for millennia and continues to remain relevant through all the cultures and historical contexts it has traversed due to the timelessness and universality of the teachings themselves and because of the continuous purity of the monastic's practice of the *Vinaya Piṭaka*.

Arguably the most significant advantage a monastic has in maximizing the monastic's enlightenment project compared to a householder is the continuity that comes from practicing a codified *vinaya* that couples behavior with social and formal accountability. The *Vinaya Piṭaka* and commitment to the practice and fulfillment of it will funnel an energetic monastic towards the practices of *sati-sampajañña* in all activities directly because of its nature and its affecting consequential social contexts.

In the *Samaññaphala Sutta*: The Fruits of the Contemplative Life (DN 2), the Buddha discusses the many benefits of the monastic life with King Ajatasattu. He gets specific and, among other benefits, describes the following:

- **Solitude's delight**: For instance, for slaves and farmers
  freedom from servitude resulting in being "content with the
  simplest food and shelter, delighting in solitude" as well as
  the veneration of others.
- **Virtue's pleasure**: "[T]he monk ... consummate in virtue sees
  no danger anywhere from his restraint through virtue. Endowed
  with this noble aggregate of virtue, he is inwardly sensitive to
  the pleasure of being blameless."
- **Simplicity's contentment**: "Wherever he goes, he takes only
  his barest necessities along. This is how a monk is content."
- **Mental calm**: With mindfulness and alertness (*see sampajañña*),
  a monk cleanses his mind of the Five Hindrances [Pāli: *nīvaraṇa*]:
  - ~ Covetousness
  - ~ Ill will and anger
  - ~ Sloth and drowsiness
  - ~ Restlessness and anxiety
  - ~ Doubt
- *Jhanic* **bliss**: He attains the four *jhanic* states associated with the
  permeating of his body with rapture, pleasure, equanimity, and a
  pure, bright awareness.
- **Insight knowledge**: "[W]ith his mind thus concentrated,
  purified, and bright, unblemished, free from defects, pliant,
  malleable, steady, and attained to imperturbability, he directs
  and inclines it to knowledge and vision. He discerns: 'This body
  of mine is endowed with form, composed of the four primary
  elements, born from mother and father, nourished with rice and
  porridge, subject to inconstancy, rubbing, pressing, dissolution,
  and dispersion. And this consciousness of mine is supported
  here and bound up here.'"
- **Release from** *saṃsāra*: "His heart, thus knowing, thus seeing,
  is released from the fermentation of sensuality, the fermentation
  of becoming, the fermentation of ignorance. With release, there

is the knowledge, 'Released.' He discerns that 'Birth is ended, the holy life fulfilled, the task done. There is nothing further for this world.'"

– https://en.wikipedia.org/wiki/
Sama%C3%B1%C3%B1aphala_Sutta

Monastics are accountable first to themselves, then to the *saṅgha*, and finally to the monastic and lay community at large. A monastic who does not train in the practice of the *Vinaya Piṭaka* with wholesome intention will have a greater tendency toward heedlessness, will have to be adjudicated by their peers due to transgressions, and will be judged in the marketplace as worthy or not of veneration and alms. The *Vinaya Piṭaka* has continued to exist for 2500 years because it has worked effectively to keep monastics focused on their study and helped to ensure the social health and sustainability of the *saṅgha* by enabling monastics to be worthy of respect and generosity. It's a package deal and serves the *saṅgha* on multiple levels.

Because householders have no such *vinaya*, they also do not have a study guide to help focus their meditation practices while at home or a formalized opportunity for commitment to others aside from conventional law and social traditions. And a householder's life is, for the most part, much more complicated than a monastic's due to the need to earn a living, support a family, or both. The economic and social activity of householders obliges them to make choices and exercise preferences with more frequent unobserved reliance on habit and patterns than that of a monastic.

While ordaining is a good option for a minority of singularly motivated individuals, the life of a monastic is clearly not for everyone, just as an Ivy League education is not the best or most tenable option for all who seek to advance their careers. Many lay *yogis* don't have the specific motivations, skills, and circumstances needed to embark on a monastic life. Instead, most people live various permutations of a householder's life, and within the 'dusty life' of a householder, we use our wisdom and circumstances to live a good and wholesome life hoping this is enough to lead us, if not directly to final and complete happiness and freedom, at least towards a life that provides a modicum of satisfaction. Most of us hope that a life cultivating *sīla*, studying a little, working with a daily meditation practice, and, for some, doing a retreat now and then will be enough. We hope a sufficient depth of wisdom and compassion will become an unforced spontaneous part of our lives and eventually part of our dying.

The Role and Limitations of the *Vinaya Piṭaka*

The *Vinaya Piṭaka* is the spine of the monastic *saṅgha*.

> *The Vinaya (Pāli and Sanskrit, literally meaning "leading out,"*
> *"education," "discipline") is the regulatory framework for the*
> *saṅgha or monastic community of Buddhism based on the canoni-*
> *cal texts called the Vinaya Piṭaka.*
>
> – Encyclopedia of Buddhism
> https://encyclopediaofbuddhism.org/wiki/Vinaya

The *Vinaya Piṭaka* is a compilation of rules and practices established at the time of the Buddha to preserve social harmony between monastics and between monastics and the laity, and to help establish a self-regulating culture that supports wholesomeness and the practice of the Noble Eightfold Path in all activities. It contains the *Pātimokkha*, the 227 rules for monks and 311 rules for nuns, as well as origin stories for the rules and other teachings of the Buddha. The rules arose organically over time as the community of monks and nuns increased and conflicts and other situations came to the Buddha's attention.

It became clear early in the Buddha's *sāsana* [dispensation] that having social harmony among monastics was necessary for meditation and study to remain the focus of what being a monastic was for and about. It also provided the laity with an unchanging model of what a *saṅgha* worthy of requisites and respect should look like. Without the support of the laity, monastics would not be able to study, meditate, or preserve the teachings. A lasting and balanced system of clear social and societal checks and balances provided both communities with reasons and methods to act in wholesome and useful ways for the teachings to remain pure and stable, and to potentially flourish.

Upon ordination, a monastic makes a commitment to the practice of and training in the *Vinaya Piṭaka* for as long as they continue to wear the robes. The respective *Pāṭimokkhas* for monks and nuns instruct them how to behave and orient themselves in practice in most of their physical and social activities from the time they open their eyes in the morning till closing them for sleep at night. A monastic's 'job' is to adhere to the *Pāṭimokkha* and the 'salary' is the opportunity to study, meditate, protect the *Dhamma*, and teach, and therefore be worthy of the laity's *dāna* with regard to the four requisites. At the core of this training and lifestyle is a multi-layered intention to steer each monastic towards the liberation of the *citta* for self and for the benefit of all beings everywhere; as a natural consequence, this provides the laity an opportunity to practice generosity towards those who practice such a noble lifestyle.

Practically, the *Vinaya Piṭaka* limits personal choice and encourages restraint of the senses. By its nature, it funnels all of the monastic's thoughts, speech and actions towards virtue, concentration, and compassion. Absolutely everything a monastic does is prescribed either by the *Vinaya Piṭaka* or by cultural influences. When practiced with integrity, the *Pāṭimokkha* is not just a set of rules. Instead, like the Five or Eight Precepts the Buddha set forth for lay people, the *Vinaya Piṭaka* assists the monastic by encouraging the continuous cultivation of intention, investigation, effort, and concentration.

When the Buddha began to teach, he taught almost exclusively those who had already made a lifelong commitment to the meditative path. His first students were five men who had been ascetics, living a meditative life and dependent on alms, before coming to the Buddha to study. These men were likely of an extraordinary caliber. The *suttas* tell us how quickly they came to understand the new teachings. Several realized full enlightenment—*arahantship*—with just brief practice. After their enlightenment, the Buddha sent them to the "four corners of the world" to teach with instructions that "no two should go in the same direction," indicating the depth of trust the Buddha had in their realization and deportment. This all happened before the creation of the rules contained within the *Vinaya Piṭaka*.

In a short time, the teachings started to be disseminated to other ascetics, other schools, and householders. Quite quickly people began to come to the Buddha to study and become students and lay devotees. Only then did a monastic order and the need for the monks' and nuns' *Pātimokkhas* arise. When folks unfamiliar with the ascetic life and not sufficiently wise or trained in *sīla* started requesting ordination into the *sangha*, issues began to arise that demanded the codification of rules. In other words, the *Pātimokkha* was originally developed as a set of training rules for those who seek liberation but have yet to realize sufficient meditative wisdom to be their own arbiter of what is truly wise, what is not wise, and what is subtly self-serving. The *Vinaya Piṭaka*, in consequence, teaches anyone who trains with it social conventions that cultivate strong intention, humility, and energy towards meditative freedom.

The *Vinaya Piṭaka* makes every monastic accountable to the *sangha* in regards to their virtue and deportment. The method that provides this accountability is the mandated confession of any transgression of the rules out loud, to one another or to the community as a whole, and acceptance of the advice or sanctions they receive in return. Orally acknowledging their transgressions strengthens the monastics' commitment to their vows and provides a model of bright sincerity to the laity that inspires the laity to accept their teachings.

The relationship the Buddha created between the monastics and the laity, *i.e.*, of monastics offering teaching and modeling wholesome behavior and the laity providing whatever the monastics need, has served both communities extremely well for thousands of years. As long as the laity supports the *sangha*, the teachings are sustained from one generation to the next. The system is designed to allow the monastics to focus their lives towards study, practice, and teaching with undistracted attention; the laity learns to practice generosity, humility, and reverence.

The most significant limitation of the *Vinaya Piṭaka* is clear: it excludes non-monastics. It was not intended for, and therefore was not created to accommodate, lay practitioners or lay practice. Independent of the fact that the rules served just the monastic community, the Buddha also recognized that the *Pātimokkha* had some weaknesses in serving the *saṅgha* after his death. On his deathbed, he encouraged those in attendance to expunge it of its "minor rules." No one clarified with the Buddha which were the minor rules, so this was never done. Because it was created in the 6th Century BCE, it has, let's just say, a few archaic and perhaps no longer useful rules, not to forget the already mentioned absence of a *vinaya* for the laity.

Historical Effect of Exclusion of the Laity

The lack of a clearly defined foundational code for the laity supported many assumptions about who could and couldn't practice meditation toward enlightenment, which solidified a spiritual caste system. It affected where and from whom a layperson could get teachings, where a lay person could practice meditation, and when a lay person would be welcome in the monastery.

The instructions the Buddha offered the laity were appropriate and specific to the culture and contexts of Northern India in the 6th Century BCE. However, what was common and the norm back then is not the same today in many ways. What remains the same regardless of place, culture, or historical context is the need to practice *sīla* and to act with integrity in all areas of life. What isn't the same today is the poverty, hunger, short lifespan, caste system, frequent wars, plagues, and an environment that still had tigers and panthers lurking outside at night. Nowadays, because of industrialization and its resulting affluence, many lay people all over the world have more safety, security, and ease of life than the royals, the wealthy, or the monastics of that time. These differing circumstances have brought new opportunities and new ways for the laity to practice the core meditative teachings as never before.

The *suttas* tell us that a few householders achieved the various stages of enlightenment or high states of concentration and remained householders. Not surprisingly, those who did were almost exclusively of the upper castes, men and women who were either educated and familiar with *Vedic* practices, or in some cases, already practicing meditators. Some were wealthy and had leisure, good diet, good health and servants to help with their daily needs. Others were wandering ascetics from other traditions who would also have been schooled and trained in various styles of concentration practices.

In some ways the current state of history has taken us back to those times, but with a twist. As in ancient times, we have a leisure class that is affluent, healthy, and educated and has more flexible choices and opportunities. But unlike in times past, today the Buddha's teachings are widely available and are no longer the exclusive purview of the monastery. There are monasteries and retreat centers available to anyone who wants to study, has the courage, and can afford to go.

Nowadays, many of us have resources that allow us to not struggle as people did 2,500 years ago. Our individual and collective affluence has removed one of the critical causes for the separation that existed between monastics and the laity in ancient times. Our collective affluence and comparative physical security for many throughout the world, but especially for industrial and post-industrial societies, allows lay people who so choose to enter a monastery as a layperson for long periods of time, or wander without worry from monastery to monastery with the knowledge that at the end of their search they will not be so poor as to be at the mercy of the winds and seasons. It no longer takes an entire society to buoy the few so that they can study, meditate, and teach in relative comfort and security.

As a result of lay people taking robes and then disrobing or of practicing in monasteries for long periods of time, many of our meditation teachers are no longer just monastics, but increasingly include lay people. The present-day pantheon of teachers in many of the Buddhist traditions and schools includes young and old laypeople from many walks of life and occupations and from many different ethnicities. Many of them have experienced deep realization and learned skillful ways to share their knowledge and experience with even more lay practitioners. Western egalitarian philosophical enlightenment has met Buddhist meditative spiritual enlightenment at a time when many *yogis* could be described as having wealth and leisure equal to that of ancient princes and princesses. And like those in the stories in the *suttas*, many now want to practice towards meditative enlightenment but don't choose to take robes.

Today's meditators have a tremendous leg up in comparison to ancient lay people in their ability to get good teachings and find suitable places to practice. Residential retreats in lay retreat centers, which didn't exist in ancient times, and in monasteries, which appear to have been almost exclusively for the ordained, allowed few options for monastic style retreats for the laity. Also, given that most people lived at a subsistence level, the conditions didn't support the laity to even consider such a possibility. Until the last century or so, the best a layperson could hope for if they wanted to learn and practice meditation, was to get personal instruction from a monastic and then be left to their own wherewithal in their home. Now there are many retreat centers and monasteries available to those who wish to practice, and most retreat centers are managed and offer teachings by laypeople.

A *Vinaya* That Includes Everyone

Without the guidance of a *vinaya*, the laity remains bereft of a powerful tool that could assist their practice with practical tools and intellectual support. I now ask: What can be reasonably created for a householder wanting a *vinaya*? Can a new *vinaya* for laypeople address the conditions and lifestyle of householders in practical and useful ways now and in the future without becoming a tool for self-serving ignorance and preferences?

It would be all too easy to hoodwink ourselves into creating something that resembles the *vinayas* of the monastics without taking into consideration the differences in lifestyle and commitments. But attempts to too closely imitate the *Vinaya Piṭaka* will result in a householder's *vinaya* that crumbles quickly because it isn't appropriate or useful. It would be equally dangerous to react to the conservative nature of the monastic *vinaya* and go way too far toward liberal notions that feel good but ignore our ignorance. A *vinaya* that is too liberal will not support most of us if we truly want to realize the Buddha's promise of spiritual freedom.

This new householder's *vinaya* must not only be a practical tool, but also one that encourages householders to step up to our emerging role as co-leaders in how lay practice is taught, and to address skillfully the changes that will affect the wheres and hows of practice.

It is important not to confuse the writing and practicing of *A Householder's Vinaya* with an attempt to amend or supplant the *Vinaya Piṭaka*. It isn't, and it isn't an attempt to challenge the role of the monastic. The *Vinaya Piṭaka* and the monastic order must remain pure, regardless of how *A Householder's Vinya* is practiced. Without the stability of the monastic order, the overall teachings will lose their keel and stability; the *Vinaya Piṭaka* helps to ensure that stability. The creation of a *vinaya* for the householder is intended as a tool to advance the teachings and practices of the Buddha to a very thirsty and able audience.

CHAPTER 3

Optimal Conditions for the Journey Ahead

The Buddha's Instructions to His Son Rāhula and *Sampajañña*

After reflecting again and again, actions by deed, word and thought
should be done. . . . Before doing such actions by deed word and
thought, while doing and after doing them, one should reflect thus:
"Does this action lead to the harm [or benefit] of myself, to the
harm [or benefit] of others, to the harm [or benefit] of both?" After
reflecting again and again one should purify one's actions by deed
word and thought. Thus, O Rāhula, should you train yourself.

– Ambalaṭṭhikārāhulovāda Sutta:
Advice to Rāhula at Ambalaṭṭhikā (MN 61)

IN THE SUTTA QUOTED *ABOVE*, *Advice to Rāhula at Ambalaṭṭhikā*, the Buddha is speaking to his son, who at the time of the discourse is still quite young and only recently ordained. Rāhula is not enlightened, yet he is energetically stepping onto the path of training that he hopes will lead to *arahantship*. The Buddha's teaching is therefore tailored to his son's particular set of circumstances: young, newly ordained, and not yet enlightened.

He is directly saying to both Rāhula and the rest of us: Train your mind so that you notice as much as you can, as quickly as you can, and make the best assessment you can as to whether or not you are helping yourself, others, or both in every moment and in every situation you find yourself. He is teaching us that in order to advance the training of the mind, we must not only sit in silent meditation, but we must reflect before, during, and after we make any choice. He is quite clear in telling us not to just notice with *sati*, but to assess the qualities of the thought, speech or action, and act as quickly as possible in accordance with our best understanding of what is wholesome and what is unwholesome; to use *sampajañña*.

These are the best instructions I have found in the *suttas* on how to practice *sampajañña*. It's not a coincidence that he is offering these instructions to someone who has already made the commitment to the process of waking up and has yet to completely train the mind in either the meditative sphere or during everyday activities. Sort of like most of the rest of us, yes?

His instructions tell us to incline our thoughts, speech, and action towards wholesomeness using the best tools we have available *at the time*. He implicitly is saying that unwholesome thoughts, speech, and action will arise and be acted upon if the mind is not fully enlightened, and we can still apply *sampajañña*. He even instructs on what to do when we act due to unwholesomeness in the mind. Our job then becomes to learn from the experience so as to prevent the same result in the future — as best we can — with the tools we have at hand.

He is not saying 'thou shall' or 'thou shall not' do this or that, he is saying: "Pay attention and learn directly for yourself through your own experience." Pay attention, incline the mind towards *sampajañña*, and with wholesome intention combined with investigation, energy, and concentration, your practice will deepen and stand a greater probability of becoming more wholesome more frequently. Learning from our everyday successes and mistakes allows wisdom to develop, mature, and integrate.

I should add the Ven. Nyanaponika himself did not regard "bare attention" (sati) as capturing the complete significance of

satipaṭṭhāna, but as representing only one phase, the initial phase,
in the meditative development of Right Mindfulness. He held
that in the proper practice of Right Mindfulness, sati has to be
integrated with sampajañña, clear comprehension, and it is only
when these two work together that Right Mindfulness can fulfill its
intended purpose.

– Correspondence between Alan Wallace and
the Venerable Bhikkhu Bodhi, Winter 2006.

Those of us who have chosen to make our lives our practices closely resemble Rāhula. We both have vowed to make our lives as wholesome, compassionate, and wise as possible. We both have taken our vows with 'bright faith' and untrained minds, with an unclear understanding of how to skillfully move forward. However, an inexperienced monastic like Rāhula takes these important first steps in practice when a false start or vague teaching could lead him into unskillfulness. With the support of the *Vinaya Piṭaka* and the monastic *saṅgha* as guides, Rāhula is more likely to be guided towards a continuous lifestyle that will naturally steer him towards the intuitive understanding of the universal natures of wholesomeness and wisdom. The householder is bereft of a close-knit *saṅgha* and doesn't have anything remotely akin to the monastic *vinaya*.

The aim of *A Householder's Vinaya*—and hopefully its appeal—is to help us examine our lives and use the totality of what we think, speak, and do as practice. As a consequence, we are able to make our daily lives the field of our practice like the monastics are able to do when they apply the *Vinaya* to their everyday lives. The householder's task is to step forward with kindly determination and establish a continuity of *sati-sampajañña* within the context of lay life and, like the monastic, create the context for life's experiment. This householder's *vinaya* helps us frame that context, and, like a liquid in a funnel, we let the rest take care of itself.

Liking and Disliking as a Part of Dependent Origination

It's really quite simple: We like what we like; we don't like what we don't like. We think, speak, and act as if there were no consequences when we repeat our actions over and over again. What isn't so simple is why this happens and what the consequences are. The why, in this context, is defined neatly by the notion of dependent origination.

A short discussion of why this process of the mind is so important is necessary if we want to understand the importance of how a *vinaya* supports the deconditioning of the mind away from habit and the conditioning of it towards new wholesome patterns of mind. In brief, we examine a few concepts that hopefully will make sense to you. For many, these concepts are useful to understand intellectually but not mandatory. When we understand them, these concepts can be intuitively integrated in our practice of *sati-sampajañña*, adding another fiber to the rope of understanding and faith.

On the other hand, some meditators find these concepts and these ways of thinking either incomprehensible and therefore distracting or too interesting and therefore get lost in speculation and intellectual self-referencing. If you find the following discussion unhelpful, I suggest you skip down to the next section, *Blindly Walking in the World*.

Regardless of our prejudices or proclivities, understanding how the mind works and how we can define and language these processes is important now and for the future. These concepts have served and protected the continuity of the *sāsana* since the time of the Buddha. If not understood and integrated, whether by monastics or by lay people, that lack of understanding and integration will affect how meditation is practiced.

WHAT IS DEPENDENT ORIGINATION?

'Dependent origination' is the term Buddhist psychology and neuroscience use to describe how and why objects arise in consciousness, how and why the brain cognizes the event, and how and why the process affects the reaction to the next sense object as it arises and passes away. This process establishes our relationship with cause and effect, or *kamma*. The Buddhist understanding of how the mind works is foundational to the intellectual understanding of Buddhist meditation. Dependent origination explains how and why, through the practice filter of *sati-sampajañña*, we can decondition and retrain the mind and free it from blind habit.

THE SENSE DOORS

The Buddha taught that, as human beings, we have six sense doors to consciousness by which we experience the world:

- Seeing
- Hearing
- Smelling
- Tasting
- Bodily sensations
- Mental activity (which encompasses all qualities of thought and emotion)

Each of these sense experiences comes mechanically to the mind through one of the sense organs or receptors:

- The eyes
- The ears
- The nose
- The tongue
- The body
- The mind

Each of them, except for the mind, have external points of stimuli. For example, a bird chirps, and the sound passes through the air until it hits the eardrum, which then sends a neurochemical signal to the brain.

Similarly, a rose's fragrance hits the nose; the eye catches a color; the body feels a stubbed toe; the tongue tastes chocolate; the mind experiences a passing thought. Each of these experiences are cognized by the brain due to a neurochemical reaction in the brain, as it is hardwired to do.

Although we constantly receive all kinds of stimuli through every sense door, the mind focuses only on the most predominant object and only one object at a time. Because too many stimuli are being received at the same time, the mind takes only the sense impression that is most pronounced as a conscious object. The rest remain in the background.

The sense door delivers the chirping sound to the mind in its rawest form, simply as a sound. A sound can be loud, soft, melodious, harsh, etc. but it is just a sound. Intuitive meditative experience teaches us that the recognition of a chirping sound then arises in the brain accompanied by a feeling tone [Pāli: *vedanā*] — an experience of the sound as pleasant, unpleasant, or neutral (neither pleasant nor unpleasant). As a result of the context, the person's nature, and the effects of *kamma*, the chirping sound, like any conscious mind moment, will arise every time with a feeling tone, which will change depending on the situation. Hearing chirping while meditating might at first be pleasant, but after 30 minutes it may become unpleasant.

Once a pleasant, unpleasant, or neutral feeling tone arises in the mind coupled with recognition of a sense object, a number of processes begin in a natural progression, not unlike water flowing downstream. If a sense object is accompanied by a pleasant feeling tone, without the proper awareness the mind will begin to like it, then want it, then cling to it with varying degrees of intensity depending on several factors, including the situation, how intense the experience of the object is, and the past conditioning surrounding similar objects or even the same object in other contexts. The opposite is true as well. Should an unpleasant feeling tone arise when the sound of chirping is perceived, the mind will not like it, not want it, and will express a desire to push it away. If a neutral feeling tone arises, the tendency will be to not look carefully and miss the object entirely.

The consequence of perceiving an object and not observing the qualities we associate with it might just be a brief, passing, and insignificant sequence, or it may lead to further thought, speech, or even some type of physical action. If mindfulness is present, we might simply observe the chirping as a sound accompanied by a pleasant feeling tone, which the mind observes till the sequence completes and disappears. Equally possible, if the chirping sound is accompanied by an unpleasant feeling tone and is not observed with mindfulness, the experience might lead to the breaking of one's meditation in order to get up and close the window.

These experiences happen countless times a day and, for the most part, have only minimal impact on our consciousness. However, the accumulation of these experiences, the massive amounts of unobserved thoughts, lead to patterns and habits that become important to us. Also, those moments when intense thoughts or emotions arise that we act on that can have an impact on ourselves and others are significant. We have to go no further than remembering the times we said or did something to someone that caused harm to both when we were unaware that we were acting from an emotion such as annoyance, or depression, or envy.

Any action performed without attention to this process is intrinsically unwholesome to one degree or another. It is therefore reinforcing our lifelong habits of clinging and reactivity. This means that without clear attention to our inner experience, some amount of unobserved attachment or aversion will be present in the mindstream due to ignorance.

So, why is this important, and how does it affect whether or not we choose to do meditation and practice *A Householder's Vinaya*?

Blindly Walking in The World

When we take a step back and understand just how fast and how often the mind continuously operates in this sequence without pause, it becomes easy to see how a billion unobserved mind moments create a veil of ignorance, just as billions of grains of sand make up a beach. Left unobserved over a lifetime, these sequences oblige the mind to operate only from data that is not fully understood. The mind will, therefore, rely only on habit and conditioning, despite the conscious part of ourselves telling us that 'I' am in control and making informed choices and wise decisions. In fact, when not observed through the filters of *sati-sampajañña*, our thoughts, speech, and actions are just a stream of pre-conditioned mind moments that latch onto the pleasant, push away the unpleasant, and get confused if the feeling tone is not charged with either desire or aversion. A prison routine.

By continuing to be unobservant, we build our own prisons with the bars and locks of liking and disliking, wanting and not wanting, clinging and pushing away. In order to feel in control, we try again and again to make the feeling tones or objects we like to last, and to keep those we do not like away permanently, neither of which can be done. Then, we wonder why we always feel like we are just not getting it.

Sīla and *Sati-Sampajañña* Together

When we decide, "I will cultivate as much *sati-sampajañña* with *sīla* in my life as frequently as possible," and "I will use my every thought, word, and action as objects for *sati-sampajañña* with *sīla* to develop and mature," we begin the gradual process of supplanting mental activity that is the product of blind habit with a mind that is always inclining itself towards bare attention and wholesome intention. This is how we whittle away ignorance.

If our actions are informed only—or at least primarily—by these new habits of paying attention to our experience through the lens of *sati-sampajañña*, we begin to break the old blinding, automatic patterns described *above*. We observe the processes of mind with an emphasis on the process, not the content; we don't believe the initial reactivity. This is what the *Vinaya Pīṭaka* does for the monastic.

This type of observation opens the field for clear new kinds of choices. When observed, pleasant, unpleasant, and neutral objects and feeling tones pleasant, unpleasant, or neither. The process stops there. The liking, not liking, etc. doesn't happen; we do not latch on. It is enough for an object to be known for what it is with its feeling tone without judgment, manipulation, and reactivity.

The only way to bring about this change in how the mind works is by bringing more and more deliberate attention to as many mind moments as possible, as quickly as possible, with whatever skill level one's *sati-sampajañña* permits. The conditioning and skill of this practice become a life-changing wholesome habit in opposition to the unwholesome and unconscious habits of the past. This wholesome habit itself leads to ever more subtle intuitive understanding of the cognitive process, and consequently to the development of much quicker mental acuity and meditative skills. This allows for the space between understanding and habituated reactivity. We learn to take time for and give space to understanding what is happening before taking action.

It's helpful to remember that this new habit of mind has a maturing process all its own, and it permits a change to arise that separates these new habits from the old ones and their accompanying lifelong patterns. This deconditioning can lead the mind to independent and clearer ways of observing the internal and external worlds and to the ability to make wholesome choices. Many old habits and patterns are skillful and useful, and they will become wholesome and unaffected by ignorance when we operate in this new way.

The story of the student asking the teacher after a retreat if one hour of meditation a day will suffice to maintain or deepen the insights gleaned while on retreat is relevant here. Succinctly, this parable illustrates why it is important for us to develop as much continuity of *sati-sampajañña* as possible. The more often we pay attention to all our activities, the more we whittle away at the blind patterns of the past and invite those patterns to be uprooted and transformed by the process into a non-reactive, wise relationship with our thoughts, speech, and actions.

Balance

The practice of *A Householder's Vinaya*, whether in home practice or during a home retreat, is intended to teach us by using our everyday experiences as fields of practice. Like on retreat, we do and think many of the same things over and over again. It is precisely here with the repetition of observing that the mind can be taught to become less reactive. The experience of observing everyday experiences with increasing amounts of non-judgmental and non-manipulative perspectives by itself deconditions previous conditioning, which allows the *yogi* to become responsive and balanced.

Balance helps to make the practice of *sati-sampajañña* the cornerstone of our mental development. Like standing and walking, which needs constant balancing without conscious effort, so too does the balance of *sati* and *sampajañña* arise when intuitive wisdom begins to operate not from the conscious mind, but instead automatically. Always inclining the mind towards balance, always towards patience, always towards acceptance, these are the exercises and less patterned reactivity is the result. On retreat and in everyday householding practice, balance in this context is when the five controlling or spiritual faculties [Pāli: *indriya-samatta*] — faith, effort, mindfulness, concentration, and wisdom support one another in equal measure. We strive to incline the mind *with* balance in every situation, whether pleasant or unpleasant, painful or pleasurable, in all situations. Not over-striving and not being lazy. Remembering to bring whatever balance we have in the moment while noticing the process. It's the kindly unflinching determination that deconditions blind reactivity. Being attentive and balanced allows this process to take root.

Examining the mind-body process through the filter of *sati-sampajañña* is like being on a teeter totter. We sit on both ends and use either *sati* or *sampajañña* to examine and learn from our habit-patterned behaviors directly. As we do when playing on a teeter-totter, we have a tendency to try to willfully overcompensate when things appear to be out of balance causing quick and jerky ups and downs in the mind.

When we're learning how to ride a bicycle or to ice skate, whenever the mind moves to counteract being out of balance, the tendency is to overcompensate, and as a consequence, we fall the other way. This is natural and everyone does it in the beginning. Lessening reactivity to being out of balance begins to allow us to become stable. Everybody who learns to ride a bicycle or ice skate, or learns how to meditate, discovers it is about being present and that getting out of the way does the work.

What may not be clear about the process of learning how to balance is that the process itself is doing the work. Reactive pushing or pulling never allows the peace of balance to arise. It's the ever more gentling effects of micro adjustments that finally permit balance to arise. A pendulum at rest. What balances the mind is simply observing without judgment or manipulation from a non-self referencing point of view. By definition, self-referencing always tilts the scale out of balance. A 'self' always, in one way or another, tries to affect the environment for its benefit. Balancing that comes from non-judgemental non-self identified observation does the work.

In all activities of the body and mind, whether on the cushion or at work, the more frequently we allow moments of non-self referencing, non-judgment, and non-manipulative intention to enter the mindstream, the greater our freedom will become.

Retreat Practice

It's helpful at this point to examine why residential retreat practice is so important for the cultivation of *A Householder's Vinaya* and the development of a home practice. What is the link between a formal residential retreat and one's meditation practice at home?

A layperson attending a residential retreat at any retreat center in the *Theravāda* tradition takes the Five or the Eight Precepts before the teachings are offered and the practice begins. Why is this critical for success on retreat and later when one returns home? Lay people, in general, have only a diffuse understanding of what *sīla* is or how important wholesomeness is on any spiritual journey. They are therefore given instructions on how important the precepts are and what they are, and then invited to take them on as a practice and recite or chant them out loud.

For most of us, virtue is about being nice and not breaking the law —more or less what we were taught in grammar school and at home. But attempts at behaving morally are moving targets when they are not anchored in the training of wholesome wisdom. They can too easily be affected by history, context, and personal ignorance. Taking the Five or the Eight Precepts, making a vow of Noble Silence, and committing to restraining the senses and giving wholesome effort, become the unique and precious 'jewels' of a retreat. For many, the conditions of a residential retreat are the first time in their lives they are living with relatively pure *sīla*.

Without *sīla*, meditation is just mental training; but coupled with *sīla* meditation has the potential to open the *citta* to full liberation. On a residential retreat we are offered a big window to see this, understand it, and to do something about it.

The psycho-spiritual environmental conditions that arise as a consequence of taking the Precepts, maintaining noble silence, and restraining the senses, launch a layperson into what might be called a temporary monastic ordination. The meditative work a person does while on retreat, the teachings they receive, the opportunity for realization, and the attention to *sīla* are all the same as those of a monastic.

Now it gets interesting. In the *suttas*—in the whole Pāli Canon—it is understood that anyone can study meditation and take its training to its full promise. Many stories recount such incidents for all types of people in various life conditions, ranging from everyday people to the chief disciples of the Buddha. Where coming to realization is concerned, there are no special ceremonial requirements; no magical initiations; no fees; no gender, racial, ethnic or class limitations or restrictions. Everyone in every walk of life is promised that if we practice with precision and integrity, stay continuous, and maintain our *sīla*, the fruits are there to realize. The ancient teachings also make clear that there are certain steps we can take to maximize our psycho-spiritual and environmental conditions to support the training and increase the probability of realization. Monastics, with their *vinaya* and lifestyle, reflect the most supportive system currently extant. The retreat environment for the layperson is near to ideal, but with a twist.

As noted in Chapter 2, when a monastic ends a retreat, which is a special time given over to out-of-the-ordinary continuous formal meditation practice, and returns to their regular life, they return to a livelihood and lifestyle regulated by the monastic *vinaya*. The monastic *vinaya* is clear and concise and demands the monastic's full attention all of the time. This implicitly supports a slowing down of all mental, verbal and physical actions and contributes to continuous micro-moments of recurring levels of attention. Thus, a virtually seamless transition occurs from intense practice to a very structured *sīla-sati-sampajañña*-oriented existence which is constantly supported and shared and buoyed by one's monastic brothers and sisters.

However, whether or not a layperson has made a commitment to live by the Five or Eight Precepts in everyday life, at the end of a residential retreat, during which there are only a few societal ambiguities, the layperson transitions to a contextualized world where *sīla*, social relationships, and livelihood are not as clearly defined, and where the post retreatant doesn't have the social supports for a meditative life. It is the norm in post-retreat instructions to the laity to encourage *sīla*, social responsibility, study and respect for monastics. The instructions do not offer anything remotely resembling a formal, codified *vinaya* with its intentional rules and practical influences. The monastic *vinaya* helps to decondition the mind away from unseen habits because it demands extreme and unusual behaviors. But the laity is without a template for their circumstances, which do not demand or encourage one's everyday attention in quite the same way. As a consequence, if both a layperson and a monastic have significant progress in their study of meditation while on retreat, the probability of being able to integrate and mature the realization after retreat will likely be significantly different between the two.

After 40 years of practice, one of my most seemingly unorthodox realizations is that while bells and whistles of deep insight that often arise in retreat are vital in a *citta's* epiphany, it is equally important whether the insights are given opportunity to be tested and applied in the context of a variety of situations off the cushion. This seems simple, but all too often the current paradigm seems to say, or at least imply, "Get enlightened, and the job's done."

Conditions at Home

*It is the daily little negligence in thoughts, words, and deeds
going on for many years of our lives ... that is chiefly responsible
for the untidiness and confusion we have in our minds. This
negligence creates the trouble and allows it to continue. Thus the
old Buddhist teachers have said: "Negligence produces a lot of
dirt. As in a house, so in the mind, only a very little dirt collects
in a day or two, but if it goes on for many years, it will grow into
a vast heap of refuse.*
     – Nyanaponika Thera, *The Power of Mindfulness*, p. 106

Many lay *yogis* live alone, some live with partners or others who practice or support practice, some live with partners or others who do not support practice, and still others have awkward living situations in which their meditative goals are seen at best as odd and at worst as a personal threat or a sin. In all situations, there are ways we can approach our lay lives to support and give our retreat-realized meditative wisdom opportunities to mature and even deepen. Home practice combined with home retreats offers many perspectives and practical techniques that actively support one's everyday meditation practice and allow it to mature.

And yet . . .

A contemporary lay *yogi* still faces many hurdles when seeking to practice with integrity and continuity. We still have work, complicated family responsibilities, and attachments to people and objects. Except for the very few of us who have deep realization, we have an incomplete understanding of practice. We also may have a willingness to organize our lives towards our meditative goals, but the willingness is shaky and the understanding imperfect. Sure we want to live morally and with wise kindness, but who has the time or really wants to study and meditate when there are other things to do that are more fun or must be done? Who has the energy? In other words, some of the 'dusty life' still remains regardless of the security and potential leisure our current lives offer. Too often, too quickly, in the conditions described *above*, our practices get relegated to a second-tier priority.

We learn on retreat that when our *sati* is more continuous our *sati* becomes . . . more continuous, a loop that feeds itself. Equally in the reverse, off retreat when we remain non-attentive to *sati* and *sampajañña* in our everyday lives, the more our minds whittle away at the continuity of our attention and the loop gets interrupted and broken. The mind will increasingly latch on to subtly unwholesome, distracting, temporal, and pleasant and unpleasant mental states and activities in order to navigate the duties of daily living. These modes of reverting to and relying on past behaviors often not only lead to the erosion of wholesome attention, and the reinforcement of non-attention, but also put the householder on the slippery slope of choice, which unchecked and unobserved leads to passive avoidance of meditative perspectives.

When the mind stays unprotected by *sati-sampajañña*, each of us will find our little pleasures, our places of zoning out, such as watching TV, reading novels, consuming intoxicants, or casually engaging in wandering and planning types of thinking. Each of us have our places of actively and passively zoning out. It is not the activity alone that we do in our lives that makes or breaks our continuity of attention, it is the quality of *sati-sampajañña* with which these thoughts and activities are approached that makes the difference. Allowing states of inattention to be the rule and not the exception is more insidious and worse for our enlightenment project than the unobserved reactivity that comes from one or two intense episodes.

Another layer to this level of inattention affecting the health of minds and hearts is doing our daily activities with the inner certainty that we are paying attention and in control when in fact we are not. The mind telling us, and us believing, that our regular way of being, our assumptions are accurate and true, when in fact they are not, is where our confusion really gets its momentum. These unstated and unseen assumptions underpin our way of experiencing the external world, the way we relate to and believe our thinking, and therefore, the ways we think and act towards self and others.

Take the example of a modern-day equivalent to King Milinda's discussion with Buddhist scholar Nāgasena about the nature of a chariot and its existence, as recorded in the *Milinda Pañha* [Questions of King Milinda, KN Bk. 18] circa 100 BCE and 200 CE. When we walk down the street, we unconsciously assume that objects we are seeing are cars. But are these objects really cars? If we were to separate it into its component parts, would there still be a 'car' there, or would we see a 'fender,' a 'hood,' a 'motor,' etc.? In reality, 'car' is a concept with which we label what we're seeing, which is actually a combination of sensory impressions and concepts. It suits us to label things as they appear on a superficial level for safety, convenience and as useful when communicating with others. So yes, in relative terms, what we see is a car; but ultimately, we almost never understand that the object we see through the eye door is not really a car. The concept is not the reality.

Slowing Down and Paying Attention

EFFECT OF THE PĀTIMOKKHA FOR MONASTICS

The *Pātimokkha*, as mentioned, is the foundation for a spiritual livelihood and at the same time a complex social contract with oneself and others, a total way of life that constantly obliges one to pay attention as continuously as possible to small and seemingly meaningless details.

On the surface, many of the rules seem to have nothing at all to do with livelihood or virtue or mindfulness, and instead appear to be about rules, appearance, external behavior, and culture. A few quick examples:

Should any bhikkhu have a felt [blanket or rug] made of a mixture containing silk, it is to be forfeited and confessed.

– Thanissaro Bhikkhu, p. 235

Should any bhikkhu have a needle case made of bone, ivory, or horn, it is to be broken and confessed.

– Thanissaro Bhikkhu, p. 505

I will not teach Dhamma to a person with an umbrella in his hand who is not ill.

–Thanissaro Bhikkhu, p. 541

What does this have to do with sustaining and deepening one's virtue or concentration? How do these practice rules and ones similar to them help a monastic in their meditative life?

To see how these rules do help monastics to sustain virtue and concentration, it's necessary to look at the whole set of rules and not get caught up in cherry picking the ones that may appear to us to be archaic or silly.

Just like a householder, a monastic is bombarded by billions of sense impressions during a day. Without a keel to reorient themselves over and over towards the purity of the commitment of one's vows, the monastic will likely become overwhelmed and lose track. Many of these rules can, therefore, be seen as wake up bells scattered throughout a monastic's day for the purpose of reminding and training them to stay alert and attentive to all thought, speech, and action as often as possible.

Maintaining attention on a seemingly arbitrary set of training precepts not only stimulates the cultivation of effort, it also supports the maturation of different types of focus. The required attention to details forces a monastic to slow down and become increasingly deliberate in speech and action. One might see the monastic *vinaya* as a controller, regulator, or limiter between the acceleration of thought and the speed of speech and action. Slowing down gives the monastic time and the opportunity to reflect or bring mindfulness to an action of body, speech or mind. Bringing reflection or mindfulness to a thought before speaking or taking action is the bedrock of a lifestyle that supports a field of potential learning 24/7. This is exactly what *A Householder's Vinaya* will help you do should you give the practice a similar priority.

LAYPEOPLE

Similarly, lay students must slow down their speech and actions if they are to skillfully master the continuity of the training and be able to look at things more carefully. When the mind is focused on a single object it ignores everything else. In effect, when the mind is concentrated it has achieved an intense level of restraint of the senses. It isn't being distracted by memories, plans, desires, aversions, doubts, etc.; it is just focused. When we invite and cultivate concentration, we create conditions to allow it to arise. Example: We don't do our work while playing volleyball; we do our work in environments that support that type of attention.

Slowing down and choosing to limit what we do with our minds and our actions affects our ability to concentrate. On retreat in the *Theravāda* tradition, *yogis* are instructed to not engage in speech and to keep their eyes averted to avoid eye contact. Both activities, when unguarded, stimulate the entry of huge amounts of data into the mind, which the mind cannot track without difficulty and therefore will easily distract us from the continuity of our *sati*. Instead of allowing unbridled looking around and speech to occur whenever the impulse strikes, the mind is given a special opportunity to watch without unnecessary or uninvited stimuli interfering.

To best restrain the senses, we must slow down physical movements and limit what we take in through the sense doors. It takes significant ongoing intention and continuity to do this well, but it provides a two-fold gain on the path towards maturing one's meditation practice:

1. It simplifies experience, which slows the cascade of the mind towards unconscious liking and disliking and the proliferation of more and more liking and disliking.
2. It demands the continuous exercising of wholesome intention and effort. The simpler our experience is, the more clearly we can observe each moment, which concomitantly strengthens our practice. This process serves us while we are on retreat and in our everyday lives.

Reflecting Before, During, and After

After reflecting again and again, actions by deed, word and thought should be done... Before doing such actions by deed, word and thought, while doing and after doing them, one should reflect thus: "Does this action lead to the harm [or benefit] of myself, to the harm [or benefit] of others, to the harm [or benefit] of both?" After reflecting again and again one should purify one's actions by deed word and thought. Thus, O Rāhula, should you train yourself.

– Ambalaṭṭhikārāhulovāda Sutta:
Advice to Rāhula at Ambalaṭṭhikā (MN 61)

THE THREE-LEVEL REFLECTION

In the Buddha's instructions to his son Rāhula, he sets forth a three-level approach to what is to be done with all activity of body, speech, and mind:

1. Before acting, we should discern where the action will lead:
   To or away from the benefit or harm to ourselves, others, or both.
2. While acting, we should discern where the action is leading:
   To or away from the benefit or harm to ourselves, others, or both.
3. After acting, we should discern where the action has led:
   To or away from the benefit or harm to ourselves, others, or both.

THE 'ABOUT TO' MOMENT

Examining our intentions before performing any activity establishes a mental habit that helps to mitigate and hopefully eventually eliminate some of the blind habits of preference and avoidance.

Conscious examination of what we intend to do slows us down both mentally and physically, which dampens preference-based impulsivity. Slowing down our willingness to speak or act only after reflection provides us with what I call an 'about to' moment. These moments allow time and space for *sati-sampajañña* to enter into the field of attention as choices and actions are formulating. Slowing down is critical to the practice of *A Householder's Vinaya* and the development of a wise and compassionate spiritual practice.

REFLECTING WHILE AND AFTER ACTING

As we also learned from the Buddha's instructions to Rāhula, should our wisdom be insufficient to restrain us before speaking or acting, we still get two more opportunities to cultivate restraint and support our commitment to our *Householder's Vinaya*:

1. We can pay attention as we do the activity.
2. We can reflect afterwards.

This three-level approach to all our thought, speech and action — the before, during, and after — creates a constant opportunity to bring *sati-sampajañña* to whatever is happening. The more frequently we cultivate the before, during, and after approach to our thoughts, speech and actions, the more we establish a pattern that creates a seamless, almost effortless approach to polishing our virtue, allowing for ideas of generosity to occur, and cultivating patient attention. Polishing up our choices based more and more frequently in *sati-sampajañña* simultaneously strengthens the linking of accompanying mental factors with wholesome patterns and increases the potential for wise choices to arise in the moment and in the future. Creating a norm in which investigation, intention, and effort are linked to wholesomeness supports the establishment of continuous bare attention, strengthening and making bare attention and wholesomeness more accessible during our everyday activities.

Even if You're Busy, Just Incline the Mind

For a householder, the obvious and most common question becomes: "How does a person like me, with a busy schedule and multiple responsibilities, realistically establish a mindset that is always inclining itself towards attention and wholesomeness?" The most important word in this question is 'inclining.' Inclining does not mean that every moment of every day we have to maintain bare attention through the practice of *sati* or constantly filter our speech and actions through *sampajañña*. Yet, we try, and if we fail we learn from the experience and start again.

The answer to the dilemma of being busy is to take one moment, one minute, one hour, one day at a time. To begin again and again after losing the way, maintaining a friendly, firm yet gentle, re-efforting attitude imbued with kind patience is the way to success. Inclining the mind with whatever wisdom and skill we have in *this* moment is the recipe that works right now and all the way through to enlightenment.

The Tire and the Road: A *Kalyāṇamitta's* Encouragement

It took the awareness that you wish to improve the quality of your *citta* for you to start your meditation practice and subsequently find your way to this guide. It is rare that anyone has the necessary inner and outer conditions to find their way to their starting gate. Most people just follow what is familiar and comfortable. And yet you are here!

General overview and context are important, but the doing and applying are more important. To do anything well, one must know how to begin; and to perfect what we begin, we must learn how to follow through. Starting with good intention and sustaining gentle but determined follow through will provide any meditator with a greater probability for wholesome outcomes to arise at all times both in the living moment and through the dying process.

In the introduction I suggested you read a few commentaries explaining Buddhist philosophy and material explaining *sampajañña,* and listen to a few recordings that offer the basic instructions in how to practice *sati.* This is a good place to remind you that all are useful, all are valuable regardless of how advanced you think your practice is. Please consider and reconsider, and if you haven't yet done the reading and listening, give it another thought.

I offer this encouragement with respect because of my experience with many of my teachers. Each of them, in their own way, repeated their teachings, sometimes word for word, many times over. My experience was similar to what Mark Twain was supposed to have said about his father:

When I was a boy of fourteen, my father was so ignorant I could hardly stand to have the old man around. But when I got to be twenty-one, I was astonished at how much he had learned in seven years.
– Attributed to Mark Twain

Good advice takes on new character depending on the context and circumstances. The suggestions about reading and listening to recordings, and many of the suggestions throughout *A Householder's Vinaya,* will have different meanings depending on who you are and when you read or practice. Providing yourself the foundation by doing the required work gives the circumstance and context the next time around a better chance of making a difference.

Continuity of Practice

I emphasize continuity of practice frequently. Skillful continuity leads to the goal. What does this mean? What does "skillful continuity" mean? It means that, as an example, whenever you can remember to bring your attention to brushing your teeth, you do it like this: Pay careful attention to the intention to start; then pay careful attention to each intervening action as well of the intention that precedes each action: The touch of picking up the brush, the reaching for the toothpaste, the thought to grab the toothpaste, the reaching, the touch of the cap on the toothpaste, the squeeze of the tube, the putting down of the tube, the intention to turn on the faucet, the sensation of the faucet, the turning of the wrist and the faucet, the sound of the water, the wetting of the brush, the lifting, the opening of the mouth, the pressure on the gums and the teeth, the taste, etc.

Until we are fully enlightened, at times we will lose touch with our intention to maintain skillful continuity, interrupting our ability to maintain an uninterrupted flow of attention. For example, while doing formal mediation, the intention is to keep the attention, *sati*, on the activity or object of attention from its beginning, through its middle, and its end, and to continue the attention without interruption into the next breath. But all too often, we can't maintain the continuity due to a wandering mind. Anyone who has tried to develop continuity of mindfulness during formal meditation will probably be familiar with this.

We sit and bring our attention to the sensations of the breath. We notice the stretching and expansion of the in breath as it affects, say, the abdomen; we notice how the abdomen fills with air to a maximum point. Perhaps we notice a pause in the movement; we then notice the experiences of the out breath, and how the new breath begins. We do this with micro attention as much as possible. We try to keep an eye on the characteristics of the experience, the quality of the breath as permanent or impermanent, whether we are satisfied or not, and if there really is someone controlling the breath or if it is happening on its own. We also notice the qualities of the breath: We notice whether it is smooth or ragged, soft or hard, pleasant or unpleasant, etc. But for how long? For most of us this lasts for a breath or two, maybe a minute before the mind wanders or gets distracted with some concept or identification and gets consumed and lost in the memory, the plan, the fantasy. Occasionally this distraction lasts only a moment or two but, if you are like most of us, this will happen more times than we would like to admit and longer than we would think possible. Sitting there lost in thought.

Whether it takes a few seconds or a few minutes to realize that the mind has been lost in thought, eventually, for most of us a sequence occurs: We notice we've been lost, which is an awakening moment of meditation. This is quickly followed by either a conscious or intuitive self-postured thought of, "Darn it, I'm such a bad *yogi*; I'm lost again." And then dutifully we drag our attention back to the breath almost like a beaten dog. This process, this getting lost, waking up, forgetting to pay attention to the waking up, and instead having the mind fall yet again into patterned self-judgement, is where and when we frequently apply both *sati* and *samajañña*, we begin to train ourselves to stay attentive to the whole process. Not forgetting to attend to the waking or the self-judgement or the dragging of the attention back to the breath or the beginning of a new breath. Paying attention to all equally with the same flow of attention, the same investigation, the same interest. The more often we learn to keep the continuity of mindfulness through all the ups and all the downs of our everyday lives and in our formal meditation, the more we bring into our lives the most common denominator, wisdom.

In many similar activities throughout the day we can do this. The example of brushing the teeth takes 3-4 minutes at most, time that would otherwise be given to automatic habitual activities like judging your face for acceptability and aging, planning, or simply staying numb. Other simple examples might include picking up your wallet or keys before leaving the house, opening a door, getting in and out of the car. There's a million of 'em. Our days are littered with automatic behaviors that we can use for moments of applied *sati* and *sampajañña*.

Our lives are our experiment. We can train our mind with inattention or attention.

As your *kalyāṇamitta* on this path, I suggest you don't dawdle and don't sell yourself short. Take as few of what appear to be attractive shortcuts as possible, and try not to compromise the continuity of your intention and effort. When your meditation gets tough or the practice of *A Householder's Vinaya* begins to feel like a chore and you need a break, figuratively get up, shake yourself off, and carry on. Meditation is a path *and* a process with many ups and downs. Starting and stopping is inevitable just as remembering and forgetting. The important lesson in both scenarios is to take a deep breath, step back, and start again.

> *Just as the ocean has a gradual shelf, a gradual slope, a gradual inclination, with a sudden drop off only after a long stretch, in the same way this Doctrine and Discipline has a gradual training, a gradual performance, a gradual progression, with the penetration to nibbāna only after a long stretch.*
>
> – *Uposatha Sutta*: Uposatha (Ud 5.5)

Paying Attention to the Small Things

To contextualize the emphasis I'm giving to the small things having more importance to our overall spiritual journey than we normally would give them, I'd like to share a story I once heard about an observant Orthodox Jewish man. Observant Orthodox Jews have many rules governing almost all aspects of their behavior throughout the day. Just as the *Vinaya Piṭaka* governs the life activities of Buddhist monastics, the *Talmud* tells an Orthodox Jew when and how to pray, how to dress, what to eat, when to rest, etc.

This particular Orthodox Jew was asked, "What does your practice do for you?" His response, after a pause, was, "It reminds me, from the moment I wake in the morning until the moment I go to sleep at night, that I am a Jew in relationship with my God." Though some of the rules prescribing the daily activities of this Orthodox Jew may seem ridiculous to an outsider, they serve him well. He is consciously and constantly training his heart and his mind by exerting investigation, effort, and attention to many small details throughout his day. Within the purpose of finding and establishing his relationship with his God, he develops his relationship with his God.

A Householder's Vinaya points the practitioner in the same direction, using investigation rather than rules as the spark of intention. *A Householder's Vinaya* creates both a mental and social environment that encourages the mind to intimately examine every detail of every waking moment from a non-judging and less personal perspective. It is only in this way that the accumulation of the ten thousand cuts will stop and be given a chance to heal. Paying attention in each moment frees the mind and the heart to learn to become equanimous in each and every thought, word or deed.

CHAPTER 4

The Categories of Practice

Analyzing Life Activities

A Householder's Vinaya, in practice, begins by consciously analyzing the things we do and how we do them, then points us in skillful ways to do practical things that help rewire the *citta*. By experimenting with both successes and failures, we intuitively learn what is skillful, what isn't, and how to become wise and compassionate in the moment.

When we break down our life into categories that delineate both our mental and physical activities, we give ourselves the chance to take a first step back from automatically repeating the same thought, speech, or action from the same states of previous reactivity. Instead, we use ourselves as an objective tool of investigation, which gives our attention something to actively investigate and then potentially act upon.

Having an overview of our mental activities without being caught by the story or the situation gives the mind permission to look at what we think, what we say, and what we do with less identification, less clinging, less reactivity. With a decreased level of identification there is automatically less reliance on habit in moments of arising, acting, and reflection. An examination in our daily life of our patterns and habits, activities and urges, as if we are taking data from our lab of everyday life, is the first step on the path of disidentification. In the moments that

we observe what's going on internally and externally with non-identi-
fication, we are not reconditioning our old habits and patterns; we are
instead deconditioning old habits and patterns while conditioning new
and wholesome habits and patterns.

Introduction to the 15 Categories and the Chart

A Householder's Vinaya breaks our life's activities down into 15 categories. These categories take into account the combination of genetics,
personalities and societal patterns of habits that arise as a consequence
of being a human being in lay life.

The householding life has a momentum that often trumps wholesome or creative intentions. We get too busy, or the roles we play and
the busyness itself become the pattern that trains us to unconsciously
become our assumptions of ourselves — who we think we are and what
it is we need to do to live our lives. These types of patterns become a
burden. The mind begins to lean into each moment not with attention
to the moment at hand, but rather with the sense that whatever we are
doing must always get done as quickly and done as efficiently as possible.
A constant inner striving.

However, there is a middle ground. Yes, we are busy, and yes, we
act as if we are our jobs or roles a good part of our lives. But there are
ways to make these roles and ways of life our practice. *Below*, I offer a
chart that summarizes what it is like to live a householder's life, to be a
householder practicing with *A Householder's Vinaya*, and to do a home
retreat. Each section of the chart gives the reader a simplified render-
ing of the discussions in the following chapters and hopefully an easily
accessible go-to cheat sheet.

The intention and hope that engendered these efforts was due to
my personal practice struggles at home between retreats. I found all too
often 'going with the flow' and adapting to the societal norms was easier
than trying to maintain a retreat-like attitude. Because I had nothing to

support me or guide me between retreats, retreats became ever more important in order to maintain and deepen my baseline of meditative wisdom in everyday life.

Now, with this effort, there is the potential that every aspect of a lay person's everyday life can be examined and practiced through the meditative lenses of *sampajañña* and *sati* without having to drop everything and go again to the monastery. I've discovered using this system that a natural metamorphosis takes place. Instead of being mindlessly busy or having to stop my everyday life in order to mimic a retreat in my home, I realized that practicing according to a householder's *Vinaya* utilizing the 15 categories is like . . . but different from . . . being on retreat while naturally and seamlessly moving my intention, investigation, and effort to new heights. As a consequence, I could observe a marked improvement in my spontaneous virtue and an exponential leap in my being able to observe preferences of mind, habits, and patterns while being able to do something about them! These practices in everyday life have provided me with a practice that if not applied, I now know, will lead to the old habits and patterns becoming the norm yet again.

As powerful as this practice can be, it promises for most of us a way to discover and integrate the practical aspects of our retreat-realized wisdom. In no way am I suggesting that this practice should be used instead of retreat unless there are no other choices. Instead, I see it as a tool to be used between retreats or by those who can't attend retreats, and as an everyday template to how we live our lives.

The Chart

STYLES AND INTENSITY OF PRACTICE

The chart presents each of the 15 categories that delineate both mental and physical activities under three styles and intensities of practice:

1. Common Morality: What normal good-hearted people aspire to.
2. *Householder's Vinaya*: For those of us wanting to make *A Householder's Vinaya* our home practice.

3. Home Retreat: When the practice of *sati-sampajañña* is ramped up for short intensive periods of time.

With each practice, I present highlights of how to practice that category depending on one's intention and circumstance. I suggest you use this chart for quick reference and as a reminder throughout your day, week, and life.

GROUPING OF CATEGORIES

The categories themselves are split into four sections that mimic and take inspiration from the principles of *dana, sīla, and bhāvanā*:

1. The Preliminary Group:

This group parallels the *Dana* group. These practices are called out because they are not emphasized formally in the texts and, in my opinion, are not explored with much detail in the *Vinaya Piṭaka* or the Noble Eightfold Path and are therefore not taught as often. The category included in this group is:

- Generosity
- Cooperation
- Patience

I see the conscious practices of generosity, cooperation, and patience as threads that in large part stitch and then hold together the concentration factors of the Noble Eightfold Path: Right Effort, Right Mindfulness, and Right Concentration. Generosity is the underlayment of cooperation and patience. Cooperation and patience are expressions of generosity, and generosity at its most elemental is the heart and mind's tendency towards non-self. When these mental factors are mature and balanced, the mind naturally becomes open, joyous, and calm. It takes an open, calm, happy, and non-reactive mind for wisdom to arise. As in everyday life and in similar ways, it may also be said for being a good parent, co-worker, or friend.

For instance, exploring how we give, when we give, and what constitutes giving will open a rich field of practice. Ask yourself: *"Why do I
give this?" "Who is this really for?"* Depending on the motivation and
the intention, the action will have different observable effects on the body
and mind. It is okay if the motivation is a bit confused. When we practice
generosity time and again, even though our wisdom is not perfect, the
expression of generosity instructs and galvanizes by degree our intention
towards freedom. The entire nature of meditation and *A Householder's
Vinaya* is to incline, train, and practice better understanding and greater
compassion in our everyday experience and our everyday trials.

Practicing generosity with *sampajañña* is a triple win. No matter
what, when these practices are applied, they will provide a framed and
easily observed experience of before, during, and after. Applying generosity through the filter of *sampajañña* allows you to investigate a rudi-
mentary form of non-self, which is not only fun, but has the potential to
bring wholesome joy to all involved.

Cooperation and patience are two additional fingers in the open
hand of generosity. Both have at their base a willingness to be present
for self and others with as much available wisdom and compassion as
can be mustered in real time. Patience, the quality of *citta* that can listen
and reflect, gives cooperation its ability to move beyond working with
others for personal gain to something greater, toward work as a currency
in the marketplace of cooperation. It serves both self and others. These
qualities of *citta* are further discussed in more detail in Chapter 5.

2. The Virtue Group

This group parallels the *Sīla* Group. It is rooted in virtue and volitional types of speech and action as detailed in the Five Precepts and the
Noble Eightfold Path. The categories included in this group are:

- Harmlessness
- Materiality
- Sexuality

- Speech
- Intoxication

3. The Preferences Group

This group parallels the *Bhāvanā* group. It encompasses the grey areas of lay life not explored in depth in the classical teachings and addresses the constant reconditioning that occurs on a continuous basis if *sati-sampajañña* is not active in the mind stream. This group describes most of a householder's life. Subtle yet ever-present, and arguably the most frequently overlooked part of our lives and therefore the most important for creating continuity of *sati-sampajañña*. The categories included in this group are:

- Meals, eating
- Livelihood
- Family, friends, community
- Activities of daily living (ADLs), maintenance
- Style preferences
- Entertainment
- Creativity

This group challenges us to examine our preferences, our unexamined mental patterns and blind habits that constantly confront us while navigating everyday life. In order to develop a meditative continuity in a lay life, we must give the space where habit and preference take hold much more wise and careful attention than we normally give it. It is here that many of the rules of the *Vinaya Piṭaka* governing what could be considered less important activities of daily life, such as a rule relating to needle cases, oblige monastics to stay alert in subtle yet very active ways. As householders, we can use these rules as encouragements for our lives and practices, understanding that they invite us to pay continuous attention, help to fill in the blanks of inattention with attention, and lead to the perfection of our mental development.

Most sincere spiritually-oriented people don't have frequent thoughts of murder or larceny. However, ask yourself how often you choose one shirt or pair of pants over another or experience long periods of internal planning on subjects like what you want to eat for dinner, what you will do with your leisure time, or what you hope your bonus at work will be this year? A casual inspection will show you that you spend much more time with small, seemingly inconsequential choices and patterns of mind throughout the day than with big decisions or over-whelming mental unwholesomeness. We spend more time conditioning our minds and hearts with ten thousand small cuts than we do with large ones. It is precisely here that *A Householder's Vinaya* expands the prac-tice and its promise to make householding practice horizon-wide for the lay practitioner.

4. The Tool Box group:

Like a tool box, this group provides a structured practice that ties all of the previous categories of the chart into a system and encourages the practice of keeping the cleaning and the use of our tools continuous in wholesome and in directed ways. The categories included in this group are:

- Choosing a spiritual tradition
- Practice, study, ceremony

Without a tool box or continuous attention to our tools, their upkeep, and their organization, our tools will be all over the place and often in a poor or broken condition. A disorganized, unclean set of tools will often rust and get misplaced, making it difficult to find and use the tools in skillful ways. Despite all our best intentions, without a structure there is a much higher likelihood that without a tested and proven practice offer-ing guidance and accountability, the tendency of the ignorant mind is to get caught in the blind habits of grasping the pleasant and rejecting the unpleasant, in effect a mental attitude that scatters and misuses our tools.

Finding the right practice and then creating a daily structure to help remind and support us in achieving our goals is more important than most individualistic-minded folks may want to hear. Taking a practice and sticking to it is not about giving up our individual rights and privileges. It is, rather, an opportunity to explore our assumptions about ourselves and what we think are our rights, to see ourselves in new ways, which helps us practice heartfelt compassion for ourselves and others.

QUICK STORY:

Towards the beginning of my exploration of meditation, I was one of those who might have been described as 'individualistic.' Never one for taking orders or doing what I was told, I was proud of my unique ability to see things differently. Some years into the practice I began to notice on retreat how much time I spent on inner discussions arguing with myself about notions regarding practice: how to practice, whether or not the practice was right, whether or not I was making progress, etc. In a moment of epiphany, I acknowledged how many of these patterns were simply habits and patterns of mind and how much time I was wasting. That day I made a vow to listen to my teacher and do what the teacher instructed, which I've kept to this day. I acknowledged to myself with an inner sly grin that I would do it while on retreat and *then* examine and consider later, a compromise that has held me in good stead for years. The joke, of course, is on me. Over the years I've discovered that allowing the practice to mature while on retreat instead of thinking and arguing with myself provided a mental framework and a freedom that made thinking and arguing with myself after retreat unnecessary.

A commitment to a practice and a qualified teacher based in accountable trust are two of the plaits necessary for this type of braided freedom to be available. *Below* I describe in more detail the reasons why these two categories are included in the list, and tips on how to utilize them when explored.

COMMON MORALITY	HOUSEHOLDER'S *VINAYA:* HOME PRACTICE	HOUSEHOLDER'S *VINAYA:* HOME RETREAT
The Preliminary Group		
1. Generosity, cooperation, patience: Act within social and legal conventions. Try to cultivate generosity, cooperation, and patience with all beings.	Act within social and legal conventions. Try to cultivate generosity, cooperation, and patience with all beings. Using this guide, consciously apply these qualities in a few interactions throughout your day.	Act within social and legal conventions. Try to cultivate generosity, cooperation, and patience with all beings. Using the guide, consciously apply these qualities in as many interactions throughout your day as possible. Remember to include yourself.
The Virtue Group		
2. Harmlessness: Act within social and legal conventions. Try to cultivate kindness and compassion for all beings.	Act within social and legal conventions. Try to cultivate kindness and compassion for all beings. Practice the *Brahma-vihāras* [divine abodes] as part of your daily meditation practice. Reflect before, during, and after any speech or action and apply *sampajañña*.	Act within social and legal conventions. Try to cultivate kindness and compassion for all beings. Practice the *Brahma-vihāras* as part of your daily meditation practice. Reflect before, during, and after any speech or action and apply *sampajañña*. Cultivate sense restraint and sit as often as possible.
3. Materiality: Act within social and legal conventions. Exercise wise restraint regarding use of money. Practice generosity and take care of personal possessions. Marshal resources for the benefit of self, family, friends, and the community. Examine your livelihood from both a personal and social perspective.	Act within social and legal conventions. Exercise wise restraint regarding use of money. Practice generosity and take care of personal possessions. Marshal resources for the benefit of self, family, friends, and the community. Examine your livelihood from both a personal and social perspective. Do not take what is not given whether it involves an object or a service. Examine your livelihood from both a personal and social perspective, and if possible make your livelihood congruent with your spiritual life.	Act within social and legal conventions. Exercise wise restraint regarding use of money. Practice generosity and take care of personal possessions. Marshal resources for the benefit of self, family, friends, and the community. Examine your livelihood from both a personal and social perspective. Do not take what is not given whether it involves an object or a service. Be meticulous about this. Examine your livelihood from both a personal and social perspective, and if possible make your livelihood congruent with your spiritual life. Exercise restraint in all uses of money while on retreat. Restrain your senses when appropriate. Simplify. While on retreat limit your workload and bring your practice in as many ways as possible to your workday.

COMMON MORALITY	HOUSEHOLDER'S *VINAYA*: HOME PRACTICE	HOUSEHOLDER'S *VINAYA*: HOME RETREAT
4. Sexuality: Act within social and legal conventions. Pay kind attention to the needs of your partner.	Act within social and legal conventions. Pay kind attention to the needs of your partner. Explore celibacy and restraint. When engaging in sexual activity bring mindfulness to the entire experience.	If possible practice celibacy, otherwise follow the home practice instructions.
5. Speech: Speak, read, watch, etc. within accepted social conventions. Try to be kind and truthful.	4th Precept: *I undertake the rule of training not to gossip, use false, harsh, or injurious speech and to maintain Noble Silence when alone.* Apply as often as possible the Five Keys to Right Speech. Practice *sampajañña* as often as possible. Use entertainment wisely.	Practice Noble Silence as much as possible. 4th Precept: *I undertake the rule of training not to gossip, use false, harsh, or injurious speech and to maintain Noble Silence when alone.* Apply as often as possible the Five Keys to Right Speech. Practice *sampajañña* as often as possible. Limit or exclude all types of reading, listening, or watching entertainments.
6. Intoxication: Act within social and legal conventions. Abstain from intoxicants. If abstention is not an available choice, observe the intention to imbibe, smoke or use, and observe the planning, the doing, and the effects of intoxication on the mind and body during and after. Examine the effects of intoxication on those around you.	Abstain from all external and internal intoxicants.	Abstain from external and internal intoxicants.

COMMON MORALITY	HOUSEHOLDER'S *VINAYA*: HOME PRACTICE	HOUSEHOLDER'S *VINAYA*: HOME RETREAT
The Preferences Group		
7. Meals, eating: Eat whenever, no restrictions. Eat regularly and healthily.	Eat regularly and eat healthily, lightly in the evening, or, if convention calls for a meal with others, use the opportunity to be filled with care for the food and the social interactions. Eat slowly and mindfully when appropriate. Apply *sati* and *sampajañña* to preparing, consuming, and cleaning up. Explore undertaking the 6th Precept: *I undertake the training not to eat after the midday meal.* Chant before the meal.	Eat regularly and eat healthily, lightly in the evening, or, if convention calls for a meal with others, use the opportunity to be filled with care for the food and the social interactions. Eat slowly and mindfully when appropriate. Apply *sati* and *sampajañña* to preparing, consuming, and cleaning up. Explore undertaking the 6th Precept: *I undertake the training not to eat after the midday meal.* Chant before the meal.
8. Livelihood: Choose a livelihood that does no harm to individuals, to the wider community or to the planet as a whole. Examine your livelihood from both a personal and social perspective.	Choose a livelihood that does no harm to individuals, to the wider community or to the planet as a whole. Examine your livelihood from both a personal and social perspective and if possible make your livelihood congruent with your spiritual life. As frequently as possible apply the many techniques described in this guide to your daily life. Become an alchemist and change your daily life into your daily practice. Make your practice as much a part of your livelihood as is your work. Do formal meditation as regularly as possible. Bring your practice in as many ways as possible to your workday.	Choose a livelihood that does no harm to individuals, to the wider community or to the planet as a whole. Examine your livelihood from both a personal and social perspective and if possible make your livelihood congruent with your spiritual life. As frequently as possible apply the many techniques described in this guide to your daily life. Become an alchemist and change your daily life into your daily practice. Make your practice as much a part of your livelihood as is your work. Do formal meditation as regularly as possible. When not working, frequently partake in home retreats. While on retreat limit your workload and bring your practice in as many ways as possible to your workday.

COMMON MORALITY	HOUSEHOLDER'S *VINAYA*: HOME PRACTICE	HOUSEHOLDER'S *VINAYA*: HOME RETREAT
9. Family, friends, community: Participate fully with as much *mettā* [loving kindness] as possible. Fulfill your responsibilities.	Participate fully with as much *mettā* as possible. Fulfill your responsibilities with as much attention to the activity as possible. Try to avoid mindless patterns. Volunteer advice, money, and time to others.	Participate fully with as much *mettā* as possible. Fulfill your responsibilities with as much attention to the activity as possible. Try to avoid mindless patterns. Volunteer advice, money, and time to others. Try to limit, but not exclude, the amount of interaction with others as much as possible. Invite your family and friends to support you while on retreat. Give them the chance to limit contact. Attend to anyone who might be hurt by your absence.
10. ADLs, maintenance: Live your life within your understanding of moral speech and action. Try to cultivate and demonstrate kindness and generosity in all situations. Try to live simply.	Live your life within your understanding of moral speech and action. Try to cultivate and demonstrate kindness and generosity in all situations. Try to live simply. Slow down all physical actions and bring *sampajañña* into the word or action. Maintain a regular formal meditation practice.	Live your life within your understanding of moral speech and action. Try to cultivate and demonstrate kindness and generosity in all situations. Try to live simply. Slow down all physical actions and bring *sampajañña* into the word or action. Increase your formal meditation practice. Reduce or eliminate all unnecessary activities until the retreat is over.

COMMON MORALITY	HOUSEHOLDER'S *VINAYA*: HOME PRACTICE	HOUSEHOLDER'S *VINAYA*: HOME RETREAT
The Preferences Group (continued)		
11. Style and preferences: Live as moral convention teaches you. Try not to allow personal preferences to harm others. Try to live simply.	Live as moral convention teaches you. Try not to allow personal preferences to harm others. Try to live simply. Reduce consumption, try to live with restraint and simplicity. Bring attention to the arising of preferences and to acting on them. Pause before acting, observe while acting, observe afterward. Simply notice. If judgment arises, notice judgment. Try to act skillfully for self and others. Apply *sampajañña* as often as possible when a choice arises.	Live as moral convention teaches you. Try not to allow personal preferences to harm others. Try to live simply. Reduce all types of consumption. Exercise restraint of all sense doors when safe and appropriate. Formally sit as frequently as possible and watch the process before, during and after a sit. Bring attention to the arising of preferences and to acting on them. Pause before acting, observe while acting, observe afterward. Simply notice. If judgment arises, notice judgment. Try to act skillfully for self and others. Apply *sampajañña* as often as possible when a choice arises. Avoid any shopping other than for groceries or necessary items for the maintenance of your life and property. Bring strong attention whenever eating or drinking. Eat or drink in moderation. Notice your speech and posture while engaging with others. Be mindful of all activities and give pause, when possible, before, during and after all speech and action. Take note of the most common default tones of voice and postures when with others.

COMMON MORALITY	HOUSEHOLDER'S VINAYA: HOME PRACTICE	HOUSEHOLDER'S VINAYA: HOME RETREAT
12. Entertainment: Allow what you want, when you want it: TV, radio, movies, newspapers, magazines, fiction and (non-Dhamma) nonfiction, unlimited internet or phone, etc. Engage within the societal standard with an eye towards health and moderation.	Exercise restraint and wise reflection when making entertainment choices. Try to use entertainment to support wholesome patterns in the mind. Practically speaking: limit exposure to radio, podcasts, TV or streaming to one hour a day, limit non-Dhamma reading. Attempt to study or do formal meditation instead of consuming entertainment. Explore reasons for entertainment choices with an eye on boredom or discomfort. Make distraction and boredom objects of examination. Limit obsessive screen checking.	No reading, radio, TV, or listening to non-Dhamma related recorded material. Very careful attention to all choices. Cultivate a continuous mental posture towards restraint of the senses.
13. Creativity: Try to cultivate and share the fruits of your creativity with others.		Intentionally train intention towards using creativity to serve others. Observe the feeling tones of creativity and the reactivity that comes with its highs and lows. Bring *sati-sampajañña* to the experience in both the body and mind when 'ah-ha' moments arise and action is required. Observe the creative mind with *sati*.
The Tool Box Group		
14. Choosing a spiritual practice tradition: Recognize your mentors and show respect to and support them as you can.	Recognize your mentors and show respect to and support them a bit more than you feel comfortable. Stay with your chosen practice through high and low. Don't flit about. Watch doubt and try not to judge your practice when doubt is in the mind.	Choose your chief mentors and show respect to and support them a bit more than you feel comfortable. Listen and follow their instructions even if your conscious mind is arguing. Stay with your chosen practice and go to your edge. Don't flit about. Watch doubt and try not to judge your practice or your abilities when doubt is in the mind.

COMMON MORALITY	HOUSEHOLDER'S VINAYA: HOME PRACTICE	HOUSEHOLDER'S VINAYA: HOME RETREAT
The Tool Box Group (continued)		
15. Practice, study, ceremony: Keep to your pattern with the intention to do the right thing.	Live normally and train the *citta* to filter your life through *sati-sampajañña* as much as possible. Incline the mind towards formal practice and make time for it. Use your ADLs as objects of *sati* or *sampajañña* as often as possible. Keep an eye out for micro-moments of bare attention. Cultivate them by briefly pausing and acknowledging them. Make space for their quick comings and goings. Study meditation by reading or listening to Dhamma talks. Take the investigation beneath the surface. Attend *saṅgha* gatherings. Offer teachings if qualified and circumstances allow. Chant the Precepts or offer·your formal meditation for the benefit of all beings before or after your formal sittings.	Train the *citta* to filter all activities through *sati-sampajañña* as much as skillfully possible. Sit at your scheduled times for formal practice. Use your ADLs as objects of *sati-sampajañña* as often as possible. Read *The Home Retreat Guide* and, as much as you can, follow the instructions. Attend *saṅgha* gatherings when available and appropriate. Add a meditative ritual such as chanting before meals or before or after a meditation session, take the Precepts daily.

PART TWO

The Vinaya

CHAPTER 5

Generosity, Cooperation, Patience

THE FIRST CATEGORY OF PRACTICE of *A Householder's Vinaya* is generosity, cooperation, and patience. They play active roles throughout our spiritual and normal everyday lives, and all three are excellent foundational practices on which to rest the entire enlightenment project.

This first category of practice could be described as societal or even evolutionary. These qualities were as necessary to our ancestors' survival as hunter-gatherers and later as agrarians, as they are to us today, mostly industrialized and post-industrialized city dwellers. They must be present in sufficient depth for people to work together, live together and effectively address outside threats together.

Without generosity, cooperation and patience, we cannot flourish as individuals either. As a consequence, here we begin our intentional attention towards the cultivation of the *citta*. Being kind, generous, clean, good citizens, and being present for others whether we like them or not, is not only what moves a society towards wholesomeness, it moves the individual as well towards establishing an attitude of compassion for self and others. What we invest in our community supports us on the personal level, while it also serves others.

Throughout the practice toward enlightenment, the process is about service to and for all beings everywhere. To cultivate this practice, we apply common sense and *sampajañña* again and again. We give, volunteer, show up for others, with an eye always to our intention, attachments, and judgments.

Generosity

Generosity can be described as the place where we see the first glimmer of the freedom of non-attachment. In any generous thought, word, or deed there is an element of offering what we can for the greater good, often at some — even small — risk or sacrifice to ourselves. It is a glimpse into what the state of one's heart and mind might be like when one acts without any sense of the fear of personal loss and without the action referring back to a notion of self.

These types of acts, this type of practice, serve us throughout our everyday lives and throughout our spiritual journeys. Act on your generosity. Give time, give money, allow risk to arise in the heart, and be present for your intention, action, and results. Giving without regard to consequences is child's play. Be aware and cultivate a generous heart.

A parable: The king decided to offer a banquet for his family, friends and advisors with the intention to conduct an experiment. He separated the people into two rooms and gave each room exactly the same food, dishes, cutlery, music, and entertainment, along with chopsticks that were too long to use skillfully from bowl to mouth.

The night of the banquet the king sequestered himself from both rooms and instead observed. He found and took delight in the differences between the groups. In the first room the guests were complaining and making a mess of themselves, each other, the food and the settings of the table trying as they might to use the chopsticks as they would normally. They argued, complained, and shouted at each other when food dropped, which only served to increase their frustration and unhappiness. In the second room there was only laughter and singing and the murmur of contentment. "How can there be such a difference?" the king asked himself. What he observed was quite simple and delightful. In the second room, instead of trying to feed themselves with the oversized chopsticks, they were feeding each other!

Bill Gates has been the richest man in the world and continues to be among the top few. Some years ago, he and his wife Melinda decided to start offering philanthropic donations to a variety of causes with the intention of giving away the vast majority of their wealth before and after they died. They discovered that their money was a powerful force to make positive changes for women globally and make a significant impact on the health of entire populations in some of the poorer regions of the world. Their contributions and involvement in both areas, among many others, have had a direct and tremendous impact on the health and welfare of millions of people all over the globe.

As a consequence of discovering the joys of giving they began to recruit others into the practice. As part of their learning curve they established the Giving Pledge, which is a pledge each individual makes to give away their fortune. To date, 204 of the wealthiest people in the world have signed. These rich one-percenters are not obliged or legally bound to give the money to any specific cause, or for that matter, to follow through; but even so, the seed has been sown. Warren Buffet, another of the world's richest men, got on board and is actively giving away quite a lot of his money. I think he summed it up well when he said, "Someone is sitting in the shade today because someone else planted a tree long ago."

Our own practices of generosity and selfless wise giving have the same effects. The more we give of ourselves with wisdom and compassion, the more others will benefit, and the more we are given the chance to explore and live with selflessness as part of our intention.

Giving back involves a certain amount of giving up.
                                                        – Colin Powell

The power of generosity affects us all. Colin Powell, Warren Buffett, and Bill and Melinda Gates are all householders, and each in their own way has found the way to this sacred and ever so valuable practice.

Because generosity is about a practice of the heart, it isn't only or always about just reaching into your pocket. Giving of oneself comes in different forms. What follows is a story about a different type of generosity that may feel closer to home. Not all of us are rich, and in any event, we may choose to give not just with money.

Venerable Maha Ghosandanda was one of the few Cambodian monks who survived the Pol Pot genocide. With his country torn apart and with every single person of that country having experienced incredible loss and suffering, Maha Ghosandanda was pressed into a leadership role. It was not entirely because of his wisdom, but because he was a surviving monk of a country that had a rich 1500-year history of monastic Buddhist practice. The people looked to him for leadership and hoped that in some way he might offer a beginning to the healing in the aftermath of the horrors they had just collectively survived.

In this story, the first time Maha Ghosananda was brought to a Cambodian refugee camp in Thailand, he saw the people gathered in awkward silence before him, not in little measure, simply because he was the first Cambodian monk any of them had seen in years. Pol Pot had murdered the great majority of monastics. Instead of speaking and lecturing, Maha Ghosananda chose to just chant the *Karaniya Mettā Sutta*: The Buddha's Words on Lovingkindness (Sn 1.8), which teaches us to open our hearts not only to our loved ones, but to our enemies as well. The assembly wept openly with what appeared to be both the sorrow of loss and the joy of the beginning of forgiveness.

For some years after, even during the subsequent Vietnamese invasion and inevitable civil war, Maha Ghosananda and his followers marched throughout Cambodia bringing the message of *mettā* everwhere, whether the bullets flew or not. Venerable Maha Ghosananda walked through Cambodia with hundreds of other caring folks chanting the *Mettā Sutta* again and again, putting their lives at risk again and again.

WARNING:

If we form the intention to give something, we need to follow through. If we don't, the conditioning toward and the consequences in the mind are significant. If memory serves, Joseph Goldstein told us in a Dhamma talk that, "If I think of giving something to someone and if I'm in a position to do it, I always give." He had observed thoughts of whether to or when to give, and noticed himself debating with himself on how much to give. He saw he was deciding to give less or not give at all. From then on, he made the commitment that he would always give and opt for the more generous choice.

Cooperation

Cooperation is a component of generosity, which at its most elemental and sublime is an expression of non-self. In order to cooperate we must sometimes lead, sometimes follow, sometimes observe. An element of cooperation is the ability to be wise when we do not have answers, as well as when we seem to have them all. Cooperation is also when we don't confuse being stronger or smarter or more anything than others with being better.

For most of us, the comparing mind is natural when we are with others, but especially when working with others. One extreme of the comparing mind is: "I'm the leader. I know more than they do!" The other extreme is: "I'm not good enough, I don't know enough, I'm not the right one to lead!" The ground between the two may be: "I'm just as smart and as good as them!" These types of mental postures occur until our minds are free from identifying with self. It's fine; it's just another practice. When we compare ourselves with others, we must just notice and ask ourselves: "Is this useful?" and "Is this lasting or not?" and "How much of this is just story?"

Allow yourself to be of service to another or to the group with as much wisdom as you possess, and keep an eye on your comparing mind. Identifying too strongly with comparisons compromises our ability to cooperate with skill and compassion.

Patience

In Buddhism, patience is one of the "perfections" [Pāli: pāramīs] that a bodhisatta [Skt: bodhisattva] trains in and practices to realize perfect enlightenment. The Buddhist concept of patience is distinct from the English definition of the word. In Buddhism, patience refers to not returning harm, rather than merely enduring a difficult situation. It is the ability to control one's emotions even when being criticized or attacked. In verse 184 of the Dhammapada it is said that enduring patience is the highest austerity.

— Acharya Buddharakkhita

Contrary to what some might think, patience is not about waiting or 'grinning and bearing it.' Instead, it is the posture of the heart and mind that with loving firmness allows us to develop a proactive way of meeting difficulty and unpleasantness—as well as pleasantness—with calm, investigation and energy and a proactive attitude of providing wholesomeness to the situation. Patience can be cultivated by examining our mental attitudes when things are or aren't going our way. We tend to experience either anger and resentment or get puffed up when we're taking credit for something, all because we weren't paying attention.

Patience is, as described *above*, the currency of cooperation. It is also a subtle and an oh-so-sweet type of *mettā* and *karunā* [Pāli: compassion]. Patience is like a drop of water in a slow-moving river at a calm sunset, the embrace of a loving grandmother. When universal and unlimited compassion, which is the state of mind wishing that those who suffer be freed from their situation, combines with the action-oriented state of mind of unlimited loving kindness, patience is birthed in its most profound aspects.

What is going on in the *citta* when you have to wait an additional 45 minutes at the dentist's office, or when stuck in a traffic jam, or when you hear your partner tell the same story for the hundredth time?

Let's say another person is talking and you have heard it all before. If you remain interested in your reactions and not interested in what the other person is saying—their stories and complaints— then you will have something interesting to do while the person drones on. No matter what the situation, in this way you'll always learn a lot as you listen.

— U Tejaniya

Countless times in a day we can check in to see what's happening when patience is called for. We can also check in during our formal meditation practices. How often in meditation are we meditating to get or get rid of some mental state? How often are we meditating just to do it?

It is precisely here, in these moments, when a deep breath, a giggle, and a mental image of the river at sunset might be useful. Moments when patience is not present are the perfect opportunities to try to cultivate . . . patience.

Patience cultivated is a sublime form of generosity to self and the world. Generosity is like a dance with a brilliant and willing partner. Almost always there is an embrace of giving and receiving. For a dance to be beautiful and to flow, having patience and cooperation makes the dancers' movements just like the music that inspires the dance.

CHAPTER 6

Harmlessness

THE NEXT ASPECT OF A HOUSEHOLDER'S VINAYA is the practice of harmlessness [Pāli: *avihiṃsā*]. The practice of harmlessness is entwined in everything we do. Therefore, it must be defined and carefully examined from an overall perspective.

> *After reflecting again and again, actions by deed, word and*
> *thought should be done . . . Before doing such actions by deed*
> *word and thought, while doing and after doing them, one should*
> *reflect thus: "Does this action lead to the harm [or benefit] of*
> *myself, to the harm [or benefit] of others, to the harm [or benefit]*
> *of both?" After reflecting again and again one should purify one's*
> *actions by deed word and thought. Thus, O Rāhula, should you*
> *train yourself.*
>
> – *Ambalaṭṭhikārāhulovāda Sutta:*
> Advice to Rāhula at Ambalaṭṭhikā (MN 61)

Harmlessness is the performance of any thought, speech or action that leads to the ultimate reduction in suffering for self, others, or both. The practice and cultivation of harmlessness includes everything from bringing wholesome attention to one's thoughts in order to not fall prey to unseen habits that harm self and others, all the way to abstaining from perpetrating any type of physical injury or killing. For the purposes of this guide, harmlessness thus is the practice of engaged compassionate wisdom, the practice and cultivation of *sati-sampajañña*. It is not passive or submissive, but is a dynamic, engaged way to approach life where the intention is to always be in the courageous service of wise and compassionate action.

For harmlessness to mature and become of service to self and others, patience, generosity, cooperation, kindness, and wise restraint must develop as skillful means and become second nature. We ought also to be aware that, as descendants of nomadic hunter-gatherers, we have a number of compelling impulses that can lead to harm, which necessitates special care and forgiveness when examined against our ideals.

'Harmlessness' means different things in different contexts, depending on one's wisdom. Giving in to the demands of a whining child can have a mixed, not entirely harmless, result: It brings relief and quiet to parent and child in the moment, but also teaches attachment to both parent and child, which results in suffering for both. What 'harmlessness' is in this context needs to be examined and practiced within the context of developing healthy family and social ties, and through the lens of our deepest current spiritual understanding.

The same applies to social action and political engagement. Not considering the potential consequences of social or political action can result in harm despite one's best intentions. How often have we seen the best and most noble notions go awry due to ignorance? One of my favorite examples is President Johnson's War on Poverty and the New Frontier in the 1960's. With noble intentions, the federal government built tens of thousands of new modern housing units for the poor, which, due to architectural flaws and social engineering failures, created ghettos never before seen on this continent. Consequences that are still being felt four generations later.

The concept of harmlessness becomes even more complex and even paradoxical when considered in the world we currently live in, the global economy of the 21st Century. We live in a time when activities as simple as buying a pair of shoes, or driving to work, or buying a banana affect others in what can be minute and often harmful, yet powerful ways. This *vinaya* does not intend to propose or promise answers to questions like whether to buy organic bananas or fair-trade shoes; neither does it suggest or encourage you to ride a bicycle to work. It does offer you a way to examine how and why you make these decisions and then use the training to give birth new ways of doing things. Example: I garden . . . a fairly big and complex garden where I need to pay careful attention to things like the compost pile, aphids, squirrels, wind, arid conditions, etc. Each of these conditions puts me in direct conflict with the needs of other species and with the elements. I turn the compost, and worms and grubs get disturbed and killed; the raised beds are often treated by birds and squirrels as if they were a drive-in restaurant; I face the question of watering in an arid climate that has finite resources. Each conflict can have a variety of solutions, each at my current level of understanding. My plans to solve the particular conflict involve an inner process of reactivity and wisdom playing out. Over the years of practice, I've noticed that, although the process is not perfect, the reactivity has decreased, allowing for more willingness to allow outcomes that I wouldn't have thought possible. The reactivity to it being 'my' garden has subsided to a degree that the garden has become more of a place than a thing that belongs to me.

Careful attention is necessary when engaging in any act of body, speech or mind. Check in with your body, check in with your mind to see if there is resistance or a desire for a shortcut. If there is, consider not acting or acting with the firm knowledge that you are doing your best but might be off the mark.

QUESTIONS FOR THE *YOGI:*

- Is this thought, speech, or action serving the overall intention of cultivating harmlessness in this moment and in future circumstances?
- Does what I did, am doing, or intend to do have a clear purpose towards that end?
- What skills can I bring to this situation that will help facilitate a skillful and wholesome outcome, in word or deed, for self and other and both?
- Is the intention based on wisdom or is it arising out of self-serving habituated unseen patterns of mind?
- Can I be present with generosity, patience, and forgiveness for myself when I don't measure up to my best understanding at the time?

CHAPTER 7

Materiality

Understanding Our Relationships with Materiality

*Rūpa is not matter as in the metaphysical substance of materialism.
Instead it means both materiality and sensibility—signifying, for
example, a tactile object both insofar as that object is made of
matter and that the object can be tactically sensed [that which can
be cognized through the 5 material sense doors; seeing, hearing,
smelling, tasting, and physical sensations]. In fact, rūpa is more
essentially defined by its amenability to being sensed than its being
matter: just like everything else it is defined in terms of its function;
what it does [in the mind], not what it is. As matter, rūpa is
traditionally analysed in two ways: as four primary elements
[Pāli: mahābhūta: earth, wind, water, fire]; and, as ten or
twenty-four secondary or derived elements.*

— Lusthaus, p. 183.

'Materiality' in the context of *A Householder's Vinaya* and our everyday world denotes our relationship with the physical world, including
how we treat our bodies, our possessions, the possessions of others, our
livelihoods, the needs of our family, community, nation, planet, and
other species, etc. The second Precept teaches us to not take what is not
freely given, only to take what is freely given. This simple Precept is the

most common contemporary understanding of how one is to relate with materiality. Whether on home retreat or living a daily life of practicing *A Householder's Vinaya*, a wholesome understanding of materiality can start with and become rooted in the Precept of taking only that which is freely given.

But isn't it much more complicated than that? Doesn't our basic existence play havoc with clear and simple notions of what is and what is not freely given?

The complexity of many of the situations a householder navigates will force a wide range of choice and interpretation regarding the simple notion of only taking what is freely given. What are the wholesome and skillful responsibilities we have to our bodies, our possessions, the possessions of others, our livelihoods, the needs of our family, community, nation, planet, and other species? To begin this inquiry, it will be helpful to notice that these relationships present a never-ending learning curve, and a simple 'one size fits all' may not be in the cards.

When engaging with complex situations, such as buying something or financial exchanges, it becomes useful to slow down. Affluence and freedom of choice put us in the cross hairs of buying and accumulating semi-valuable or semi-useful or downright useless objects and doing activities just for stimulation to avoid boredom or gain status.

QUESTIONS FOR THE *YOGI:*

When preparing to acquire material possessions or engage in activities, ask yourself:

- Do I really need this?
- Is this necessary for my health, safety, and wholesome contentment?
- Will my accumulating of this deprive others of necessities?
- What motivates this desire?
- Do I need 10 pairs of shoes, 15 of this, or 20 of that?

- Is having so much stuff "taking what is freely given?"
- Is accumulating things a skillful practice and wholesome way to live when our minds and the atmosphere of the planet are getting polluted as a consequence? Is accumulation the best way to train the mind away from clinging?

The goal behind asking these types of questions is not to create guilt or shame. If we want to practice on our meditative journey, these questions must be asked consciously and examined carefully throughout the day. The practice of *sati-sampajañña*, from a grand perspective, is a wonderful way of establishing a relationship to all material objects through a filter that challenges what may be seen as normal for everyone else.

Maturing a wholesome relationship with the various forms of materiality can be assisted with two reflections:

1. Can I develop a relationship with materiality that fosters restraint, generosity, and patience?
2. How much of this intention to act am I genetically engineered to experience?

If we constantly abuse ourselves with criticism and judgment, especially when our minds are genetically engineered to react in a particular way, our minds will react and rebel. On the other hand, if we allow mindlessness to be our highest bar for the development of our meditation practice, we are training the mind to be lazy, greedy, and inattentive.

Like all other species, as humans we have unconscious hardwired motivations that help us survive. The types of motivations that support our survival tend to blind us to the nature and consequences of our actions. Examples of actions grounded in these types of motivations include having sex to reproduce, finding and eating food, sleeping, ensuring our safety, etc. All of these activities were evolutionary answers for questions facing the survival of hunter gathers on the savanna in Africa, not for us today as post-industrial citizens of the world. We still have many of the same survival motivations as our ancestors, but the environments in which we live—both physical and cultural—are different. And so, when we eat that extra piece of pizza or want our partners to pleasure us in ways they don't want to perform, we can have a cascade of inner and subjective self-judgment that conditions us in countless ways when we are obliged to do other things in our lives. We condition ourselves to doubt and judge ourselves.

The practice of mindfulness teaches us techniques that allow us to watch desires as they arise and to decide how we choose to respond to them. The practice then teaches us to use exactly the same tools to observe how the intention, the act, and how the results affect our near- and long-term conditioning. Mindfulness untangles this cocoon of a universe and lets us take a step back to observe with an interested, non-judgmental point of view. This perspective frees the mind in the moment and trains the mind to be free in other moments as well.

Dependent Origination and Non-Self

The Buddha's instructions are clear, simple, and effective: Practice *sati-sampajañña*, and this meditative training will decondition the mind from old habits toward greater wisdom, compassion and lasting happiness. He gave us two notions to explain how these trainings work, detailing the underlying conditions that give *sati-sampajañña* the power to completely decondition the unwholesome parts of the mind. Both of these notions are subtle, and for many can be confusing and counterintuitive at best, hard to see, and off-putting at their most severe. Their subtlety and potential for confusion is probably why these most basic tenets of Buddhist philosophy and practice are not often taught or emphasized to lay people. Because of their subtlety and their counter-intuitive qualities, they beg a bit of textual elaboration.

> *The Dhamma I [the Buddha] have attained is profound, hard to see*
> *and hard to understand, peaceful and sublime, unattainable*
> *by mere reasoning, subtle, to be experienced by the wise. But this*

generation delights in attachment, takes delight in attachment,
rejoices in attachment. It is hard for such a generation to see this
truth, namely specific conditionality, dependent origination.

And it is hard to see this truth, namely, the stilling of all
formations, the relinquishing of all acquisitions, the destruction
of craving, dispassion, Nibbāna. If I were to teach the Dhamma,
others would not understand me.

– Ariyapariyesana Sutta: The Noble Search (MN 26:19)

With *sati-sapajañña* we see how to realize these truths directly for ourselves, not as notions or intellectual constructions, but in ways that intuitively affect our relationship with the world. When experienced and known, they become second nature. When we do not realize dependent origination and *anattā* through the realization of *nibbāna*, our minds cling to the notions of having a soul or an abiding self, which become the default filters of our lives. This default position of mind creates a sense that whatever we are has a quality of materiality. This in turn directly affects how we think, speak, and act.

DEPENDENT ORIGINATION

The first notion, dependent origination, I addressed in some detail in Chapter 3. I discussed how ignorance affects the mind when pleasant-ness, unpleasantness, or neither unpleasant nor pleasant is present; how that ignorance leads the mind, due to inclination and blind habit, towards habituated reactive patterns in thought, speech and action. As subtle as this process is, it can be observed, directly experienced, and intuitively known fairly early in practice.

NON-SELF/ANATTĀ

The second notion—non-self—is more subtle, more difficult to intuitively experience and grasp; yet it is central to the foundation of the under-standing and the effects of the Buddha's teachings. *Anattā* is the unique notion in Buddhist philosophy that teaches us there is no abiding self, soul, ego, or even a theistically styled god moving the thought, speech, and actions that happen as a consequence of us being alive and in a body. This way of experiencing our existence addresses the question of reality and unsatisfactoriness at the most basic neurological level, and simultaneously the deepest ontological level. *Anattā* is directly addressed in the first three truths of the Four Noble Truths:

- The reality of unsatisfactoriness
- The cause of unsatisfactoriness
- The promise that there is an end to unsatisfactoriness

Yes, most religious traditions — and most people — nowadays will say that the self or soul is not material, but the mind has no option but to conceptualize the self or soul as having some type of materiality, because the nature of our conditioned thinking makes the notion of a soul or self material in the mind. Even if the self or soul is given amorphic qualities, it is what the mind does to the notion that is important to understand. The notion of 'my soul' or 'me' refers back to something that is a de facto entity in the mind and gives the notion a form. When the mind takes any object as a 'thing,' it automatically creates a relationship to it as being something separate.

"So what?" you may be asking. Well, in fact, these mental processes are a very big deal. Seeing the world from the perspective of having a soul or being a 'me' steers the mind towards grasping onto notions such as 'my soul,' 'this is me,' 'this is mine,' etc. Being an entity automatically obliges the mind to experience our inner world as one that separates everything into 'I' and 'thou.' This, in turn, forces the mind then to think of itself and the outer world as distinct, unique, special and separate. If 'thou' is separate from 'I', then both are material in concept and both have a relationship to each other materially. This forces us to behave in thought, speech and actions rooted in those perspectives. Again, materiality.

In the discussion of dependent origination in Chapter 3, I discussed how pleasant and unpleasant and neutral experiences, when unobserved, cascade into sequences of thought processes that have significant consequences for each other. For example, pleasant sensations lead to liking, wanting, then clinging.

The Buddha intuitively experienced that if pleasantness arises and is noticed with a non-self-referencing, nonjudgmental and non-manipulative mind, the experience of pleasantness simply arises and passes. This easy to see and understandable meditative experience directly affects how we begin to see the world. However, the truly subtle part is what doesn't exist underneath the processes of the mind. Under any object of consciousness, the pleasantness that co-arises, and the consciousness of knowing these objects and processes is . . . *no-thing*! There is no Wizard of Oz, no soul, or no self pulling the strings. It is just process. The intuitive experience of 'nothing underneath' again and again allows the mind to find ways to experience reality without attachment or the need to create the notion of the soul. The mind loses the need to create what isn't there in order to feel comfortable with how the mind and the world function.

We live in illusion and the appearance of things. There is a reality.
We are that reality. When you understand this, you see that you are
nothing, and being nothing, you are everything. That is all.

— Kalu Rinpoche

Consciously being with the object and the feeling tone of pleasantness, for example, allows the mind to begin deconditioning, and as consequence the mind frees itself and, with the heart, is able to be present for what is. Being present without an 'I' integrates that realization into our thoughts, speech, and actions without trying. In other words, when there is no 'I' there is less or no attachment to anything material. Another great Buddhist aphorism:

No self, no problem.
— Anonymous

A Householder's Vinaya seeks to point the practitioner in the direction of finding out whether one embraces and is actively applying these practices throughout the day. For me, there is so much in meditation that reminds me of how we biologically and psychologically mature as humans. A child in the sandbox doesn't know the joys of later stages in life, nor do they care; an adolescent doesn't know or really care that they are in the throes of a maturing process; an adult does not perceive what is happening in our maturing towards death, to name just a few of many developmental changes that happen to us whether or not we know it or even like it.

It is the same with meditation. Whether or not we understand or embrace the notions that form the conceptual foundations of practice — dependent origination and non-self — they are still manifest, and when we are doing the practice our understanding of them matures along with the development of our meditative wisdom. If we find wholesome usefulness in the practice of *sati-sampajañña*, the practice itself is training the mind to be progressively less attached, with the probable outcome that there will arise a nonconceptual understanding that there is nothing to attach or cling to.

Livelihood

One of the Path factors of the Noble Eightfold Path is Right Livelihood. The importance of this applies to monastic and laity alike. The principle of Right Livelihood instructs us in no uncertain terms to make sure we do not commit our adult life to the active and direct suffering of self, others or both.

Note: Although our relationship with livelihood constitutes a type of materiality, it is its own factor in the Noble Eightfold Path and therefore examined in greater detail in Chapter 12.

As noted *above*, when monastics take vows they embrace a livelihood, and, because of the particular nature of this livelihood, it steers all
who embrace it towards wholesome speech and action either by social
convention or by spiritual realization or both. For the monastic, many of
the ambiguities of the householder's lifestyle are removed, which makes
it all the more relevant to us as householders that we examine and try to
make our livelihood choices very carefully should we wish to mold our
lives in ways that support our spiritual goals.

As lay people, work affects who we are. For most of us livelihood
occupies more time than any other single activity in our adult lives and
deserves very careful examination should we want a clear and complete
picture of what we do to ourselves. To better understand and predict
what comes next, what the consequences might be for this action or non-
action, we need to be clear and honest with ourselves about what it is we
give ourselves permission to do and what that does to condition our ways
in the world. Here it is helpful to remind ourselves that until we attain
full enlightenment, we are practicing and assessing everything with limited wisdom. So it is that we are always in a grey area when exploring or
doing anything. In the grey area of livelihood, *A Householder's Vinaya*
invites each of us to look carefully at what we do, how we do it, with
whom we do it, and why we do it. To support our enlightenment project,
it is vital that we assess our livelihoods to make sure what we do is congruent with who we want to be.

The *suttas* give us some direction to what Right Livelihood means.
The teachings tell us a few basic things flat out, like that becoming
a monastic constitutes Right Livelihood and that butchering is not
Right Livelihood. Other examples of wrong livelihood in the *suttas*
include selling slaves, poisons, intoxicants, or weapons or making a
living through butchery and animal husbandry. There are places in the
suttas where the Buddha admonishes the rich and the royal to care for
their employees, slaves, and subjects by building hospitals, being fair
in taxation, planting trees, giving time off, and being generally kind
and generous. And, throughout the teachings we are reminded over

and over again that how we train our minds, the environments we allow our minds to dwell in and be conditioned by, and how often we do something with or without *sati-samajañña* will all have a lasting impact on our ability to see clearly, and therefore act with wisdom and compassion.

However, in order to suss out the nuances and determine the broad stroke of what Right Livelihood means for the laity, we must braid together a number of inferred strands to make the rope of Right Livelihood. Having a perfectly suitable livelihood in this day and age is often a grey area. The economies of Northern India 2,500 years ago were simpler and much more delineated than those of today. They didn't have multinational corporations that manufacture both life-saving chemotherapy drugs and poisons that slowly kill millions of beings daily, or sell goods and services that appeal only to whetting appetites and inflaming more desire.

Right Livelihood is not just about what type of livelihood one does, it is also about the environment of your work situation. Two tines of the same fork: the work and the environment. For monastics, *the Vinaya Piṭaka*, among many other things, is about establishing and maintaining concord in the *saṅgha*. Without concord, cooperation, and social routines, practice will be challenged. The same can be said for our work situations.

QUESTIONS FOR THE *YOGI:*

As a householder, imagine, or reflect on your work situation:

- If you work with people who are unkind, uncooperative, and vengeful, how does that affect you there and then later at home?
- What happens to your productivity and the conditioning of your *citta*?

Once we examine our livelihoods from a *vinaya* perspective, we can choose to make do with the situation we have or work towards changing the situation in small or large degrees. Changing a work situation does not necessarily mean changing jobs or finding a new career; it starts by examining the situation and bringing the best tools we have to make whatever situation we are in more wholesome.

Perhaps you discover your livelihood is wrong livelihood, and you have the opportunity and willingness to change it. If this is the case, I suggest you carefully consider working towards that end with small, conscious and graduated practices. Making the choice to change a job or career can take time. Be patient. Making the choice and working towards the change is the first step in drawing together this part of your practice.

In my twenties, I was living an unwholesome life. It was easy to assess and to see how it affected my relationship to myself, how I saw and treated others, and how it affected my meditation at home and when I went on retreat. I chose to change my profession and never regretted the effort, the adventure, and the fruits of the changes I made. It took me almost six years from the time I decided to do something about my situation until I passed my exams and got my license to practice nursing. Six years was a long time. During those six years an underused set of skills and *pāramīs* were slowly maturing and supporting momentum towards wholesome results in personality, livelihood, and meditation practice. If some magical deity had come down and waved a wand and all of the sudden I was a registered nurse, I would not have had the wisdom or patience to do the work with the character, skill and patience necessary. The process helped me develop many practical skills, the same skills that furthered my meditation practice later on.

Please carefully examine your livelihood *and* your attitude toward what you're doing as a livelihood. Use your wisdom to become proactive in support of your home practice. Every moment is important in the deconditioning of a lifetime of habit.

CHAPTER 8

Sexuality

SEXUALITY IS CONFUSING, complicated, and often compelling for almost every human. In certain ways this particular aspect of being human, being a mammal, is intensely wrapped up in our genetics and is therefore more primitive and compelling than any other drive, after we have reasonably secured the basics of food, hydration, and safety. All sentient beings who procreate are hard-wired to try to get their seed or egg into the gene pool regardless of sexual orientation. As a consequence, many of our urges and behaviors are genetically engineered to compete with others to achieve this goal. Even those of us whose sexual orientation means we are not competing quite at this level compete with each other in order to be chosen and so behave in much the same way. Get the seed out or in, be chosen, win. The consequences for the vast majority of humans, in real time, are influenced by strong hormonal drives that often make no seeming logical or lasting self-benefiting sense. When we are not attentive to these drives, they often oblige us to move into areas where unwholesome thoughts, speech, and actions have the potential to arise without conscious invitation.

Our cultural and societal conditioning—both nature and nurture—affect our attitudes, thoughts and behaviors surrounding sexuality almost as much as our genetics. We all carry many of our parents' attitudes either lock, stock and barrel, or we have conflicts with those attitudes in both conscious and unconscious ways. Because our engagement with those attitudes often results in extremely deep-rooted patterns and habits, they offer us rich and often very complicated objects to explore both with *sati* and with *sampajañña*.

One's relationship to sexuality in the context of home practice and home retreat has many facets. It is helpful to decide if you are on home retreat or doing home practice before you set your intentions in this arena.

Home Practice

When doing home practice, *A Householder's Vinaya* is pretty simple:

- Watch your impulses.
- If sexual thoughts or sensations arise, notice them.
- If indulging in fantasy, notice as quickly as possible and bring bare attention to the process.
- Observe how you use language with your sexual partner(s) when sexual thoughts or feelings are present.
- Notice if objectification arises. Movies, TV, advertising, magazines, music, and other visual and auditory stimuli are often designed to stimulate latent sexual appetite or keep obsessive sexual appetites whetted.
- Notice what objectification does to your mind stream and capacity for empathy.
- Watch this process as often as possible.

QUESTIONS FOR THE *YOGI:*

When doing home practice and normally engaging in the sexual arena as a partner or as a candidate, watch your intentions, your actions and the aftermath and ask yourself:

- Is this motivation for the benefit of self, for the other, for both?
- Can I provide my body, my seed or egg, for the benefit of both?

- Can I maintain attention to the process and allow pleasantness and intimacy to arise?
- Do emotions such as loyalty, shame, anger, love, seem to arise over and over again? Can I observe these emotions without attachment or rejection?
- Is it possible to engage in courting and sex for nonprocreative reasons in ways that serve self, the other, and both?

Bring as much attention as possible to the whole process while trying to cultivate a skill set that will serve, in as wholesome a way as possible, the cultivation of intimacy and relative love.

For those of you who are really curious, watch with mindfulness the entire process of the sexual act. Bring careful attention to how the mind and body become stimulated with desire, notice the automatic and planned strategies that come to mind to get what you want, the movements of both you and your partner's bodies, the touching and being touched. Notice the momentum of urge, notice the beginning of one's cascade towards orgasm, see if you can pay attention with mindfulness throughout the dance and into the release afterwards. Warning: If you choose to examine your sexual experience in this way, you may discover that it isn't the same as when normally just engaging to pleasure yourself or your partner.

Home Retreat Practice

Monastics take a vow of celibacy and make this particular vow, which is one of only five that, if broken, will lead to automatic expulsion from the monastic *sangha* for the remainder of this lifetime. I suspect this emphasis comes a bit from historically-influenced cultural contexts between men and women; for example, in the *suttas* and *Bhikkhuni Pātimokkha* women are implicitly identified as needing protection from men's uncontrollable behaviors. I suspect it also arises from the wisdom that came from knowing that any active indulgence in sex while living as a monastic will distract in ways that overwhelm one's ability to practice meditation with continuity. Not just the act of sexual interaction, but the whole process: the fantasy, the planning, the engagement, the aftermath.

Sexual activities are not isolated incidents. They have a beginning, a middle, and often an indeterminate ending as shown by, for example, jealousy of one or the other partner or a third party, or by pregnancy or increased desire. Sex almost always involves complication and emotions that are counterproductive to the cultivation of balanced concentration and development of meditative wisdom. Indulging in sex as a monastic will also create divisions with one's colleagues due to comparing and jealousy.

The intensity and importance monastics give to celibacy is a useful pointer for us when doing a home retreat. I suggest being celibate, but if not, following any relevant practices detailed *above* when doing a home retreat.

CHAPTER 9

Speech

No OTHER SEEMINGLY NORMAL and inconsequential activity in our daily lives has greater influence on what can lead to wholesome or unwholesome conditioning than speaking. Every human activity, be it an action, a thought, or speech, leads to wholesome or unwholesome activity depending on a wide variety of factors, the most important of which is the intention and understanding with which it is performed. However, because speech is so quickly and so often used throughout our day, it leads to more conditioning than any other physical behavior.

We use speech to find our place in the group, which defines our ability to get food, shelter, and a mate. In other words, speech in many ways defines our ability to survive and thrive, and is therefore a very obvious object for attention, and at the same time, incredibly subtle.

The answers to the questions of what we say, how we say it, and why we say it are each a symptom and a cause: A symptom of the underlying mental state, and a cause of both internal and external consequences. If not attended to carefully, speech will limit our capacity to deepen our meditative growth.

Exploring how often and why we speak can be a rich and demanding field of practice. Because we speak so often and speech has such profound linking consequences to action and further thought, the repeated application of *sampajañña* as often as possible when we choose to speak gives us the chance for close examination of the process before, during, and after.

Guidance from the Texts

I find the texts of the Pāli Canon are both the most forgiving and the most demanding guides on how to practice the training of Right Speech in everyday life because of their simplicity and clarity.

And what is right speech? Abstaining from lying, from divisive speech, from abusive speech, and from idle chatter: This is called right speech.
   – Magga-vibhanga Sutta: An Analysis of the Path (SN 45.8)

Speak only the speech that neither torments self nor does harm to others. That speech is truly well spoken.
                         – Subhasita Sutta: Well-Spoken (Sn 3.3)

FIVE KEYS TO RIGHT SPEECH

[A] statement endowed with five factors is well-spoken, not ill-spoken. It is blameless and unfaulted by knowledgeable people. Which five?
   It is spoken at the right time. It is spoken in truth. It is spoken affectionately. It is spoken beneficially. It is spoken with a mind of goodwill.
                         – Vaca Sutta: A Statement (AN 5.198)

Applying the Texts in Everyday Life

The training rules and keys to Right Speech [Pāli: *sammā-vaca*] set forth in the Pāli Canon offer all humans, under all conditions, a context for how to try to use speech skillfully. What they don't address is how speech, when not attended to, often leads to reconditioning of unwholesome mental patterns. Unwholesome speech is not just about lying, slander, and abusive or idle chatter. It's also about how unseen patterns and blind habits condition the mind.

Probably since the beginning of language, most folks, most of the time, have used speech for survival. But when it's not being used in that way, it has served to reinforce notions of self-referencing or for entertainment or for the avoidance of boredom. For pleasure. It only takes a short examination to realize that, like training in non-harming, most of our speech is not as often about the BIG transgressions but has more to do with the ten thousand cuts. Each unobserved unwholesome thought or speech acts like ten thousand small cuts would to its victim. Whether it is one big cut or ten thousand small ones, *A Householder's Vinaya* is a tool to avoid both. A continuous attention to *sati* and *sampajañña* in our daily lives makes each time we speak an opportunity to not only avoid the unwholesome, but instead, develop the wholesome.

QUESTIONS FOR THE *YOGI:*

I suggest you watch your speech for a day without trying to limit what you say or restrict your behavior:

- How often do you speak simply out of the desire for pleasant sensations?
- How often do you make sounds to distract yourself from uncomfortable mental or physical experiences?
- Is what you have to say beneficial and wholesome to yourself, others, or both? Check this out as often as possible.

We frequently speak with limited wisdom, and the result is often a mixed bag. Simply be aware and notice. Acknowledge the mixture of service and self-service and carry on. The attention itself will slowly begin to affect your willingness to speak and the ways in which you choose to speak. Careful attention to intention, action, and results is what we practice in all aspects of *A Householder's Vinaya*. With speech, more can be seen and worked with more creatively than in most of the other categories.

Gossip and Idle Chatter

The texts are emphatic and clear. Gossip and idle chatter are not Right Speech, and yet . . .

As a householder I've examined Right Speech from both the context of everyday life and on retreat. On retreat it has become absolutely clear that limiting speech to almost silence is beneficial to the continuity of one's concentration. And, on retreat, if one is obliged to speak, it is important to speak only that which must be spoken in order to learn *Dhamma* or to attend to the immediate needs of the body and the environment.

However, in everyday life householders use language simultaneously on many levels. In fact, when gossiping and engaging in idle chatter, a householder is also giving and receiving information about who they are talking to, what role that person plays in the community, and whether or not that person can be trusted, among a myriad of otherwise not easily seen pieces of information. These are all vital pieces of information in a householder's community, and types of information that a monastic following the *Vinaya* does not have to confront.

And, yes, mixed in the normal flow of chatter are all the challenges detailed *above*. And, yes, both perspectives are useful when examining Right Speech. It is a big practice, and there must be room for both perspectives in order to have balance in our social interactions. Gossip and idle chatter áre often part of the fabric of community. The more wholesome the speech, the more wholesome the community.

Retreat Practice

Because speech is so complex and subtle and potentially distracting, it is common and seen as very useful to take a vow of Noble Silence while on retreat. Noble Silence is not just the restraint of speaking, it also includes refraining from unnecessary reading, unnecessary writing, and even unnecessary wandering of the eye and use of the body to communicate messages or to distract oneself. Silence on retreat means restraining the senses with as much external concept and engagement as possible. This includes gesturing to others or involving yourself in passive communication such as offering gifts, wearing attention-seeking clothing or making eye contact.

Silence supports meditative concentration on multiple levels. Everyday speaking or communicating stimulates the proliferation of distracting thought. By remaining silent, we reduce that stimulation so that fewer distracting thoughts arise and we are less likely to take action based on them. It stops us from planning to speak or the inevitable reflection that comes after speaking. Speech almost always reinforces self-referencing. To support our meditation with as little self-referencing as possible, it is best to remain silent for the prescribed committed time period.

If we don't engage in extra reading, writing, glancing around, and outright speech, there will be more opportunity to develop a stronger and deeper continuity of *sati* because we are giving the mind the opportunity to develop focus with fewer interruptions. Each time we willfully pick up a book, write something, or glance around, we are supporting a willfulness that is often rooted in unobserved boredom, aversion, or restlessness. By staying focused, we are offered the chance to watch why and how it is we make so many choices to distract ourselves. Having more opportunity to be with the causes for distraction allows us to become more familiar with the process and to learn to be less reactive.

Chanting

Between silence and talking is another category of speech: chanting. Many traditions and many people use chanting as part of their spiritual practices. Chanting offers those who chant the opportunity to develop and cultivate the wholesome intention that underlies the chant. In this tradition, the intention could be any number of wholesome intentions including:

- Paying homage to the Buddha
- Taking refuge in the Buddha, *Dhamma*, *Saṅgha*
- Taking the Five or Eight Precepts
- Chanting the *Karaniya Mettā Sutta* or other *suttas*
- Saying the *Pāramīs* silently to oneself or out loud

Chanting also teaches and strengthens a number of mental factors depending on the quality of the mind with which one does the chanting. Chanting done by rote with little reflection or little attention is little better than a wandering mind, but a mind imbued with the meaning of the reflection with an eye to the quality of the supporting mental states can both inspire and deepen both *sati* and *sampajañña*.

CHAPTER 10

Intoxication and Clouding the Mind

Using Intoxicants

USING INTOXICANTS CLOUDS THE MIND, which often leads to varying degrees of heedlessness in thought, speech and action, and therefore increases the potential to harm self and others.

On another level, when we give ourselves permission to have just one glass of wine, there are many subtleties to consider. By thinking the thought, by engaging in the intention, by exercising willfulness to treat ourselves in this particular way, we are reinforcing a variety of mental factors that support identification with self and thus cloud the mind to non-self. Each time we identify with the choices we make, whether wholesome or unwholesome, pleasant or unpleasant, we reinforce identification with the notion that we are in control, that our thoughts are who we are, that we know what's best for ourselves.

Intoxication, like any willful behavior, plays an important role in whether we maintain continuity towards a non-self-referencing attention or not. Compared to, say, accumulation of material stuff, intoxication adds an additional layer of clouding. This is not a value judgement — far be it from me to say or have a value judgment about activities that I engaged in heavily for many years.

Many of us, due to character or station in life, choose to intoxicate ourselves with substances or activities. A few of the most common, of course, are drugs and alcohol. But there are also those pleasant attachments to opinions that give us the rush of self-righteousness, or the reaching for the smartphone at every moment of boredom, or just letting our minds wander to places of pleasant daydreaming and fantasizing, just to name a few of the ways we intoxicate ourselves. We can also intoxicate ourselves with sex, exercise, and risky behaviors, just to name a few more.

SUGGESTIONS FOR PRACTICE:

Intoxication for many is not just a meditative question; it is about health and general well-being. If this is the case for you, pay attention!

- Pay attention to the thought that stimulates the event that results in intoxication.
- Pay attention to the preparation for the event.
- Pay attention to the action.
- Pay attention to its consequences during the event, the immediate aftermath, and the following day.
- Assess as best you can.
- Ameliorate the activity as much as possible if you can't stop the behavior.
- Take vows for temporary abstinence and examine the results.
- Do retreats.
- Should this behavior be interfering with your life on the most basic levels such as your relationships, your work, or your health, seek treatment as soon as possible.

Wherever and whenever we intoxicate the mind or body, we should try to attend to the desire, intention, process, and consequences. For those types of intoxication in which we can choose whether or not to engage, we should incline the mind towards the beginning of the sequence, check to see if a feeling tone of pleasant, unpleasant or neither is present, and then apply the reflective powers of *sampajañña*. The wholesome qualities of the observing mind will effect a change in our relationship to the activity. Repeated attention will bring wisdom.

Recreational Drugs

My suggestion regarding the use of recreational drugs? Be very careful and try to understand your motivations for doing them.

PSYCHEDELICS AND MDMA (ECSTASY)

Many people use psychedelics as part of their spiritual path. A variety of spiritual traditions have long and honorable histories of using psychedelics as vehicles towards spiritual wisdom. A few things seem common to most people and schools who use psychedelics skillfully:

- They use psychedelics with strong wholesome intentions to build and deepen spiritual practice.
- People taking the drugs are mentored in safe environments in sessions led by skilled and compassionate teachers and guides.

For many years, I would use the occasional psychedelic for spiritual reasons. But after years of not using them, I know that, overall, I used them more to prove things to myself and to be part of the group than to open doors to deep insights. Although there is no question in my mind that having done psychedelics as a practice did lead the way to deep benefits, not until I had a fairly mature *vipassanā* practice was I able to get a more wholesome result.

TIP AND CAUTION

The Fifth Precept tells us that it is unwholesome and unskillful to consume any substances that alter the consciousness, which psychedelics clearly do. However, should you choose to use them:

- Apply *sati-sampajañña* as often as the mind will permit and ask yourself afterwards whether the experience served the cultivation of wisdom and compassion for self and others.
- Establish a safe and mentored environment where the experience is about learning and not just going for a ride.
- Should the spiritual school in which you choose to practice espouse the notion that the drug experience is all that is necessary to find the way to freedom from suffering, run the other way. No matter the practice, our engagement with our everyday lives matures our insights.

CANNABIS

Nowadays, a large number of people are using cannabis for medical reasons: pain, sleep disorders, glaucoma, nausea, etc. Another razor's edge. If you are using cannabis for medical reasons or recreational reasons, question why you are using it and ask yourself if there is a treatment that is an alternative to getting high. I suggest you try to find alternative treatments or, if possible, use cannabis delivery methods without the THC. The THC in cannabis clouds the mind and undermines the continuity of wholesome mental development. Again, no judgment.

OTHER RECREATIONAL DRUGS

All need attention, and all need to be viewed as potentially very dangerous to health and the conditioning of the mind.

Alcohol

In most First World or industrially developed societies, the use and abuse of alcohol play a significant role both socially and emotionally. In less developed societies, the use and abuse of alcohol also play a role, but often due to cultural and historical conditions the society relegates its use more to abuse rather than as a vaunted and respected part of the social fabric.

Drinking alcohol is so accessible in the cultures that accept it, and yet it has consequences that are real both in short- and long-term use. The way most modern societies currently embrace alcohol use is very much like how they embrace the consumption of food. For many of us, alcohol — almost like food — has come to be a currency for bonding, celebrating, and acceptable self-medicating. Just as we use food, most people use alcohol within the boundaries of what is socially acceptable and even encouraged. And again, like food, this way of looking at alcohol can be dangerous for a meditative practice and our health. For example, despite an obesity epidemic in the United States, many folks continue to eat and overindulge with very little attention to the quality of the food they eat or the consequences the overindulgence has on their health or the environment. Contemporary society appears to increasingly accept obesity as the norm. It isn't. Just like the obesity epidemic, alcohol consumption is having an often unacknowledged and collectively-denied impact on our health.

The people we socialize or work with can have enormous effects on what we give ourselves permission to eat and drink, as can the entertainment media with movies, ads, and any number of implicit invitations to use alcohol. Often, adults drink alcohol and do not notice the effect of their alcohol consumption on their behavior with family, friends, and work. As an extreme example, alcohol has a special place in the culture of many college fraternities, which affects what people associated with them allow themselves to choose to do.

Some may say the examples *above* point to extremes, but do they? Is obesity an extreme or the norm? Is alcohol use, despite its clear effect on consciousness, an acceptable norm or is it seen with a clear eye for what it is and its consequences?

One cannot drink alcohol without it affecting consciousness. This is established in the habit pattern that permits the choice, the process of getting the alcohol, and the imbibing, not to mention its very real effects. The habit of blindly choosing to use alcohol supports the same mental patterns that inhibit our ability to decondition the mind towards greater meditative wisdom. The use of alcohol, even in small amounts, affects our consciousness in complex ways that can loosen our tongues and affect our physical abilities to do simple everyday tasks such as driving or using our bodies. Plain and simple: *Alcohol is a very dangerous drug and should be seen as such.*

Being offered a drink—a glass of wine, or a beer—is often a chance to pay attention. Should you choose to have that glass of wine with dinner or the beer with friends while watching the game, be aware of what you are doing. Examine the entire process and assess the effects against your intention to realize your enlightenment project. Restraint and more importantly abstinence in the consumption of alcohol supports wholesome intention and can provide the mind a brief clear field of focus when alcohol is socially offered.

Both the casual use of alcohol and the chronic abuse of it have their effects. I suggest, if possible, that you abstain. Should you be self-medicating with alcohol for anxiety, depression, boredom, or the inability to break the habit, I suggest you take a careful look and get help.

QUESTIONS FOR THE *YOGI:*

With alcohol use, ask yourself:

- Is this what I want to do with my time, my life?
- Do I really ever examine this activity with a clear and non-attached perspective?
- Is my behavior affecting others in ways that I just don't or won't own?
- Are there activities that I see as more beneficial to self and others that this use of alcohol makes difficult or impossible?

If you frequently use alcohol with others ask yourself:

- Are these the people who inspire me or keep me in place?
- Are these friends I would have if I wasn't drinking?

Caffeine

Sorry . . . caffeine is also a drug that affects all who use it. All too many of us use caffeine like we do food and alcohol. We simply see it as part of who we are, part of being human, and deny that its use and abuse could be a problem in our lives or on a meditative journey. Caffeine can make us unable to sit still and to speak without restraint. Caffeine can affect our ability to concentrate, making us distracted and restless during meditation.

I remember a teacher telling me the story of a *yogi* who was on the cusp of her first enlightenment experience, but it just wouldn't happen. Day after day her practice seemed to have stalled for no logical reason. With just a little investigation the teacher discovered that she was having an extra cup of coffee with breakfast. When she restrained her desire and stopped taking the second cup she quickly realized her first enlightenment experience.

Many of the instructions and questions offered for use of intoxicants *above* can also be applied to the use of caffeine:

- Watch the thought.
- Watch the desire.
- Watch the intention.
- Watch what happens during the period of use.
- Watch the after effects.

QUESTIONS FOR THE *YOGI:*

- Is this necessary?
- For what reason am I doing it?
- What result am I reaping?
- Can I experiment with refraining from using it, and if not, with moderation and judicious use?

It isn't just about the drug, alcohol, food or caffeine. It's also about our intentions and willful identification and manipulation of our consciousness that is being affected by indulging or over indulging in these socially acceptable forms of intoxication.

Prescription Medications

Mind-altering medically prescribed medications are a grey area. Many medications that are necessary for life or health maintenance can affect the mind stream. Some of these drugs are critical for health, and regardless of the effect they may have on the mind, need to be taken. In these cases, I suggest the householding *yogi* take the baseline mental environment the drug causes and use *sati-sampajañña* to meet that consciousness where its effect and your skill base meet.

PAIN MEDICATIONS

Drugs that assist in the temporary relief of pain, such as episodes of back pain, strained muscles, and the like, can also cloud the mind and need careful attention. I suggest finding alternative treatments that do not affect the mind, and, unless the situation is extreme, avoid these types of medications.

On the other hand, many people who use mind-altering medications to treat chronic pain can establish a meditative attention. I suggest you find your baseline and bring your *sati* there. It is more difficult, but can be done. If possible, always try to find other less mind-altering treatments that leave the mind clear.

MOOD MEDICATIONS: ACUTE MOOD CHANGE EXPERIENCES

Yet another type of medically prescribed drug falls into the very challenging area of taking meds to affect emotions. Medications prescribed for chronic emotional and mental disorders and distress such as anxiety, fear, depression, etc., are discussed *below*.

Depending on the severity of the symptoms, I suggest vigilant and frequent experimentation as to whether or not you should use them. Clearly, if the mind is overwhelmed, not just annoyed, and you have a medically prescribed medication that will break the cycle of an oppressive emotional pattern and unwholesome reactivity in the mind, take it. At times when the symptoms arise and you can bring attention to the symptoms with *sati-sampajañña,* I suggest you do that.

At the same time, begin a very careful examination of the precursors to the arising of the intense symptoms and bring as much continuous non-reactive investigation as possible to the sequences. Watch carefully with interest and as continuously as possible. And again, if the symptoms overwhelm, take your medication. Incline the mind towards skillful examination. As the drug takes effect, when possible, formally sit and watch the effects of the drug while meditating.

MOOD MEDICATIONS: TREATMENT OF CHRONIC CONDITIONS

Another category of mood medications is those prescribed for chronic conditions such as depression, anxiety, etc. These types of medications can be prescribed whether the underlying cause is physical or emotional. They work only if the drug is and continues to be sufficiently absorbed into the bloodstream in therapeutic levels to work effectively, which usually takes several days to several weeks and must be taken on an ongoing basis in order to maintain the therapeutic levels requiring that they be taken as prescribed.

CAUTION: It is critical to take your medications if your physical or mental health depends on them. You should never stop taking these medications without consulting your medical team. Stopping them without medical advice can have serious consequences.

Instead of stopping these meds, examine your baseline mental environment with the meds, and use that as your starting point for observing. Meditation is always about learning how to meet our realities where they are, not where we think they should be or want them to be.

Consult your physician or therapist before you sign up for a retreat. Make sure the retreat center and your teachers know of your condition, the meds you take and your medical history. It is always best to make an appointment with your medical provider to discuss your unique situation before a retreat or if you want to change how you take your meds. As meditators, we often have high opinions of what the practice can do for us, which may not be wise or well-informed and in reality may be higher than warranted. At times the practice itself might give us confidence that we can do anything, that we can heal ourselves with just meditation or gain full enlightenment and no longer need to take the medication. Don't listen to these voices and don't act without consulting your doctor or therapist.

Sleep Medications

Some sleep disorders are self-inflicted; many are not. Those that are not must be examined, diagnosed and treated. We can also examine, diagnose and treat those that are self-inflicted. A couple of examples of the self-inflicted variety:

1. Throughout her life, my mother thought she had to get 8-9 hours of uninterrupted sleep to qualify as having had a good night's rest. She would obsess in the morning if she hadn't had the prescribed amount of sleep regardless of her physical and mental status. She'd awaken in the night to use the bathroom after 6 hours of sleep and then toss and turn trying to regain her sleep. Unable to fall asleep again, she'd take a pill. And, yes, she'd be groggy and worried the whole next day that she'd have to take another pill in the middle of the night.
2. Similarly, I often find it hard to believe I need only 4-6 hours of sleep at night. As a consequence, often—in fact more times than I'd like to admit—I find that I want to roll over and try and grab a few more minutes of sleep when my mind is perfectly rested and ready for the day.

QUESTIONS FOR THE *YOGI:*

Worrying about sleep is often more stressful than how much sleep you actually get. These examples are an invitation for you to look at your attitudes and projections that surround sleep. Ask yourself:

- Are my expectations and attachment to notions about sleep preventing me from being present for my sleep needs?
- During my day, do real health consequences seem to be caused by insufficient sleep?
- Are there alternatives to sleep medications I could use, such as taking short naps or drinking warm milk before going to bed?

Go on a longish retreat—not less than nine days. See what you learn regarding the use and non-use of these drugs and what your sleep patterns are.

Natural Mood Chemicals

Another group of intoxicants are the ones the body itself produces: endorphins, pheromones, and adrenaline. The highs that result from their release are part and parcel of many activities throughout our day, not just in intense moments when the hormones are pumping strong. Throughout our days, we can see their presence when we flirt, reach for our phones, or when we're stressed by a deadline or other external pressure. Bringing *sati-sampajañña* into the mix as we experience both mild and intense forms of these highs during our day is a rich practice.

ATHLETICS

If you are an 'extreme' athlete, such as being a runner, rock climber, skate boarder, martial artist, etc., consider practicing a skillful approach to those activities in the context of *A Householder's Vinaya.* You may not wish to give up the highs you get from physically challenging yourself.

I suggest watching the high and the type of attachment that might also be present when the high is pumping, or watching at low energy times during your day when you yearn for the rush. Really watch, not just play with sidelong glances at the processes. Examine what and why you do what you do, what the feeling tones are, what catalyzes the intention, the effort, the rush.

I was a runner for many years and found the high was as important as the need to balance my testosterone and stay strong and healthy. I had a metabolism and character that needed to get physical to help balance and serve the other areas of my life. So I ran and paid very careful attention while I ran to the sensations in the body and the effects of the hormones on my body and mind. And I found that while on retreat I didn't need— or for that matter want—to exercise hardly at all. There are ways in which we can observe, structure, and experiment with our habits.

Sexuality, blind habit, and compulsive behaviors also stimulate the release of these hormones and chemicals in the mind and body. As described in Chapter 8 regarding sexuality, attending to the beginning of the thought and to the physical processes and staying attuned throughout and afterwards is the best way to become familiar with them. Becoming aware and familiar with them allows for the amelioration of the habitual reactivity for them to kick in, while also allowing more freedom of choice and more opportunity to act with skill and compassion.

TALKING

Whether or not you have developed the skill to identify when endorphins, pheromones, or adrenaline are present or absent in the mind stream, using speech as a 'canary in the coal mine' is a good practice to see if any of these highs are at play when choosing to speak and when choosing tone and posture when speaking. Examine your intentions to speak, the feeling tones in the body and mind when you speak, and see if you can notice any letdown or changes in the quality of the mental flow after you stop speaking. Using this practice will give you another field to deepen your awareness of the power and effect they have on behavior. Just watch as you would with any object. Watching heightens your continuity of the practice, strengthens purpose and plasticity of the mind, and could give you the opportunity to experience an 'about to' moment to enable you to make a conscious choice in the next moment.

CHAPTER 11

Food

History and Biology

FOR MOST OF THE MIDDLE AND UPPER CLASSES in industrial societies, widespread hunger has been almost unknown since World War II. So many of us take food and eating for granted. In reality, having regular, varied and nutritious food has been only true for a very brief period of history.

Members of lower classes and earlier societies have always been at risk of experiencing famine due to war or drought, of vulnerabilities to situations such as extreme poverty, disability, unprotected young and old, or being incarcerated or enslaved. Historically, homo sapiens as hunter-gatherers would spend most — if not all — of their time securing, preparing, storing food and water and the seeking of and building of shelters. Members of agrarian societies had very limited diets and, like their prehistoric ancestors, could be affected by drought, plagues, and societal upheavals almost unknown to most people in post-World War II affluent societies.

Like all species, we are genetically engineered to fear starvation and death, which makes food and water pretty darn important. We are still physically and mentally engineered in exactly the same way as our prehistoric relatives. As a consequence, our relationship to our food and water—if we get it, what it tastes like, when and with whom we eat, and how to procure it—still takes up much of our time, which directly or indirectly affects how we relate to our preferences for and identifications with various areas of our lives.

A casual examination of the activities that surround gathering, storing, preparing and eating highlights the importance and effect on our consciousness:

- We frequently have the desire for food.
- We eat frequently.
- We need to procure and prepare our food.
- We often use food as a currency in our relationships and our celebrations. A Wednesday family dinner is a much different setting than Thanksgiving or a Bar Mitzvah. The cost, presentation, and the choices of the food are often used to designate a special occasion, status, and much more often, love and care of friends and relatives.
- Our homes are designed in large part to accommodate food preparation, storage and clean up after consumption.
- Nowadays many of us equate good, tasty and attractive food with living well and having fun.

All this is in addition to our biology, which puts food and water at the very top of our hierarchy of needs once relative safety is thought to be assured.

When we boil down all of civilization and all our preferences, the human body and mind are engineered to seek out safety, hydration and food. In other words, food and hydration and our relationships to them, whether or not we recognize it, are places where basic and fundamental conditioning and preferences are molded in significant and powerful ways.

Food and our relationships to it are complicated and more of a continuous influencing factor in our conditioning than a casual glance might indicate right off the bat. It's helpful to keep in mind that any activity needed in order to live is also entwined—with very strong roots—with unseen areas of our consciousness, creating a field of conditioning that is both necessary and potentially a sea of ignorance that creates unfathomable depths of greed and aversion.

So what's the big deal? Precisely because food and its presence in our lives touch on so many levels of our needs and behavior, our relationship with these needs is critical to our conditioning. We need to take a look at some of the conditioning factors a little more closely.

A STORY THAT QUIETLY AND SWEETLY ILLUSTRATES SOME OF THESE POINTS COMES TO MIND:

Years ago, I practiced in a monastery in northern Burma, near Mandalay. In Burma, an extremely devout *Theravāda* Buddhist country, it's the custom for individuals, families and even whole villages to offer food to monasteries for the main meal of the day. The custom includes the benefactors' names being put on a chalkboard at the entrance of the dining room, and they are commonly invited to stand at a special place at the side of the dining room to watch the monks, nuns, and lay residents eat their food in silence. Normally at this well-heeled monastery the food was good, nutritious and plentiful. But one morning the meal was sparse: noodles, rice and some unknown type of stringy vegetable. My mind started down the path of unwholesomeness with thoughts like, "What the heck? . . . How am I going to deal with the hunger? . . . What's going on here?" With an angry and petulant eye, I glanced at the honored place for the merit [Pāli: *puñña*] givers. It was a humbling sight: There stood a group of ragged but radiantly happy villagers who were obviously very poor. It is believed in Burmese-style Buddhist practice that more difficult gift-giving, coupled with offering to those who are enlightened or practicing towards enlightenment, produces the most merit. The competing attitude and motivations in my mind settled into very careful attention to eating mindfully.

Monastic Practice

The amount of attention the *Vinaya Piṭaka* gives to food and its consumption points to how well the ancients understood the importance food has on our conditioning. The *Vinaya Piṭaka* is interested in providing a healthy relationship to food and our bodies beyond what the food tastes like, what the food is or isn't, or choices about when and with whom we share it.

Many rules in the *Pātimokkha* examine this aspect of being human. For example, rules dictate when a monk or nun can eat, how they are permitted to procure the food and how to share it, along with other rules that might appear to the contemporary lay person as petty.

For most *Theravāda* monks and nuns, as well as lay people on retreat or staying in a monastery, food is offered once or twice a day, generally at or around dawn and again at 11 a.m., but in any event before solar noon. You are allowed to eat as much or little as you wish and instructed to eat silently and, of course, mindfully.

Food and Eating as Practice for Laypeople

To survive we must eat. That's a big deal and one of the most important conditioning factors in our lives. Fear of hunger and starvation are fears we all unconsciously share, even if we have never been forced by severe external circumstances to miss even a single meal. Having this level of secure luxury can separate us psychologically from most people throughout history and from people not so fortunate here and in other parts of the world right now. Many people have known, and still know, that food is not always a constant or a given and that famine could be just around the corner. Many people in many places around the world still live this reality, including those living in conditions that include war, famine and poverty in underdeveloped areas of the world all the way to just a few blocks from Wall Street. And everyone still faces the realities of why and how our minds work the way they do in relationship to food.

We need to respect unconscious tendencies surrounding food and use them as a field of observation. While doing home practice any activity that involves food can act as a wake-up call. Any frequent attempt to bring attention to what we do, why we do it, while directly experiencing the action and its after effects, will provide us with more moments of attention. The more we pay attention at these levels, the more that attention will affect other areas of our lives. Mindfulness around food and our relationship to it, is a practice of immeasurable importance.

I suggest we slow down and bring our mindfulness to hunger or the desire for food when the desire becomes a conscious thought. Apply *sampajañña* when we begin the process of getting the food from the grocery store, garden, or fridge, and continue that during our preparation, the eating of the snack or meal itself — whether we eat with others or eat alone — and the eventual task of cleaning up. There are so many opportunities to change our habituated patterns towards any aspect of this process, it staggers the imagination.

On home retreat or during home practice, we may have to contend with an array of choices regarding food. If one lives alone it is fairly simple to procure, prepare, eat and clean up with whatever level of attention one chooses to apply. However, many of us live with family or friends or in institutions; we share meals at work, or we are otherwise obliged by conditions and social convention to eat with others. Because of our limited wisdom, our choices in how we apply *sampajañña* become ever more important. How we utilize the understanding of how important our relationship is to food gives each of us the responsibility to plan and try to follow through with strategies that allow us to bring the utmost skill to this complicated field of practice.

Most of our experience with food is subtle, but it also provides us with peak experiences of pleasure and judgements. Here too is another level we can apply to our practice. Most of our conditioning is a consequence of an unobserved pleasant sensation leading to liking, leading to wanting, culminating in clinging; or an unobserved unpleasant sensation leading to not liking, leading to not wanting, culminating in pushing away or aversion or not seeing clearly; or neither pleasant nor unpleasant unobserved sensation leading to zoning out.

Intense liking and disliking that are often found in the consumption of food are very clear and valuable places to begin this deconditioning. Intense preferences are the mother lode of opportunity to examine these patterns and tendencies. However, the application of *sati* or *sampajañña* to any of the three mental feeling tones will give the mind space to not automatically react out of habit. This allows the meditation to mature, and teaches the mind in an incremental fashion how to enter into equanimity.

A casual examination of many common eating disorders that involve food is further evidence of how important food is to us. These include bulimia, anorexia, obesity, binge eating, etc. There is a new disorder related to food that may be shared by some who read this book to a lesser or greater degree. Although it has not been officially designated an eating disorder, orthorexia has been increasingly mentioned in the media and scientific studies. Individuals with orthorexia tend to have an obsessive focus on healthy eating, to an extent that disrupts their daily lives. For instance, they may eliminate entire food groups in the belief that they are unhealthy, which can lead to malnutrition, severe weight loss, difficulty eating outside the home, and emotional distress. Individuals with orthorexia rarely focus on losing weight. Instead, their self-worth, identity or satisfaction depends on how well they comply with their self-imposed dietary rules. (*See* https://www.healthline.com/nutrition/common-eating-disorders#other).

I'm reminded of a story offered in a *Dhamma* talk I heard many years ago at Insight Meditation Society (IMS) in Western Massachusetts. Once upon a time . . . a very sincere *yogi* came to IMS to participate in a formal meditation retreat. He became twisted into a pretzel of suffering because the food didn't meet his expectations and desires. He had been a baker and a self-appointed nutritionist. His practice during retreat was getting stuck and complicated by his aversion and his sense of victimhood arising from his not being able to 'eat right.'

His interviews with his teachers were about what IMS should do in order that he and all *yogis* could eat food that was better and healthier, which, at the time, in his mind, would serve them on their paths to enlightenment. One day his teacher asked how much suffering or freedom he experienced as a consequence of trying to control his own food and the food of others. Over time, the *yogi* began to understand and adapt to the diet served at IMS. If memory serves, some years later he ordained as a Buddhist monk.

QUESTION FOR THE *YOGI:*

- How much suffering are you causing yourself in relationship to food?

Formal Retreat Practice

I have found the conditions surrounding food on formal meditation retreats extremely helpful for practice, because food is only offered between dawn and the solar noon at monasteries. At retreat centers, I practice Eight Precepts, which means that I only eat between dawn and the solar noon. Eating is predictable; there is enough to eat, and, at the retreat center, I don't have much choice about what I eat.

Because there are approximately 18 hours between lunch and breakfast, the body experiences the ups and downs of having eaten and a bit of hunger. Episodes of hunger are valuable objects of meditation that are not actively or often chosen. Experiencing hunger with a meal still hours away provides an opportunity to examine mild unpleasantness for longer than just a brief passing glimpse. A truly wonderful practice.

Eating and Speech and Behavior

When we observe our own behaviors, it won't take long for us to realize that food is not just about the tasting and chewing and swallowing of food. It is also about inserting whom we believe ourselves to be into the experience and trying to get our secondary goals met, in whatever social environment we find ourselves. The story of the *yogi* at IMS *above* illustrates this.

Thus, how we behave while we eat deserves our attention. Right Speech will come into the mix as will the question and examination of whether we are eating for intoxication, for socialization, for a sense of control or for health. *Above* we discuss how we eat alone, with family and friends, and on various levels of retreat. In each of these there are different parameters and customs regarding what we do with our bodies and our speech while we eat. A few examples:

- Eating with family: Most families sit in the same places around their table for years. This has an effect on how and to whom we speak, whom we touch, whom we rely on to support us. In effect how we behave during meals has a tremendous impact on our socialization and how we begin to think of ourselves.
- A first date: How we use our eyes, the tones of our voices, whether or not we touch, the types of foods eaten.
- Retreat: On most formal retreats there is no talking, we avoid eye contact, and there is no touching even though we will be eating with many others.

Using just these three examples of how speech and body language are a part of our eating experience if others are present gives us cause to examine our inner intentions and watch the resultant pleasantness or unpleasantness in the variety of situations in which we find ourselves eating.

QUESTIONS FOR THE *YOGI:*

When eating with others, ask yourself:

- Under what conditions am I eating, and do these conditions affect how I behave?
- Is this food more about socialization and fun than about sustenance?
- When with others, am I tasting the food or just waiting for an opportunity to say something?

For more details and further examination of the use of food during home retreat, *see The Home Retreat Guide.*

CHAPTER 12

Livelihood

EARNING A LIVELIHOOD is one aspect of materiality, which is discussed in Chapter 7. However, I have made livelihood its own category in *A Householder's Vinaya,* because I find it surprising and somehow bracing that the Buddha included this very necessary human activity — working to earn a living — in the Noble Eightfold Path as a separate factor. I believe he understood in very real time that the single most time-consuming activity in our adult lives has an effect on our ability to study and practice the other seven Path factors. I believe he understood that how we carry out our most frequently repeated activities affects our conditioning and how minds and hearts work, and how these conditions affect our *kamma*.

Earning a livelihood is a householder responsibility that is not addressed in the monastic *Vinaya*. A householder must choose a livelihood, unlike monastics whose livelihood is prescribed in their *Vinaya* and defined by their relationship to the laity.

Because of its importance in our lives, as householders we need to ensure that our livelihood is itself wholesome and that the environment in which we work is wholesome as well, whether we work out in the world or at home. What we do affects how we see ourselves and how others view us, and the conditions in which we do it are often what we become. Our livelihood is a supremely important part of our spiritual path and deserves to be examined with care.

QUESTIONS FOR THE *YOGI:*

Livelihood as materiality:

- Doesn't my relationship with my livelihood constitute a type of materiality?
- Isn't my relationship as an employer or an employee confusing and a grey area at the best of times?
- When there is a relationship that is based in payment for time and labor, am I doing either the giving or the receiving freely with an open heart?

Livelihood and our spiritual practice:

- Is this work wholesome?
- Is my work environment wholesome?
- Does this livelihood support my benefit, and the benefit of those dependent on me, the community, and the earth?
- Does my work environment support friendly wholesome relations between co-workers or is it competitive or unnecessarily anxiety-provoking?

Most of us live in some grey area regarding our livelihoods. Even if we have a wholesome livelihood, we may have unwholesome intentions. For example, a friend who was trained as an attorney began her career working as a litigator. Even though she only worked on cases she believed in, she saw that her livelihood thrived on suffering and conflict. She also realized that she and fellow litigators whose intention was to help people—like legal aid attorneys and public defenders—did their jobs to win and were often angry about the situation they were trying to fix and very dependent on the outcome. She left litigation and became a legal editor, which also was a grey area. She was glad to help lawyers help people by making sure they had the appropriate and updated tools of their profession. At the same time, especially working with materials for litigators, she was helping them be in conflict by taking on the conflict of the client and by being dependent on the outcome.

SUGGESTIONS FOR PRACTICE:

- Examine your own situation carefully and try to assess with as little judgement as possible whether your work is of benefit to yourself, others, or both.
- If it isn't, or is in a grey area, pay close constant attention to what effect your livelihood is having on your heart and mind, your relationship with the world, and your meditation practice.

If your situation is obviously creating unwholesomeness in your *citta* and not contributing to the benefit of the world at large, I suggest you do your best to effect changes in the existing situation or consider finding a new livelihood. Yes, examining your livelihood against your ideals and your common sense is a hassle; and yes, it may take time and cause risk to yourself and your family to change working conditions, jobs, or careers. However, not to do so will have a deep and lasting unwholesome impact on not only your life, but the many lives you are responsible to and for as well.

Remember, you have only this moment and maybe only this life. Is it worth your life and potential for wise happiness to expose yourself to constant unwholesome conditions? This activity, which occupies more time than anything else in your life, will have an obvious and very lasting impact on how you navigate your spiritual life.

CHAPTER 13

Family, Friends, Community

Family

THE *SAṄGHA* IS A MONASTIC'S primary family and community. When a monastic takes ordination, the family of origin is relegated to a satellite status and the *saṅgha* becomes the center of the monastic's life. All historical and cultural ties are filtered through the *Vinaya*. The relationship a monastic has to their *Vinaya* affects how they will act with their peers, family of origin, lay friends, and the outside community. The *saṅgha's* way of doing things supplants the old way of doing things.

An example that may make us lay people scratch our heads is told by my teacher Sayadaw U Vivekananda. His mother lived in Germany before her death, and he made it a point to visit her each year when he was traveling and teaching abroad. The visits were cherished and celebrated by both mother and son, but came with some adjustments. Because of U Vivekananda's adherence to his *Vinaya*, even though he was visiting his mother, he could not sleep under the same roof as her because, well, she's a woman, and the *Vinaya Piṭaka* does not allow a male monastic to sleep under the same roof as any female. So each time he came to visit special accommodations needed to be made, including transportation issues, because a monk isn't supposed to ride in a car alone with a woman. Meals too would take on an unaccustomed character, with questions arising such as where he could sit for meals, whom he could touch, when he could and could not eat, and what and how much he could eat, or whether he could express preferences for food and beverages.

Each of these circumstances is not shared with the intention of highlighting the awkwardness of U Vivekananda's choice to supplant his *sangha* as his primary family and community. Rather, they are windows into how the rules in the *Vinaya Piṭaka* affect every waking moment of the lives of monastics who have embraced their vows. A shared commitment and adherence to the rules such as those of monastics naturally condition the individual towards their new family and support out of the ordinary diligence and attention.

For householders, like livelihood, family can be a consuming part of our lives. Spouses, partners, children, in-laws are like leaves on a tree; they become a part of the life process without any way around them. Because human beings cannot survive without connections to others, our commitments and our human connections are extremely important and strong, whether they be wholesome, unwholesome or disinterested. They are therefore more clearly present and appear much deeper and, at times, are even harder to see.

When my parents were still alive, my two brothers and I would occasionally visit them in Florida as a family. Often I shocked myself by some of the things I would say and do during those visits. It was almost as if at times I was 12 years old again. The triggers were unclear and unseen but clearly there. My father, a child of struggling immigrant parents who grew up during the Great Depression, had some predictable attitudes about spending money. When I was a child, he would meet my expression of a preference when we were eating out with some kind of cutting admonishment like, "Allan always wants the best for himself." We're talking about egg foo young instead of kung pao chicken. I can remember as a 50-year-old having dinner with the family at a restaurant. It was some kind of celebration, an anniversary or birthday. So, a fancy and expensive restaurant. As a 50-year-old looking at the menu, I was overwhelmed with anxiety. I can't remember exactly what I ordered, but I probably chose the hamburger.

This particular aspect of lay life deserves special attention and special focus. It's one thing to apply *sati* or *sampajañña* to speech or action at work or in our everyday encounters; it's quite another to apply them at Thanksgiving dinner when an uncle gets drunk and becomes less than polite, or while reading *Curious George* to your three-year-old before sleep.

I suggest that whatever the conditions, be they mildly or intensely pleasant, unpleasant, or neither pleasant nor unpleasant, facing our reactions at a family dinner is an opportunity to cultivate patient and reflective compassion for yourself and others. The particular skills you develop will be yours. What is important is that in these types of moments, you bring frequent intention to your enlightenment project and wake up for just that moment.

As a householder, you need to live your life normally, and at the same time and as often as possible examine any thought, emotion or sensation that leads to speech or action with the help of *sampajañña*. Using reflection, practice patience and forgiveness as much as possible for yourself and others. If you are like me, you'll discover how habituated you are to allowing reaction to be your default behavior mode. With *sampajañña* we give ourselves the opportunity to condition the *citta* towards wise active responses as opposed to a quick reactive habit. The more often we pause and give reflection a chance to mix with the situation, the more likely our speech and actions will become kindlier and more skillful.

Friends

When we begin a formal spiritual journey, whoever we are and regardless of the tradition we choose, we come to our path with our family and our current friends in tow. In the West, a person who embarks on a spiritual journey in meditation often finds that many old friends fall away as the practice matures. It just comes with the territory that our friends change as a consequence of our changing priorities. As we begin to change, the values of our practice and the transformation in our behavior become more of a common expression and they begin to have an effect on those around us. For most of us, the more we practice in a given tradition the more we begin to associate with and rely on our peers. Also, if the tradition places a strong emphasis on some quality of everyday life that is not currently practiced by the general public, we begin to be seen by our old friends as not being the same person they became friends with, and therefore there is a natural cooling in the old relationships.

My experience has taught me that the most important friendships, the ones that are rooted in native and natural wholesomeness and/or are inexorably linked to our history, endure. But those that are more or less based on entertainment and *quid pro quo* attentions fall away. The cooling of those friendships along with this developing transition can be seen as a wise and wholesome development; it may sometimes feel awkward, but it is definitely wholesome. In fact, it can be useful to consciously allow these changes to develop.

Kalyāṇamitta, the quality of friendship that inspires and leads us towards deeper wisdom through modeling and inspiration, occurs by exposure and opportunity.

> *There is no companionship with a fool;*
> *It is better to go alone.*
> *Travel alone, at ease, doing no evil*
> *Like the elephant Matanga in the forest.*
> — *Nagavagga*: Elephants (Dhp XXIII 330)

> *"No, Ananda," the Buddha told him, "having good friends isn't half of the Holy Life. Having good friends is the whole of the Holy Life."*
> — *Upaddha Sutta*: Half (of the Holy Life) (SN 45.2)

In the first quote, the Buddha is warning us that should we continue to hang out with people who, for example, behave unwholesomely and unskillfully when our wisdom is not yet solid, it is inevitable that we will be affected in negative ways. In the second quote, the Buddha isn't speaking about intimacy in the way that most people understand friendship. He is talking about *kalyāṇamitta*. When we cultivate our friendships following the Buddha's advice, over time we learn that our *kalyāṇamitta* near and far offer us immeasurable support.

Community

Community plays a similar role on our spiritual path as family and friends. Community is where we learn how to give and take with skill and gratitude regardless of the situation. It is also where we work, where we play, where we practice. It can be temporary or long lasting.

Being in community is when we are obliged to be present for multiple people with varying agendas that demand compromise and compassion. Community is a place that can confuse or inspire. A community is more than a place like a country or a town or village or even a monastery. It is a place in time where, because of the confusion and the conflict that comes from being with many humans, we practice and bring our *sampajañña* to maturity.

QUESTIONS FOR THE *YOGI:*

- Does this community support the cultivation of *dāna*, *sīla*, and *bhāvanā*, or does it hold me in the grip of a mixture of unwholesome convenience and unwise intentions?
- Do I have the skill and wisdom to associate for extended periods of time with the unwholesome and unskillful? If not, what can I do about it?

HELPFUL CAUTION:

In many ways, a householder's life is the householder's *sangha*. As householders we may have a number of implicit contracts with our family and friends that may help or hinder our practice. We may celebrate birthdays together, observe Christmas, maybe watch the Super Bowl. Some of these implicit contracts serve a lifelong purpose. They build lasting affection, teach patience and compassion, and serve everybody in the moment and set the frame of serving each other in the future. There are times when it is skillful, kind and prudent to participate with as much wholesomeness as you can muster, even if the activity itself is not as wholesome or as skillful as you would normally like it to be. Use your *vinaya* in service to others and yourself now and in the future. Use *sampajañña* to determine if the activity in the contract is something you can do skillfully, and if not, see what alternatives you can offer so that you continue to meet your obligations without damaging your practice or the group.

CHAPTER 14

Activities of Daily Life, Maintenance of the Body, Health-Sickness, Exercise

Advice from a Guru

ON MY WAY TO BURMA many years ago I visited a celebrated Vedanta guru in northern India. His school of practice uses language and instructions such as, "You don't have to do anything; you are already enlightened." His tradition espouses the notion that making effort and working towards the goal of enlightenment or stressing about it or even considering thoughts such as, "My goal is to get enlightened and I intend to do something about it," pushes realization out of reach.

This guru's school of Hindu practice teaches that having such notions will just reinforce the tendency to deepen attachment to self-created goals and serve the tendency for self-serving strategies to arise, the exact opposite of the goal. The seeker, according to this school, gets caught in trying to control outcomes and pushes what is native to the *citta* further away simply by making energetic effort towards those ends. Striving and trying to control outcomes is a common hindrance at one time or another for almost every spiritual seeker, whether their tradition teaches that they are already enlightened or has a detailed psycho-spiritual template of the path. These pitfalls come with the territory of learning how to balance the *citta* while on the spiritual path.

During my brief visit, I asked him a couple of questions based on having read his autobiography and knowing something of his teachings.

In his autobiography, this guru declared that he had his own enlighten-ment experience in mid-life, in his 40's or 50's. So first I asked, "Until you had your transformative enlightenment experience, what was your spiritual and meditative life and practice like?" I knew beforehand that throughout his life he was a very sincere family man with a wife and children, had a career as an engineer, and was a full and willing partner with all that comes with being a typical Indian family man. In other words, he was like most of us, a householder. His answer to my ques-tion was both surprising and not. He said something like, "Every single moment that my mind was not otherwise occupied with the life activities that demanded my attention I said my mantra over and over again." The second question I asked was, "Does investigation, effort and concentration serve one on the path to enlightenment?" He answered, "Yes, absolutely. *Yoga*, *seva*, and *samādhi* are integral to the arising of enlightenment. All very good practice."

I share this story because this guru was an ordinary householder who—while living his family life, raising children, and going to work—was able to train himself to get and stay focused on his spiritual path whenever the opportunities allowed him to turn his mind in that direction. He obviously didn't see his householding life as a barrier to integrating his deepest spiritual and meditative aspirations. I'm certain that with many ups and downs, periods of boredom and failure, he simply got out of the way and let the practice become his teacher.

What he described in his practice's language is the practice of *sati-sampajañña*. Lay practitioners of this school of practice have the opportunity to do the same as the guru. It is only a matter of understanding, intention, investigation, and effort as frequently as conditions permit.

Micro-Moments of *Anattā*

A micro-moment of *anattā* is when the mind does not refer back to *I, me, mine*, and yet continues with a task or a thought. These moments do not resemble moments when the mind zones out and remains blank. Quite the opposite, these are moments of uncommon clarity. Many of us experience moments of *anattā* throughout our day. This is as true for an experienced meditator as for someone who has little or no meditation experience. The only difference is in how often they appear and whether they are noticed.

Most people don't notice these moments. They're there; we just need to notice. These moments and contexts and their usefulness can be explored as they arise. For those who have had significant training in meditation, these moments can happen quite frequently and be intuitively known, but equally as often are ignored or shuttled to the side of consciousness due to external or internal circumstances.

I suggest you give these moments their due and bring attention to them should circumstances permit. Willing the mind to go to the experience will almost always happen too late to experience the moment as it arises, and willing the mind to observe will push it away. Yet the effort to bring attention to and the remembering of the moment establish a greater opportunity and greater invitation for these moments to become a more frequent and welcome part of our consciousness.

Inclining the mind to give permission for micro-moments of non-self to arise assists on two counts:

1. It cultivates the permission for these non-attached moments to become more frequent, which helps to decondition the normal flow of the conditioned mind.
2. It can dramatically affect their frequency and power during formal meditation when the mind has a continuity of effortless mindfulness present.

Micro-Moments of Bare Attention

Anyone can cultivate the habit of bringing micro-moments of attention to a thought, word, or action. In fact, in many ways, that's all we're doing when we try to formally practice on the cushion. Most of us are able only to string together short bursts of clear unencumbered sequences of *sati* while we meditate.

We can also add moments of unencumbered *sati* into our daily lives without the intention or the expectation that the moments will or should last. Just do it. The inclining leads to a stronger more focused intention, which heightens effort that results in the more frequent 'waking up' moments. This process and these moments add a frame to our entire life. The nature of the mind is to take one moment at a time in order to truly know it. Each time we incline the mind towards wholesomeness or the observing of one moment at a time, we've inclined the mind towards skillful means. This is the practice of the wise.

Nature of Activities of Daily Living (ADLs)

ADLs—activities of daily living—are the mortar to the bricks of building a householding life. These are the activities we must do to live and to navigate our lives.

Anyone who has read this far will likely have a variety of other activities in their life that demand extraordinary effort. Maybe you are a single mom with two jobs and going to school; or maybe you are a musician or some type of artist or hobbyist; or maybe an athlete; or maybe taking care of a loved one. These and many other activities of daily living will mirror and teach some aspects of our meditative life and as a consequence can be used consciously for both our everyday life and our meditative life. The effort, diligence and patience it takes to achieve a level of maturity in just one area of your life can serve you in all the areas of your life.

In formulating the Noble Eightfold Path and the Five and Eight Precepts, the Buddha separated some activities of daily life out from the collective of everyday activities to help us focus on the activities that have the most impact on our enlightenment projects. *A Householder's Vinaya* treats those activities as separate categories and in their own chapters:

- Speech, Chapter 9
- Livelihood, Chapter 12

- Sexuality, Chapter 8
- Intoxicants, Chapter 10
- Meals and food, Chapter 11
- Spiritual practices, Chapters 18, 19

Throughout our days we spend a significant amount of time performing activities to ensure our lives flow and support ease, comfort, health, and safety. Our bodies offer us frequent opportunities to step back and observe our reality from perspectives that we usually don't want to see or fail to see. These are all moments and activities that can be integrated into a whole set of micro-attentions that will dramatically support your enlightenment project.

Some of these activities are done involuntarily and others voluntarily. Most of us every day have to urinate, defecate, breathe, swallow, blink, scratch, and sleep, to name just a few of the involuntary activities of the body that give us a chance to see how we are not in control, how we are not our body. Each of these activities is stimulated by automatic bodily processes we don't dictate. Each offers us an opportunity to step back and observe with a meditative eye the action and the causes of the action. We also voluntarily do things to simply maintain and take care of the body, such as eat, wash, brush the teeth, shave or cut hairs from various parts of the body, cut finger and toe nails, put on and take off clothing, wash clothing, clean house. . . . I think you get the picture.

Many of these activities, should we be able to do them, are often done without attention; they are chores or activities of the body to get done and get through in order to move on to the things we think are important or we want to do. Many of these types of activities are treated as checkboxes on a list with the goal to go to bed at night having checked off as many as possible.

ADLs can be broken down according to their complexity. In their simplest forms, ADLs are activities that are required to physically navigate our day such as walking, sitting, getting up from sitting, feeding ourselves, and managing our toilet. More complex activities, which then require a series of more complex connecting intentions, include such activities as cooking, washing dishes, doing laundry, and cleaning. The most complex ADLs are things like driving, shopping, socializing, and work or hobbies, which need many types of intention, investigation, effort, and concentration in order to achieve one's goal. These activities are complex. We often have mixed agendas for engaging in them, and at times we're not even aware we're engaging in them. However, how we perform them and how we attend to our *citta* during such activities will make or break the continuity of our home practice and will or won't support us in our enlightenment project.

> *Think of your home as a retreat center. Begin by altering the way you see your home. When you begin to view your home in the same way that you view a meditation center, your practice will become smoother. Keep checking your attitudes and views, your thinking and your background ideas.*
>
>   – U Tejaniya

Frequent gaps in attention, with subsequent relapses to modes of automatic non-attention, cause practice to falter and fail. If we train our minds to become alert to these gaps of attention, and train ourselves to wake up and use *sati* and *sampajañña* in those moments, the meditative life becomes second nature.

Rules in the *Vinaya Piṭaka* for Monastics

For monastics, living according to the rules of the *Vinaya* establishes a baseline of attention and requires continuous attention, vigilance and effort that can lift a meditation practice. The monastic who takes the *Vinaya* seriously is more likely to develop the habit of paying attention to all activities and give their meditation practice a boost, not to mention that they also appear to the laity as one who deserves support.

Householder Practice

By applying effort, investigation, and concentration during everyday activities, as householders we develop a deeper, more continuous practice. With this understanding and intention, we can utilize *A Householder's Vinaya* and home practice or home retreat and make better use of them than if we didn't pay close attention to the details of our everyday lives. The Hindu guru in the story *above* was able to weave a balance between his everyday activities and repeating his mantra. Doing his daily activities, when not doing his mantra, was not a break or an interruption; they were part of his practice. His everyday life became an uninterrupted whole.

It is comparatively simple to try to sustain attention during formal meditation versus being able to sustain a constant meditative perspective in everyday life. I did say 'comparatively.' There is a quality of purpose that heightens our intention, energy, focus and investigation when we choose to formally sit; not so often or so much when we are washing the dishes or taking out the garbage.

Remember, all trainings are a process. It takes time and effort for the marathon-like strength and endurance needed to even learn how to incline the mind towards attention on a continuous basis during everyday activities, let alone establish it and then maintain it. What is often lost on the Indian guru's students is the understanding that striving only pushes away wisdom when it remains striving. Balanced effort is not striving.

Moving Focus 'In and Out'

In the everyday world thoughts, speech and actions are happening very quickly; in fact too quickly to attend to their changing nature with continuous unbroken *sati*. Instead one can take an object and know it briefly with simple bare attention: a color, pleasantness, a sound, unpleasantness, etc. But they happen too quickly to stay with the process, such as the hand already moving towards the tomatoes because you are in the veggie section of the food store.

In some of the examples of practicing with ADLs throughout this chapter, the instruction is given to move one's bare attention or *sati* 'in and out.' This means not to let your attention rest on the object. In this type of situation, we can move our attention to the reflection of whether we are reaching for the tomato because it's on the list or because we didn't notice liking arise when the thought, "How beautiful they look" entered the mind. Here one can either switch back to bare attention to the coolness of the tomato in the hand or the color, and again to a reflection of whether it was unnoticed pleasantness that inspired the sequence. The next step back might be a reflection on whether the tomato will be put into the basket.

Among other secondary benefits, moving attention to and from an object keeps the mind sharp and forestalls the potential of falling prey to the traps of unseen pleasantness or unpleasantness. Exercising this type of practice strengthens intention, investigation, effort, mindfulness, concentration and wisdom from new and not often used perspectives. The more frequently we apply the tools of *sati-sampajañña* to more situations, the more we strengthen the individual mental factors that make up the spine of our practice. This practice helps to naturally incline the mind towards moment to moment continuity. Exercising *sati* and *sampajañña* in tandem morph the practice into a lifestyle that in and of itself is training towards balance that allows wisdom to arise.

General Examples of Practicing in Daily Life

The following list is a scattershot of things many householders do in a given day, for the most part without attention. It is not exhaustive, and each list is ultimately personal, and informed by each practitioner's daily activities.

A. Hygiene: bathing; taking care of teeth, nails, hair; going to the toilet. *Sati* or *sampajañña* can be practiced depending on the situation. Move the focus of bare attention in and out, in and out.

B. Driving: Practice with a general bare attention. There are times when focusing on too much detail is both counterproductive and dangerous. Use common sense, use *sampajañña*.

C. Exercise: Practice with a general bare attention. As with driving, focusing too intently on detail is both counterproductive and occasionally dangerous. Use common sense, use *sampajañña*.

D. Shopping, waiting in lines: *Sati* or *sampajañña* can be practiced, depending on the situation. Move the focus of bare attention in and out, in and out. Waiting in lines is especially suited to doing *mettā* meditation. Both *sati* and *sampajañña* can be practiced when looking at something on the shelf that is or isn't on your shopping list. Notice the charge of desire and wanting, notice the process of reaching, etc., notice if there is a change when the object is in your basket. This process is happening over and over again while we're shopping with varying degrees of desire or aversion, which makes the grocery store an oasis of opportunity to watch pleasant or unpleasant, liking or not liking, wanting or not wanting, clinging or pushing away.

E. Walking or resting between activities: *Sati* or *sampajañña* can be practiced depending on the situation. Move the focus of bare attention in and out, in and out.

F. Cleaning: *Sati* or *sampajañña* can be practiced depending on the situation. Move the focus of bare attention in and out, in and out.

G. Gardening: *Sati* or *sampajañña* can be practiced depending on the situation. Move the focus of bare attention in and out, in and out.

H. Small movements and posture changes: scratching, adjusting glasses, etc.. *Sati* or *sampajañña* can be practiced depending on the situation. As quickly as you can discern the intention to willfully do any small action, move the focus of bare attention in and out, in and out. Unconscious reactions to unpleasant or pleasant bodily sensations happen frequently throughout the day. Our interactions with these objects or reactions are windows to how the unconscious attempt to get rid of unpleasant sensations or hold on to pleasant ones conditions our habit patterns. Watch. Bring your attention to the process. Try to identify the arising of the pleasant or unpleasant sensation and then the process of how either habit or *sati-sampajañña* plugs in.

I. Caring for your kids or elders: Use micro-moments of attention.

QUESTIONS FOR THE *YOGI:*

While performing ADLs, ask yourself:

- Can I do any of these activities with a new and more focused attention?
- What tools and reminders can I use to help myself remember and stay focused?

Exercise, Yoga, Sports, Extreme Athletics

EXERCISE IN GENERAL

The other day, I was at the gym. I'm getting to be an old man. I used to run, but haven't in years due to injuries and surgery. As I age, the intention to stay healthy and strong doesn't change, but the techniques I use to embody that intention do. Even though I hadn't 'pushed it' in years, for one reason or another, I chose to start pushing it that day. As my pulse was rising higher and higher, and the respirations got more and more painful, I noticed the meditative mind observing the rush of doubt and aversion to the pain and the willingness to believe I could still continue to push it. The mind was calm and observant and didn't mistake the unpleasantness of the thinking and the painful bodily sensations for the reality that the body and mind were just behaving the way they do under stress.

It is precisely this type of opportunity to train and strengthen the mind that happens when we put ourselves on the edge. Use your pain, your doubt, your willingness to go the extra mile as training for your practice. Be patient and kind as well as courageous and be willing to take sensible risks. It is at our edge, whatever that edge is, where we open to the potential of learning equanimity under duress.

Having been a runner and an avid gym goer for over 40 years, I have developed a certain perspective. I've noticed that I and many others believe we have to continue doing these activities despite conscious or unconscious unwholesome intentions or consequences. Those beliefs can result from unobserved competitiveness, to attachment to either a specific self-image or to the self-generated highs, or both, and our unwillingness to abandon them. It then becomes ever more important that when engaging in these activities, we develop patience, attention, and as much *sati* and *sampajañña* as possible until our body and mind come into balance and the less wholesome intentions fall away or become non-clinging events as consequence of aging and practice. Exercise and yoga in and of themselves are neither wholesome or unwholesome. What we bring to them and how we observe them make them so valuable.

YOGA

Nowadays, for those staying active, yoga and stretching are components of normal exercise routines; this includes large numbers of people using yoga as a meditation of breathing and movement. These complimentary activities have cross pollinated so successfully that many Western meditation centers offer yoga or stretching as formal parts of the retreat; some retreat centers have designated yoga and stretching rooms for the retreatants' use during retreat. This then deserves a more than casual look.

In everyday life these practices are very useful for the maintenance of our bodies or to heal from injury. The *Satipaṭṭhāna Sutta* (MN 10) implicitly describes how to use them skillfully:

[W]hen walking, a bhikkhu [meditator] understands: "I am walking;" when standing, he understands; "I am standing;" when sitting, he understands: "I am sitting;" when lying down,

he understands; "I am lying down;" or he understands accordingly
however his body is disposed.

[A] bhikkhu [meditator] is one who acts in full awareness when
going forward and returning; who acts in full awareness when
looking ahead and looking away; who acts in full awareness when
flexing and extending his limbs; . . . [who acts in full awareness
dressing and wearing clothes]; . . . who acts in full awareness when
eating, drinking, consuming food, and tasting; who acts in full
awareness when defecating and urinating; who acts in full awareness
when walking, standing, sitting, falling asleep, waking up, talking,
and keeping silent. . . . not clinging to anything in this world. That is
how a bhikkhu [meditator] abides contemplating body in body.

– Satipaṭṭhāna Sutta:
The Four Foundations of Mindfulness (MN 10:3, 8-9)

The question and the challenge then become whether we can
apply our *sati* or our *sampajañña* to the before, during, and after of
the activity.

SUGGESTIONS FOR PRACTICE:

When on retreat:

- Be very careful that you are not doing yoga, stretching or
  exercising as a distraction.
- If you are, pay attention to how the distraction or entertainment
  affects the choice to do the exercise.
- Notice the mind quality during the activity and what are the
  consequences to your continuity of effort and investigation after.

The same applies in everyday life or when at a yoga class, but with
more emphasis on *sampajañña* than on *sati*.

SPORTS

In this day and age, people in the West engage in sports in a variety of ways. Examples:

- Competing individually against themselves in such activities as rock climbing, running, golf.
- Competing one on one in sports like tennis, or board and card games (which are not really a sport but have many of the same mental factors and characteristics at play.)
- Engaging in group sports like volleyball, baseball, basketball, soccer.

In all three examples, the beginning, middle and end of the activity can be rich with observable non-ordinary states of mind. In participating in sports, we have a treasure trove of opportunities to practice *sati* or *sampajañña* or both, as well as to observe what the activity and the consequences are doing to the mind and body in real time. Routine often blinds us; continuity is the invitation to incline the mind to stay present. Use these times not just as parts of your routine but as part of your continuity.

Competition is a very sharp-edged mental state. All too often the types of mental factors we use to meditate are similar to or the same as those we use when play sports or games. Some meditators compete with themselves; some with others. It is not uncommon while on retreat to hear oneself say silently, "I can sit as still and as long as that person," or "I'll stay mindful for the entire hour!" This type of competition can get so inflated that one may hear, or have as an unseen current of practice, notions akin to, "I will be enlightened by such and such a date." These types of thinking and subsequent behaviors generate related thoughts and behavior that can be more easily observed and have less charge when playing sports or engaging in other types of competition. If we learn intuitively what competition feels like in the body and mind in all our everyday activities, we are more likely to know it when it arises in our meditation.

QUESTIONS FOR THE *YOGI:*

When participating in sports, ask yourself and be honest:

- Am I paying attention . . . really?
- Am I just giving sidelong glances at the activity in order to allow myself to just zone into the high of the exercise or competition?
- Can I use this activity to better familiarize myself with the mind and body of what competition feels like in the body and how it affects the mental process?
- Is over efforting, striving, or heroic effort useful? What do any of these feel like? Are they cousins to competition? What actions can I take when I notice them so as to bring the controlling faculties into balance?

EXTREME ATHLETICS

Extreme sports need extreme caution, both as a constellation of mental states that condition the mind, and the general sensibility of what it is one is doing. Being present in extreme situations allows the mind to see extremes. Balance, the forerunner and the consequence of a liberated mind, arises only when the mind, in part, learns to come to a nonreactive place while adrenaline, endorphins, pain or extreme pleasure are pulsating in the body and mind.

QUESTIONS FOR THE *YOGI:*

When participating in extreme sports, ask yourself:

- Is this really necessary?
- Is it useful?
- Will this lead to less or greater suffering down the line?

Dealing with Sickness, Injury, and Aging

Off and on throughout our lives we are oppressed with a body that just isn't behaving. We get sick; we get injured; we age. Each of these conditions is a unique practice opportunity. Each of them engenders certain types of thinking and physical behaviors that are out-of-the-recent ordinary. They are precious opportunities to observe how the mind works when challenged by things out of its control.

Most of us, most of the time, assume our bodies are indeed who we are, perhaps like a fish that isn't able to discern that it is swimming in water. What is constant is often hard to see and know. Yet the fish may get thrown onto the shore in a storm. We get sick, injured, and old, forcing us out of the norm and the assumed status quo. Getting sick and old reminds—perhaps teaches—us that we really do not have control over what we have identified as 'our' bodies.

A lesson like this is easily forgotten or brushed under the carpet as soon as we either get well or get habituated to the new baseline. However, a lesson like this, explored and examined carefully as it is evolving, has the potential to teach us wholesome ways to adapt to our changing bodies and our changing circumstances. By becoming proactive in observing the changes in our bodies as we age, are injured, or get sick, we prepare ourselves for the ups and downs of meditation, the totality of a spiritual life, and our own dying process.

I suggest that when you have a cold or some type of injury, and your energy is low and the mind is saying things like "I can't" or "I don't," you observe and become familiar with what precipitated the thought and the belief. See if you can see the thought just as a thought, and see if there is room to not blindly believe what the body is telling the mind or what the mind is telling the body. I'm not suggesting that we ignore the symptoms and conditions of our bodies and further hurt or endanger our health or recovery. The more room we allow for wholesome investigation when we're sick or injured, the more likely we'll be able to learn the skills of being present when meditation is difficult or when we're dying. Training our attention in everyday life activities when sick or hurt is an opportunity that deserves our full attention.

Dying

Just a few words about the elephant in the room.

We all are dying; we will all die. Possibly apart from committing suicide, none of us know when it will happen or how it will happen. Here again we are offered ahead of time the clear and obvious lesson that we are not our bodies. Yet still, most of us choose to totally ignore this inevitable event. Our examination of it is often limited by our own inability to separate fear and projection from the normal certainty of dying.

Suffice it to say, dying is arguably the most important event of our lives because it is the one and only time we get to do it. It will be the only time we can affect our experience of this particular process by utilizing previous training. Can't really say that about birth, and can't say that about marriage, or a job or even having children, which, unlike dying happen in relationship with others or are events that we can try again and learn from similar previous experience and situations. Dying is unique in this particular way and, depending on our point of view, might be the most important moment(s) of our lives.

A life of meditation trains the mind to increase the probability we will be able to call to mind wholesomeness coupled with bare attention during the whole adventure. Of course, I can't speak to what happens after we stop breathing. But having been a hospice nurse, and having had a few near-death illnesses and accidents of my own, I can say that when the mind is well trained with meditative skill it remains clear and observant longer than when it is not trained.

In my hospice work, I have witnessed many deaths. Those who had minds and hearts that were clear and observant through the process of diagnosis, treatment, and the choice to stop treatment more often were able to stay mentally clear, open, and observant longer into their active dying process than those who hadn't been open from the beginning. I've noticed that when illness strikes now, as opposed to when I was much younger both in age and practice, I am much better equipped to be present for the discomfort and fears that arise. I'm not saying that the fear and discomfort don't arise; I'm just saying it's much more likely that while fear is present, the mind can simply be present for the fear without believing it. No control of the physical or mental events; just the skill to be able to observe with active impersonal interest what is happening both internally and externally.

CHAPTER 15

Style and Preferences

The Great Way is not difficult, for those who have no preferences.
Let go of longing and aversion, and it reveals itself.
Make the smallest distinction, however, and you are as far from it as
heaven is from earth.

If you want to realize the truth, then hold no opinions for or against
anything.
Like and dislike is the disease of the mind.
When the deep meaning [of the Way] is not understood the
intrinsic peace of mind is disturbed.
As vast as infinite space, it is perfect and lacks nothing.

Indeed, it is due to your grasping and repelling that you do not
see things as they are.

– Third Zen Patriarch

The Nature of Style and Preference

IT'S THE NATURE OF OUR CONSCIOUS MIND to constantly think it is making choices. Thus when we are engaged in this pervasive activity, we can effect a significant change in the patterns of mind habit. Choices are almost entirely based on preferences built upon blind habits.

Preferences are almost always a consequence of unobserved pleasantness morphing into liking, wanting and clinging; or unpleasantness morphing into not liking, not wanting, then pushing away; or the inability to discern pleasant or unpleasant and the mind spacing out in search of something more stimulating. These patterns of mind, the unobserved arising from a feeling tone — pleasant, unpleasant, or neither pleasant nor unpleasant — coupled with a sense object, are the root of most of our suffering. For more detailed discussion of this process, *see* the discussion of dependent origination in Chapter 3.

So, what does this have to do with style and what is meant by 'style' anyway? Style is a synonym for preferences. For most of us, style consists of the ways we express our likes and dislikes without paying attention to the cause, sequence, or consequences of our habits. All of us do this most of the time, and the householder's lifestyle supports it with very few restraints; one might say it even encourages and cultivates it: *What kind of car do I want to buy? What color shirt do I wear today? How do I want my fish prepared?* And on and on.

The Monastic *Vinaya* and Style and Preferences

The monastic *Vinaya* consciously limits the monastic's choices, therefore helping to isolate the habit of acting according to preferences when they arise and allowing the habit to be seen more clearly against the flow of restraint and attention. Under the rules prescribed in the monastic *Vinaya*, a monastic wears the same style of robes every day, having only two sets: a clean one, and one on the body; eats at the same time every day and eats only what's offered; limits entertainment and distractions; and generally leads a very regulated life with a limited amount of choice compared to that of a householder.

Monastics are obliged to do without, forcing them to be frequently exposed to varying types of choices being made for them or learning to do without, with no recourse to get the desired or needed object or service. A monastic doesn't just think and then act on thoughts like, "I think I'll turn on the television . . . have a cup of ice cream . . . buy a new outfit or car," etc. Their *Vinaya* prevents it and exposes them to their wants and preferences on a frequent basis from the point of view of restraint, patience, and acceptance.

Householder Practice

Because householders must make many more choices in their daily lives than monastics, they have many more opportunities to examine their preferences. Therefore, as householders we must give special attention to this area of our everyday lives if we want to establish an effective everyday practice. Imagine if we could pay more attention without judgment to the arising of a pleasant or unpleasant feeling tone and just learn to leave the experience of the pleasantness or unpleasantness there.

Apart from practicing the restraints and the wisdom the Precepts teach, a householder can say or do what they please, when they please, with whomever they please. Especially in this day and age, when freedom of expression is considered to be a right from birth, the issues and consequences of unbridled and unexamined choices often play havoc with notions of attachment. The way we relate to unconscious attachment affects our attention, concentration, and virtue. Every time boredom arises we can and often do reach for our smart phones, buy something or go to the fridge. We believe acting on our feelings and emotions is more important than observing, knowing and trying to effect any change to the habit.

Each of us must choose how, when and where to exercise restraint with wise reflection when a choice arises. We have too many habit-rooted choices to notice them all. Some are necessary for efficiency, safety and survival. Start your practice of bringing preferences into focus by observing which choices are survival-rooted and which have the strong fragrance of identification with bodily and mental feelings that translate into what we want.

SUGGESTIONS FOR PRACTICE:

- See if you can notice the preferences as they arise. Watch to see if you can detect how or when they arise.
- See if unobserved preferences usually lead towards or away from wholesome continuity in concentration, attention or virtue.
- In speaking or performing other acts, make determined choices to act or refrain from acting in response to the thought or emotion.
- Assess if you see changes in your automatic behaviors when applying this type of focus over and over again.

QUESTIONS FOR THE *YOGI:*

- Did preferences arise when you weren't paying attention?
- Does this practice lead your mind towards more blind habit while reinforcing old patterns, or towards having the space to act with skill and compassion for self and others?

CHAPTER 16

Entertainment

Presence of Entertainment as Distraction in Our Lives

BEING IN THE EVERYDAY WORLD and having preferences gives us many opportunities to explore and indulge in sensual pleasure whether we want to or not. Most householders, to varying degrees, include in their lives sexuality, intimacy, art, theater, literature, nature, epicurean activities, and having a family, to name just a very few possibilities of entertainment and sensual pleasures that keep our sense of self alive and vital. Even if we do not indulge in or cultivate all of these types of distraction or entertainment, we are nevertheless bombarded by a wide variety of opportunities to entertain the mind continuously throughout our day, which can be both pleasant and unpleasant.

QUESTIONS FOR THE *YOGI:*

- At a certain level, for example, isn't an advertisement in a bank about a savings account, a billboard for a new car, or a pop-up on the computer advertising a new gadget a type of creative bait for the mind because it is meant to be attractive and massage our karmic preferences?
- Aren't many of our family and social activities and obligations — both pleasant and unpleasant — entertainments of sorts?

- How much entertainment and distraction are valuable in your life, and how much is burying the practice of continuity of attention?
- How much do your patterns of preference in choosing unwholesome amusement persist even after you are aware of their impact, and how subtle can they become when you choose to distract yourself or zone out?

Our natural appreciation for pretty things and pleasure and for avoiding unpleasantness constantly distracts our attention into unconscious liking and not liking, even if just for a millisecond. And as humans we like liking and we don't like not liking. As householders we train ourselves to be distracted off and on throughout our days, leaning again and again towards what we like and away from what we don't like. But we also consciously invest a fair amount of time in structured distraction that might be called social responsibilities. These would include work-related social events we are required to attend, children's athletic or art events, extended family gatherings, political gatherings and organized athletics. These activities come with the territory of our contemporary ways of life.

The list of activities we do to engage with life through our senses by relaxing and entertaining ourselves is a very long one. In simply being out and about in the world, we exercise our likes and dislikes, for example, by allowing our gaze to linger a millisecond longer on that attractive person, that antique in the store window, that new Subaru. Furthermore, we actively choose, for example, to watch TV, read magazines or novels, go for nature walks or take vacations, or get married and have children. The reasons we give ourselves to do what we like are equally endless. We give ourselves a break or a rest; we call what we're doing being 'right' or 'righteous;' or, for no clear reason, we turn away from unpleasantness and grab at something fun and distracting. As adults we know from experience how often we've chosen an easy distraction and lost the momentum for something that had much greater value and reward.

If by renouncing a lesser happiness one may realize a greater
happiness, let the wise man renounce the lesser, having regard for
the greater.

                    Pakinnakavagga: Miscellaneous (Dhp XXI 290)

SUGGESTIONS FOR PRACTICE:

- Consciously choose your structured entertainment.
- Watch the arising of the thought for entertainment, the intention, the preparation, the doing.
- Reflect afterwards by assessing your body and mind to see if the entertainment, in fact, did relax or distract in useful ways, or if it just added another very subtle layer of anxiety or distraction to an already distracting pattern.
- Ask, or even experiment with, whether there is something more wholesome or skillful you can do that will provide better results.

FAMILY

I discuss family life in general in Chapter 13. However, I'm including this discussion of family in the discussion of entertainment, even though it seems counterintuitive to include having a family with activities like going to an art gallery as a type of distraction or entertainment. But is it? The unexamined life has obliged people the world over to mimic and to seek the pleasures and rewards that our parents and society have taught us and expect of us, and to obey the invisible influence of the genetic command to reproduce. One of the chief lessons we learn as children is that we will grow up and have families, and for the most part this is true whether in Europe or Asia, or whether Muslim, Buddhist, or Christian.

What isn't seen and isn't often examined from a meditative perspective before we are funneled into family life is whether we chose to participate in these activities or whether we have succumbed to the expectations of our parents and society in general. Without examination from a meditative perspective, we cannot determine if they readily serve the cultivation of clinging or non-clinging.

Most of us cannot extricate ourselves from the notion that having a family is the right and righteous thing to do. We give ourselves inflated notions of our importance because we are now responsible for the health and welfare of those who cannot fare for themselves. It may be true, but being a responsible mentor and clinging to being a provider are two different realities. Clinging to the notion of being the provider is a profound distraction and can be amazingly entertaining. For example, how many times have you had to look at the picture of an infant from somebody's wallet, or listen endlessly about what their kids are doing? How is this not entertainment based on unobserved clinging?

QUESTIONS FOR THE *YOGI:*

- How, as a family person, can I use my circumstances to see how I can use the experience of having a family in the development of *sampajañña*?
- Are there ways I can use my circumstances to observe how I can use the experience of having a family as a way to cultivate *mettā, karunā, muditā, upekkhā,* and the *pāramīs*?
- Do I use having a family as a method to check out of the meditative level and bathe in the notions of being and doing the right and righteous thing?

Play and Humor

Humor and play are challenging areas of practice both at home and on retreat. They can be extremely valuable, but in my experience they are often not examined or encouraged. Having experienced the effects of a misunderstanding grounded in personal ignorance, I have come to recognize that both of these avenues of practice are fraught with marked levels of unwholesomeness. However, I can't help but give a nod to their usefulness.

The attitude of play, the joy of unbridled investigation coupled with the absence of fear of failure, may be one outstanding mental factor not delineated or emphasized in many meditative traditions. Play teaches us what it is like to be in an avalanche experience of investigation, effort, and awe. As adults, we lose this skill. Not only do we lose it, we forget we ever had it.

Everyday practice is by its nature a recipe for 'failure' like baseball, where the greatest hitters in the game have always failed at least 60% of the time. Thomas Edison said, "I have not failed. I've just found 10,000 ways that won't work." Everyday practice combined with investigation and fun is how and where we learn that 'failure' is not a reason to stop or hesitate; it is the place where we learn from our mistakes and start again with a grin.

Many times during difficult periods of my practice or difficult periods of my everyday life, stepping outside myself and putting on my 'Groucho hat' has had benefits beyond the obvious chuckles. Making myself or the situation a tad less personal has often translated to letting in a moment without as much attachment. The chuckle, smile, and ironic compassion that come from seeing myself and the situation like a good joke or a funny movie can help to balance the spiritual faculties.

Obviously this type of practice is not for everybody. I suggest you experiment. Humor is part of play and play is integral to balance. Balancing our practice is the key to deepening our wisdom.

CHAPTER 17

Creativity

CREATIVITY IS THE MOST DIFFICULT of the 15 categories to discuss. Because creativity is about activities that are not only pleasant but often benefit self and others when embarked with wholesome intention, they tend to be areas that many a *yogi* have difficulty looking at simply as an object of observation. All creativity is not wholesome; but whether wholesome or unwholesome, creativity comes with a pleasant feeling tone, making it a particularly hard nut to crack. Also, creativity comes in gradations. It can express itself in being able to perform a simple task or by discovering the best tomato at the grocery, all the way to curing cancer or playing Chopin one handed.

In other words, creativity plays an important role in our everyday lives and happens frequently throughout our day. This discussion is about pleasantness and attachment when creativity is unseen or when it is strong. Creativity requires a specific type of mindset, and it can be accompanied by subtle and at times intense joy. The process of creative thinking plays an important role in our adaptability to each other and to our environment. It is one of the great gifts of being human. Plain and simple, creativity is fun.

Creative acts, such as getting lost in activities like transplanting parts of your garden or planning your kid's college education, might have functional applications and could, in fact, be necessary in your householder's life. However, even when the action is necessary, there may also be an unseen attachment to pleasantness, which is a wake-up call. While observing that unpleasantness can wake us up to reactivity, we need to observe pleasantness as well with the same open-handed intensity as unpleasantness.

If attachment co-arises, creativity could be likened, to some degree, to preferences (*see* Chapter 15) because of the unseen pleasantness and almost instantaneous ownership of the experience. But it is more than just pleasantness unseen. There is something inherently human about putting two numbers together and coming up with the total, or seeing a problem and the fix, or having a totally new beautiful idea arise out of nowhere.

Becoming familiar with creativity's characteristics and qualities will support you in more easily accessing the creative mind as well as not getting caught by the ignorance of attachment. This noticing with less attachment and greater attention will serve the meditation and everyday practice when the mind is happy, joyous, or equanimous. At those times in meditation and in our everyday lives when we don't notice these very intense happy and pleasant states of mind, we begin to identify with them as *me* and *mine*. If this happens, either in every-day life or on the cushion, the natural tendency is for the mind to cling, to identify with that state. Knowing those states, one is better able to be present.

In our gradual progress towards freedom from reactivity, quite a few insights arise. Some of them are extremely pleasant and some very unpleasant. In either case, they are creative moments, and the mind will naturally get stuck to varying degrees in the joy of having discovered something new, even transformative. Knowing the qualities of our rela-tionship and tendencies towards attachment to creativity can assist us with letting go with greater ease. The more we are familiar with the workings and tendencies of the mind, the less likely we are to attach to them for extended periods of time.

QUESTIONS FOR THE *YOGI:*

- What is creativity?
- How does it affect my life?
- How can I use it as an object of attention?
- How can I use it skillfully without getting lost in it?
- When does a creative thought become 'my' creative thought?
- When do creativity and any accompanying pleasantness arise in formal practice, and do I get caught in the pleasantness?

HELPFUL CAUTION

This examination could get overworked, especially during a home practice or on a home retreat. If that happens, simply be aware that the process itself has the potential to undercut the creativity needed for the task at hand. Trying too hard can create loops of thinking, which, if not noticed, condition old patterns and usually dampen creativity.

SUGGESTIONS FOR PRACTICE:

Say you have to go to the grocery store, then you remember the hardware store is right next door saving you time and effort if you do both on one trip. This applies all the way to, for instance, solving an equation or observing an object of consciousness while being present without any self-referencing:

- Be aware of this quality as it arises even in its most subtle manifestations.
- Attend to these types of 'ah-ha' moments and bring your attention to both the body and the mind to see if there are qualities you have never noticed before.
- If so, to see if you can know them, try to feel them and be present for their passing.

CHAPTER 18

Choosing a Spiritual Practice Tradition

WE'VE DISCUSSED *ABOVE* THE NOTION that we all have spiritual practices in one way or another. Some see their family life as a spiritual practice; some might see rooting for the Dallas Cowboys as fulfilling their spiritual needs; and some will consciously choose a religious practice and look for the best way to cultivate it to attain the promise(s) it offers. These more formal types of spiritual practices are varied.

Some schools of thought offer you happiness in the next life, some right now, and some offer a gradual training towards enlightenment. This chapter offers seekers of the gradual approach a few pointers on how to choose the right practice for themselves.

Before practice-based wisdom arises, almost everyone has a much too high opinion of their own thinking, which is both surprising and not. What is surprising is just how often our minds are just plain silly, unwholesome, uncontrolled, and flat out wrong, yet we continue to believe what they tell us about the world and our lives. Without the sensible filter of spirited incredulity, we often make silly mistakes misperceiving things through the sense doors while making wrongful and often hurtful assumptions about other people's motives and even our own. All the while we seem to find ways to conveniently file away these frequent and often damaging misperceptions and harmful behaviors of mind, speech, and actions into places that appear totally immune from memory or the deduction that what we may be thinking is incorrect, unwholesome and plainly misguided. Even with all this data, most of us still have the inclination to think that what we think is accurate and right or at least to our benefit. So we just forge ahead heedlessly. When we patiently embrace the inarguable facts that our minds aren't always providing accurate data and, in fact, are frequently giving us false information, we are in a much better position to begin to change the patterns and habits of a lifetime.

Using the self-awareness described *above*, we put ourselves in a much better position to make a wise decision regarding the choice of our spiritual tradition and practice, along with what effort we want to give over to this enterprise. A soft and compassionate incredulity is ever important in areas where our unobserved blindness and preferences are intersecting with dogmas that are pleasing and are being taught by charismatic folks with all types of agendas.

Why Choose a Spiritual Tradition?

Everyone chooses and practices a religion or a spiritual tradition with varying degrees of conscious intention and intensity. In this case, 'religion' or 'spiritual tradition' means those activities we believe will make our lives better right now, in this life, or — for some — in preparation for death and the afterlife. Even agnostics and atheists choose a way of thinking or believing that provides solace when addressing the future and the unknown. It all boils down to some type of belief for the purpose of soothing our ways of walking into the unknown. In other words, everybody has a spiritual practice. Even the football-loving couch potatoes doing what they think will provide them with happiness can be said to have a type of spiritual practice.

What to Look For

It makes sense to choose your spiritual life with a conscious investigation that includes some built-in checks and balances if you want to achieve the promise of your choice. The wisest choice would be a spiritual tradition that has a history of wholesomeness and integrity, requires accountability for the practitioner and the leadership, and has many lay practitioners who exemplify the qualities you want for yourself. Assessing whether the teachers or leaders of the tradition can 'walk their talk' is a good first step towards finding a practice or school that will point you towards achieving your personal spiritual goals.

A tried and true spiritual tradition offers a balance and buffer to our confused and often mistaken ways of thinking and assumptions about the world. A good tradition both offers support when things are difficult and tempers us when we are overly excited about our progress, success or worldly happiness. That the members and teachers exemplify kindness, restraint, virtue, and humility will be signs that this practice or school might offer you tools and community that will support your enlightenment project.

Due Diligence

I am reminded of the Arabic saying:

Believe in Allah, but always tie your camel to a fencepost.
                                              – Sunan al-Tirmidhi̅ 2517

Despite any window dressing, all too often in the world of spiritual promise there are charlatans and self-deluded self-appointed 'guru' types. It serves us well to cull the chaff from the wheat before we invest our precious wholesome intentions in a practice.

With effort and time, you'll be exposed more and more to the subtleties of the practice, and you will begin to meet those around you who best exemplify the teachings. Some of these people will become friends, and some will become teachers. The more we establish carefully constructed relationships based in reciprocal wholesomeness, the more our practices will benefit through the osmosis of mutual goals and respect.

When choosing a spiritual practice and a mentor, a few cautions and practical steps are in order:

WHAT DO YOU WANT?

First and most importantly, make sure the practice you are considering is promising the results you think you want.

QUESTIONS FOR THE *YOGI:*

- Do you want meditative success?
- Do you want a ticket to heaven?
- Do you want a supportive social community?
- What do you want from the training of your *citta*, your life?
- If training the mind is not that important to you, what do you want from your spiritual life?

WHERE WILL YOU FIND WHAT YOU WANT?

Once you have a sufficient first answer to the question of what you want, look for a practice that seems consistent with the goal you've stated for yourself. Try to make sure it is harmonious with your character. This may involve going to where the practitioners meet, such as a community center or retreat center, a number of times before you make your commitment. Take some time, but don't dawdle in wishy washy arguments with yourself. Caring is different from doubting.

QUESTIONS FOR THE *YOGI:*

To optimize your investigation into religions or spiritual traditions, do some research by asking the following questions. Each of these questions is a window into the integrity of the practice. These are, after all, the criteria for whether the time, trust, and generosity you invest in the practice will have a likelihood of being wholesomely rewarded:

- How many students are realizing the promise of the practice?
- Who is benefiting from the money the organization collects?
- What is the emphasis on morality, and do the teachers and students walk their talk?

- Does the practice appear to free the student or does it bind
  the student to the practice and school in a psychological or
  financial way?

Butterfly Syndrome

Buffets are popular in affluent societies. The massive choices of a buffet
seem to me to be akin to and as popular as thinking, "I know what's best
for me." The converging influences of choice with abundance will often
lead to a plate overflowing with more food than we can comfortably eat.
A flower garden is a butterfly's buffet. Just as a butterfly flitting from
flower to flower never gets to know any one of the flowers, because we
made so many selections of dishes at the buffet, we don't get to know
any one dish intimately.

Today, especially in the West, there are many noble and wise meditative traditions available to practice and study. At first glance, this might
be seen as a spiritual buffet. The allure and the excitement of so many
ways to practice and so much to study, for some, can be likened to TV
'channel surfing,' which when practiced condemns you to never taking
the time to get to know the details of what you're watching. Staying on
the surface, if that. Never resting, always inserting your will and sense
of control.

Like diners at a buffet, many spiritual practitioners take a bit of this
practice and a slice of that thinking, "This is truly wise; this is truly
important; this will be useful." They do not consider that each 'wise,'
'important,' and 'useful' bit or slice is always offered in a context that is
special to that tradition. "So what?" you may say, "It's important stuff."
And it often is, because it is part of a larger whole. We often separate
practices or notions from the whole of the practice because we just happen to like those practices or notions. A meditative tradition relies on
what is unpleasant as much as what is pleasant for the *yogi* to learn what
the tradition is trying to teach.

We've discussed the nature of the untutored mind clinging to what
is pleasant and turning away from what is unpleasant, which is the

often-unseen weakness of a spiritual seeker who gaily accumulates a bag of tricks from a variety of traditions. For the wisdom of a school or tradition to shine forth one must know it from all its highs and lows, ups and downs, and successes and failures. Then the bits and slices will make progressive sense and become realities—not just ideas—in one's consciousness. Filling one's bag of tricks from various traditions without follow-through serves only to support clinging and aversion. This is why it is so important to find a tradition that has integrity, suits your character and provides you with the basis for a willingness to stick to it through both hard and good times. Should you wish to achieve the promise of any practice, you are going to have to be in it for the long haul.

All traditions will lead an adherent towards and then into what Christians call the 'dark night of the soul.' This is a time in practice when everything is dark and impossible. One has to live and learn while in the dark night of the soul so as to touch what is impossible over and over again, to learn how to be with what seems to be impossible to hold with equanimity and patience. If we choose our spiritual practice based on what we like and don't like, we will never discover for ourselves the meaning and reward of embracing without aversion both the bliss of freedom and the dark night of the soul.

Doubt

After you've done your due diligence, it's time to pay careful attention and watch out for doubt if and when it arises. Sensible doubt helped you to choose the practice; now a different type of doubt, known as skeptical or subjective doubt, may prevent you from benefiting from your choice. Doubt about your choice will prevent you from making a full wholehearted commitment to any of the practices at every point along the way: the beginning, in the middle, and near the 'end.' It is the nature of spiritual practice and the nature of doubt.

By its nature, doubt consumes the mind and engages it like a clutch slowing the car and preventing forward momentum. To allow the pressure on the clutch to ease, we must observe and at the same time compartmentalize doubt from the full-hearted exploration the practice is calling for.

The mind is not shy about masking massive doubt with distraction. Step back, observe and remind yourself that whatever is distracting will have some element of doubt. The more subtle our ability to recognize these masks, the more we will not get distracted by them. Often for thinking types—and Westerners tend to be thinking types—discursive intellectual analysis of what's going on is a prime example of doubt masquerading as useful thinking. Comparing yourself to others or your practice to another's is another example. An especially common type of doubt that masquerades as wholesome is a thought like, "I'll do some *mettā* now to calm the mind." This type of thinking is a trap to divert mindfulness from the object.

CAUTION:

Doubt has as many faces because our ignorance is deep.

SUGGESTIONS FOR PRACTICE:

- For a committed and prescribed time, abandon believing in your doubtful thoughts. Just know doubt as a passing thought process, and give yourself over to the study and practice that are offered.
- Say to yourself, depending on your choice: "I will go on a ten-day retreat [or engage in study sessions], listen and do what is instructed, and not add anything except my investigation and effort."
- At the end of the prescribed time period, assess what you've learned. Should it appear to have not just led towards bliss and pleasantness but also to have steered the mind and heart towards wisdom and compassion, stick with it.

QUESTIONS FOR THE *YOGI:*

Assess your practice during this period by asking:
- What has this done for my understanding and practice of virtue?
- What has this done for the opening of the heart, concentration, and wisdom of mind?
- Has this practice tended to lead me in the direction of its promise?

For me, the first criteria of the success of the practice is two-fold:

1. Has my morality and virtue before, during, and after this period been improved or not?
2. Is the quality of mind showing signs of greater generosity, virtue, concentration or wisdom?

If you can answer both of these questions sufficiently with a *yes*, commit for another longer and more energetic period of time with more study and more practice. Then reassess again, always watching carefully for whether doubt is a reflection of wisdom or ignorance. Thinking will not be the best marker. The marker will be the answers to the two questions *above*.

Notice I don't ask, "Am I happier than before?" Happiness on a spiritual journey comes and goes till it finally comes and stays. Asking, "Am I happy?" will often be a question hiding doubts.

Ups and Downs

Remember: Pleasant practice is not always good practice. This aphorism is especially relevant for those who choose meditation as a practice to change unwholesome patterns of mind. Happiness—true happiness—comes and stays when there is room for and equal acceptance of both the pleasant and the unpleasant.

In order to grow, to gain wisdom and compassion, both the depths and peaks in formal practice and in everyday life must be seen and brought into an intuitive understanding. Every wisdom practice will teach this.

This reality points to the fact that every spiritual practice worth its salt demands that there be times that the practice will be unpleasant and uncomfortable and at other times filled with ease and bliss. Both. We must come with an open heart to all experience in order for freedom to arise. You will find yourselves at this razor's edge of wisdom only if you do the due diligence before choosing the practice and investing the courage to be present again and again for both the ups and downs.

Even when you are doing the practice that is right for you and your goals, doubt about the teachings, the teacher or our willingness to go the distance at this stage of practice will often be profound and unsettling. Long stretches of unpleasantness will distract, deter and often uncouple you from your intended purpose. These periods of unpleasantness can be easily noticed, because the mind is invaded by doubt, restlessness in the forms of intense wanting and not wanting, and diminished energy, all of which make an openhearted patient investigation difficult. On the other hand, if incredibly pleasant periods arise without wise attention, the mind will latch on and get stuck by wanting to keep and sustain the pleasantness.

At these stages of practice, one will hear—all too clearly and often—extremely loud internal voices arising over and over again in the mind stream that begin with phrases like: "If only" . . . "I want" . . . "I just" . . . "I got it!" The types of thoughts that begin with these types of prefaces are indications that doubt or attachment or some other combination of the hindrances are present in the mind stream. Signs and symptoms that indicate that progress has stalled.

SUGGESTIONS FOR PRACTICE:

- Watch them.
- Smile.
- Make space for your reactivity and attachments with wise observation.
- Be patient with whatever distracting thoughts might be arising.

- Just go back to the basic practice and with patience observe any object, any emotion and see if you can notice their characteristics and their nature to come and go.

Community and Accountability

SUPPORT FROM AND ACCOUNTABILITY TO OTHERS

On a spiritual journey, we all go it alone . . . in a way. Sure, the investigation and effort come from us, but we are also supported by all who have walked this path before us and by those who are walking it now. Our teachers and our *kalyāṇamitta* are tremendous supports.

> *With regard to external factors, I don't envision any other single factor like admirable friendship as doing so much for a monk in training, who has not attained the heart's goal but remains intent on the unsurpassed safety from bondage. A monk who is a friend with admirable people abandons what is unskillful and develops what is skillful.*
>
> – Iti. 1.17

In the *Theravāda* texts the Buddha repeatedly stated that there is only a small difference between a Buddha and an *arahant*. It is mostly culture and history that inflamed the myth that the Buddha was greater and more special than he said he was. He said the very same freedom he intuitively realized is available to all. In other words, the most significant difference between him and the rest of us is the fact that he alone rediscovered the *Dhamma* without a teacher, while the rest of us have teachers and a tradition that point us in the right direction.

Part of the value of having a teacher, beyond their sharing of experience and technical knowledge, is having someone who you respect and honor to whom you want to be accountable. A teacher can be an individual or a community; both can provide a relationship that permits us to give our respect and gratitude for what is being offered.

Why is accountability important, and how do we best use this relationship skillfully? We are, more or less either consciously or unconsciously, accountable to ourselves; but there are ways others can support and help us in the endeavor. Being with others very often inspires us to be better than we'd be alone. We may have learned the power that comes with accountability to our family, friends, teams, or teachers. Even if not, either through our fear of wrongdoing and the repugnance of experiencing moral shame [Pāli: *hiri* and *ottappa*] or through competition, all of us have learned that we do better than we thought we could or would when in relationship with others.

On a meditative journey, almost all of us occasionally need a helpful, virtuous, wise hand to support or direct us or just be there as a model, not unlike being on a hunt or a migration when we were hunter-gatherers. Fortunately, if there isn't a specific person to offer inspiration and support, there are ways to allow the group to help, such as through *sangha* retreats for which *The Sangha Nonresidential Retreat Guide* can be of use.

MONASTIC PRACTICE

Monastic practice utilizes both the individual and the group. The *Vinaya Piṭaka* has rules that require a monastic to rely on their preceptor and on the group to help them maintain their commitment. This happens with the confessing of transgressions and, when necessary, the adjudication of them by the preceptor or the *sangha* at large. These avenues of community support and accountability have a dramatic impact on one's willingness to walk the talk.

Lay life doesn't offer the same type of social pressure or social structure as the monastic *sangha*. The reverse is mostly the case: Lay life encourages us to hide our transgressions and our failings from others and ourselves.

REPORT ABOUT YOUR PRACTICE

To support your practice of *A Householder's Vinaya*, identify someone with whom you can share and to whom you can report details about your practice; someone whose opinion and wisdom you respect. Practice here does not mean just meditation; it means your relationship to your *sīla*, and your practice of *sampajañña* in your everyday life. Make this a regular occurrence.

It is common and to be expected that when we report, most of us will soften or omit facts like being depressed or confused or just not wanting or able to find the ease of momentum. These types of reports are as important as the ones that glow and are infused with enthusiasm. Be honest; don't just paint a good picture.

FIND A *SAṄGHA*

It is also helpful to find an active and diverse *saṅgha* to be a part of. If you engage publicly with a group, your actions become practices in *hiri* and *ottappa*. Join the administration, offer *dāna*, show up to meetings, be public.

Both having a mentor and being in a *saṅgha* lift our aspirations higher and oblige us to consciously and more frequently visit our personal motivations for practicing. Both the frequency of contact and the desire to gain the respect of a mentor and community are parts of the training that not only assist us in our outward actions, but also strengthen our inner commitments.

Exposing ourselves to situations that call for humility and patience will help us practice *A Householder's Vinaya* with greater ease and success. Being in community and relationship are ways to practice that sitting on the cushion can't offer.

Stick with One Practice

Choose one practice and stick with it! Any spiritual path will have many ups and downs and engender some of the doubts mentioned *above*. Until wisdom arrives, the downs will result in doubt, which gives the mind many reasons to change practice, to turn away from the unpleasant or give up. Don't! If you've done your due diligence and begun the practice you've chosen with good investigation and effort, and the tradition you've chosen has met the outward criteria of integrity and wholesomeness, you've likely found a good match. The downs and doubts mean that the path has led you to the dark places, the difficult places, the places that keep you blind to your own ignorance. And it is here that the practice and good guidance become critical in order to pass into the freedom on the other side of ignorance.

CHAPTER 19

Practice, Study, Ceremony

What Is Spiritual Practice?

MOST FOLKS WOULD CONSIDER the components that identify the activities of a spiritual life to be practice (including prayer, formal meditation and chanting), study and ceremony. It's commonly believed that if one just does the practice, the study or the ceremony, all will be well, provided they are done with continuity and integrity. And yet, every other category that we've explored in *A Householder's Vinaya* expands the meaning of what it means to do practice, study, and do ceremony. Three aphorisms come to mind from two of my teachers that touch on this:

> *If it's easy, it's cheap.*
> — U Pandita

> *Buddhism is simple but doing it doesn't*
> *make me a simpleton.*
> — Munindraji

> *Buddhist practice is simple but not easy.*
> — U Pandita

Each of these pithy acknowledgements about spiritual practice warns us that what we are about to start, or what we are studying, is not simple or easy, and it takes sincere effort over a long haul to harvest its full promise.

All-important on the spiritual path is *how* we do whatever we do. Above all else, the emphasis in the fifteen categories discussed in this guide is how to make every-day mundane activities a part of a fully integrated practice and halt the tendency to separate formal practice from our everyday lives in our minds. Simply performing an activity doesn't mean that we are effecting neurological changes or training our hearts to open to wisdom and compassion. What moves us towards our goal is what qualities of *citta* we mix in with our intention.

Everyday life can be likened to a sailing ship: Our thoughts, speech and actions are the keel, the rudder and the material that floats the boat, while formal practice is the sails. To cross over the sea and make port, we need to be able to float, steer with good navigation and make sure there is balance and accuracy. The monastic *Vinaya* assists monastics with navigating beyond the human inclination towards staying close to home with continuous spiritual energy, effort and investigation. *A Householder's Vinaya* does the same for the laity.

QUESTIONS FOR THE *YOGI:*

- Am I striving?
- Am I doing what I do because my group or family does it?
- Am I bored and just going through the motions?

We discover through experimentation how to make our daily practices fit our lives. Each and every lifestyle, regardless of conditions, has places during the day when *sati-sampajañña* is both available and called for. We experiment by planning our practice and following through in our own unique ways. For example, the practices of a person with an infant doing home practice will look much different from that of a retiree. How we practice in our daily lives is an opportunity to actively establish a skill base of wholesome strengths that translate both to formal meditation practice and to practice in everyday life. The doing allows for a greater probability that the tools investigated, practiced and trained will begin to spontaneously arise and become useful for the rest of our lives.

Home practice, home retreat, and the practice of *A Householder's Vinaya* are opportunities to discover our choices in practice, our rhythms, strengths and weaknesses all at the cutting edge of our wisdom. A home retreat is like a formal retreat in that on a formal retreat, we learn the precise clarity of *sati* in a rarefied environment, while on home retreat we learn how to practice both *sati* and *sampajañña* in our everyday life. The information we learn in the first few retreats at home teaches the us how to make our home practices fit our characters and our circumstances.

Concentration or One-Pointedness Practices

CONCENTRATION IN EVERYDAY LIFE

At its basic level, it takes concentration to do the simplest of tasks, to do basic tasks throughout the day. Without some level of concentration, we can do almost nothing more than breathe. It even takes an element of concentration to stay standing.

Concentration can also be honed to laser-like focus with varying degrees of intensity. This isn't meditative concentration, but it is very similar. This type of concentration, like the meditative type, suppresses distracting thoughts and allows the action to happen without self-oriented thinking or distracting thoughts or moods. We know this without the cultivation of meditation. All of us throughout our lives use concentration to study, play musical instruments, perform with our bodies in very precise and complex ways, and much more. With the development of concentration, we can master very complex tasks, such as winning gold medals at the Olympics, curing cancer, baking cakes, etc.

SAMĀDHI

In meditation, *samādhi* in the practice of one pointedness happens naturally. *Samādhi* practiced in meditation will lead to skills that allow the meditator to consciously choose how and when to use it.

There is a relationship between *samādhi* and *sati*. It takes *samādhi* to stay focused on objects, whether there is only one object the mind attends to continuously or a flow of objects taken one at a time. It takes focus of mind to be aware and investigate a moment of consciousness from its first moment of arising till it disappears over and over again. These qualities of practice intertwine a little like the double helix of our DNA. Both are necessary to varying degrees at various times to realize the full fruit of *sati* and *sampajañña*.

In order to do *sati* effectively, one must develop a level of intense concentration not generally accessible to the untrained mind. To make the *samādhi* continuous, the meditator needs to be able to observe an object of consciousness arise, change and pass away, to be followed by another and another etc., without self-referencing interfering with the process. Without sufficient concentration and continuity of concentration, this level of awareness is unavailable to the untrained mind. *Samādhi* is vital to the cultivation and fruition of any enlightenment project regardless of the tradition.

JHĀNA

Another type and level of *samādhi* leads to what is called in English 'absorption' or in Pāli *jhāna*. These states of mind suppress the normal activities of mind and bring a state that is free from all distractions. The mind is free of the effects of the hindrances (sensual desire, ill will, sloth and torpor, restlessness and worry, and skeptical doubt), allowing the mind to be entirely focused and, for all intents and purposes, to be completely wholesome. A mind free of the hindrances is a mind that is happy and content beyond relative happiness of any order. A significant difference between this level of concentration and that of the scholar or athlete at their best moments is that a person who has trained and has mastered access to *jhāna* can do it at will and control the mind in and out of these states of consciousness.

BRAHMA-VIHĀRA PRACTICE

A type of practice that can be used to develop one's *samādhi* is *Brahma-vihāra* meditation practice. The *Brahma-vihāras* are four wholesome states of mind the Buddha encouraged practitioners to cultivate:

- *Mettā* [loving-kindness]
- *Karunā* [compassion]
- *Muditā* [empathetic joy]
- *Upekkhā* [equanimity]

Practicing the *Brahma-vihāras* can lead to states of *jhāna* through the development of various mental factors and perspectives that are very useful in mindfulness practice.

When these states of mind are developed and are allowed to come to maturity, they transform the mind into states of such purity of being that there is, in those moments, no separation between self and other. When *mettā, karunā, muditā* and *upekkhā* mature, the mind becomes 'universal;' we achieve a state of consciousness in which these states of mind have no ownership. Each of us has the capacity to realize these states, and when they are realized we enter into states of mind in which, while they are present, there is no self and other. The *mettā* just is, the *karunā* just is, etc.

There are specific meditative techniques the meditator uses to bring one-pointed attention towards the cultivation of these mind states. Practicing meditation in this way trains the meditator's mind to concentrate in profound ways, and it simultaneously teaches the meditator the reality and the subtlety of what *mettā, karunā, muditā* and *upekkhā* are and what they mean to the mind stream and the happiness of all beings.

A SMALL TIP:

Not mentioned in teachings or normal *Dhamma* talks at our *saṅghas*— or even on retreat in monastery or retreat center—is the little-known fact that when the mind is sufficiently trained in mindfulness, and some of the hindrances have been uprooted or significantly ameliorated, the mind and heart will spontaneously encounter the *Brahma-viharas* like a traveler finds an oasis in the desert. Suppress or uproot the hindrances and *mettā* becomes the baseline.

U Kundala, a profound meditation master and student of Mahasi Sayadaw, was called the *Mettā* Sayadaw because of the incredibly deep and manifestly gentle, loving qualities of his character. I sat with him once. He was among a very few people I have ever met who radiated kindness and a loving nature in profound ways. He was asked frequently if he did *mettā* meditation in order to realize his beatific qualities. His answer always remained the same; to paraphrase: "Mindfulness will lead you to *mettā*."

Reflection or Prayer, Chanting, Ceremony

Every spiritual tradition that I can think of relies on reflection or prayer, chanting, and ceremony as styles of practice. Each of them in their own way helps to build a home for our intentions and can offer ways to share and communicate with others wanting company on our paths through life and the dying process.

Chanting and ceremonies are shared activities that arise from tradition; they are manifestations of shared belief. They provide a framework, a physical language for inspiration and community. These are all important and useful tools in the whole of a spiritual life.

Chanting and ceremony have the greatest power when done with full attention to their meaning. Simply reciting a phrase or bowing, by themselves, have no power to effect any lasting fundamental change to the way the *citta* works. The power for change comes through the application of what the phrase, the sound, the movement means to us and others, and whether our framework for doing these activities has an impact on changing how the mind works. The reflection and the training on the meaning provides the power as does the attention to the intention, investigation, effort and *sati-sampajañña* we bring when doing them.

Reflection, chanting, and ceremony are in many ways close cousins to *sampajañña*, and in some ways they are the same. As an example, the reflection taken from reciting the Hail Mary or the *Shma Yisroel*, bowing to Allah, or repeating a mantra takes reflection to do and to benefit from. It is the reflective power that motivates and opens doors to both conscious and intuitive understanding.

Saying a phrase or bowing without reflection or paying attention is just habit and preference. For many, religious activity gains its appeal by unnoticed and unattended to attachment to pleasant feeling tones. Most religions and most of the activity of religious behavior are about belonging and sharing in tribal ways, unconscious ways of just being human and finding our place in the group and sharing pleasant experiences.

Do your practices, study your texts, and take inspiration from your ceremonies. Do them with as much *sati-sampajañña* as you can muster as often as you find you have the skill. The combination is high octane practice.

Conclusion

If . . . one habitually yields to all whims, or allows oneself too easily to be deflected from one's purpose, then such qualities as energy, endurance, concentration, loyalty, etc., will gradually be undermined and weakened to such an extent that they become insufficient for achieving that original purpose, or even for truly appreciating it any longer. In that way, it often happens that, unheeded by the person concerned, his [or her] ideals, religious convictions, and even his [or her] ordinary purpose and ambitions, are turned into empty shells which he [or she] still carries along with him [or her], solely through habit.

– Nyanaponika Thera,
The Heart of Buddhist Meditation, pp. 52-53.

NYANAPONIKA THERA POINTS OUT TO US what anybody who has grown up knows. He says that in order to develop any skill or wholesome quality of *citta*, one must practice with focused attention for the practice or skill to reach maturity. As the taxi driver in New York City said to the tourist who asked him how to get to Carnegie Hall, "Practice, practice, practice!"

A Householder's Vinaya is just sheet music. You will choose to rouse your spiritual intentions regularly or not depending on your circumstances, determination, and integrity. Your ability to alchemize the lead of your life into the gold of your practice is up to you. There are ways to use the context and nuance of *A Householder's Vinaya* and *The Home Retreat Guide* in your life by focusing on one of the 15 categories or by taking the whole as a practice. Either one or both will point you towards your goal. It is up to you.

Reflections and Concerns

Until now, a structured *vinaya* specifically for householders did not exist. By definition, *A Householder's Vinaya* is new and might be viewed by some as being radical. *A Householder's Vinaya* will likely be seen as a challenge to the old ways of doing things, the opposite of the way things have been done for thousands of years in *Theravāda* and other ancient meditative traditions. It will be the job of the laity to appreciate the consequences and be generous with their wisdom should this new way to practice as householders be met with resistance.

There can often be large consequences with things that are new. We know this simply by watching our own experience moment by moment. We know that one moment affects the next and the next and the next. We know, for example, the reaction in the mind has different intensities when we wash our hands or when we stub our toe or when the supermarket is out of tomatoes, compared to when our dog has just died. What will this moment be like when we offer a new *vinaya* to an ancient tradition? How will it affect the dissemination of the Buddha's extant teachings and the feelings of people wedded to orthodoxy who have never had a householder's *vinaya* before and see the Canon as complete and a done deal? What will be the reactions from those it affects or possibly offends? How might householders begin to see themselves in ways they didn't 50 to 100 years ago? One thing is clear, should *A Householder's Vinaya* begin to play its intended role, the voice of the monastic will be affected, ancient traditions of the role of lay people will be undermined and both wisdom and tomfoolery by many may arise in the wake of the change.

A likely consequence of *A Householder's Vinaya* will be the plucking of the strings of relationship between the monastics and the laity. A new sound will arise, a new tune. A probable outcome in the short term is that lay people will begin to marginalize the voice of the monastics, believing its own voice is as valuable and clear as that of the monastic *saṅgha*. This is inevitable and very misguided. Some monastics may see this new practice as heresy, which will serve only to alienate the laity and demonstrate in real time a weakness in an unwise and inflexible attitude between tradition and change. Both types of thinking and possible consequences are simply poor and misguided ways to meet this inevitable change.

The monastic *saṅgha* is vital to the sustaining of the *sāsana* and will remain so whether or not *A Householder's Vinaya* takes root. The monastery will remain the place where one can choose the most conducive conditions to study, learn and share the teachings. The monastics' adherence to tradition and consistency allows them the privilege of and the appropriate responsibility for maintaining the purity of the core teachings of the Buddha. Regardless of how much a householder is able to practice their *vinaya* at home, practice conditions—for the vast majority, most of the time—will remain best in a monastery. Thanks in no small part to the historical context of Buddhist monasticism and lay practice, the laity as a group is much too affected by collective ignorance to be wise enough to know and understand their preferences and prejudices. This collective blindness will limit their ability most of the time to carry the responsibility for maintaining the purity and orthodoxy of the core teachings.

Individually and collectively the lay *saṅgha* will be served by watching the encroachment of any self-inflated opinions of their collective wisdom. The monastic *saṅgha*, for the health of the *sāsana*, will continue to best serve their responsibility by collaborating with changes that are putting pressure on archaic traditions.

Collaboration and the Future of *A Householder's Vinaya*

It took decades for the Buddha to create the *Pātimokkha*. We no longer have a Buddha to adjudicate conflicts and give advice and make rules. We do, however, have wise and considered lay practitioners and scholars who have a voice in instructing us how to live lay lives. In our time and age in history, collaboration and trial and error will play a role in the development of *A Householder's Vinaya*.

Neither the monastic order nor the laity have indisputable authority to say yea or nay. Buddhism does not have anything like a pope to be the sole authority. The forces of time and social change listen to no one in particular. This project, the development of *A Householder's Vinaya*, is now the property of all of us. This offering is an attempt to steer lay people towards graciously accepting their new-found positions in Buddhist society and moving forward to help create guidelines for an intensive *vinaya*-oriented practice. The edits to come are inevitable, and suggestions are invited with the hope that what comes will offer us wiser and more skilled voices than this first attempt.

May the editions to come discover and develop ways to move this notion forward and make *A Householder's Vinaya* a lasting, elastic, and relevant guide for generations to come.

PART THREE

The Home Retreat Guide

PART III: THE HOME RETREAT GUIDE
TABLE OF CONTENTS

Introduction

What Is Home Retreat?

DURING HOME RETREATS, we take a specific period of time—a specified number of days or weeks—to bring an out-of-the-ordinary attention into our everyday activities, coupled with an increase of formal meditation practice. By increasing the frequency and the total amount of time we practice *vipassanā* [insight] and *samatha* [concentration] meditation, we anchor the retreat. What ties the practice together is the cultivation of *sampajañña* [clear comprehension] in our everyday activities. On home retreat, *sampajañña* becomes the *yogi's* [meditator's] primary meditation tool when not doing formal meditation.

Home retreat is a committed, prescribed period of time in which we intensify our meditative focus beyond our usual home practice by:

1. Applying skills gleaned from residential retreats such as:
   a. Using techniques learned on retreat to support continuity of *sati-sampajañña* [insight and clear comprehension].
   b. Deepening intention by reflecting on previously attained wholesome states of mind that were realized on formal retreat.
   c. Remembering to restrain the senses [Pāli: *indriya-saṃvara*] thus catalyzing continuity of effort by embracing renunciation [Pāli: *nekkhamma*].
2. Bringing in new techniques to be explored and developed, for example:

    a. Using *vipassanā* when it is appropriate during our daily lives, and exploring the full spectrum of what *vipassanā* is.

    b. Using *sampajañña* when *vipassanā* is not appropriate.

    c. Using both during formal meditation sessions.

3. Altering our daily routines and our focus in order to bring much greater continuous attention to our daily activities, including:

    a. Following the schedule with integrity coupled with flexible kindness.

    b. Making Right Speech [Pāli: *sammā-vaca*], Right Action [Pāli: *sammā-kammanta*], and Right Livelihood [Pāli: *sammā-ājīva*] constant fields of attention and experimentation.

    c. Adding micro-moments of mindfulness throughout the day.

Who Can Benefit from Home Retreat

Home retreats are exceptionally valuable for two types of lay *yogi*:

- A *yogi* who, regardless of formal retreat experience or level of wisdom, is motivated to make spiritual practice the central focus of their life.
- A *yogi* who has done a number of longish formal retreats and finds that their lay life practice is under-supported between formal retreats.

This guide relies heavily on the Mahasi Sayadaw school of *Theravāda* Buddhist practice as a foundation, but spiritual practice is not exclusive to any one tradition. Thus, this guide can be of service to anyone who is sincere in cultivating an integrated and effective meditative life. Anyone who may be unfamiliar with Mahasi practice or Buddhist meditation practices should consider using their own spiritual tradition's language by applying the practice to their own when it appears to fit and be useful.

Pāli Words and Phrases

Words and phrases in Pāli, the ancient Buddhist scriptural language, are used regularly throughout the text. When a Pāli word or phrase is used in the text, it has been chosen because there is no adequate English word or phrase to capture the precise meaning.

Knowing or being able to use Pāli is not a necessary requirement to practice or study *vipassanā* meditation, but it does allow those who practice in this particular way to share a common language. Sharing a language specific to meditation can have wide ranging benefits; it can serve to reduce confusion when speaking with others regarding meditation practice while simultaneously creating community.

It will be especially useful to have a working understanding of these basic terms:

- *Sati*
- *Sampajañña*
- *Sati-sampajañña*
- *Yogi*
- *Vipassanā*
- *Vinaya*

Sampajañña

Sampajañña is one of the most commonly used Pāli terms in this guide. This particular Pāli term is frequently used, because it is generally not understood and often overlooked during formal retreat practice. *Sampajañña* is especially important for householder practice and a successful home retreat. In a nutshell, *sampajañña* is a mental process by which the *yogi* considers every speech and action through the filters of the Four Noble Truths, with an emphasis on virtue, and the Three Characteristics [Pāli: *ti-lakkhaṇa*]. Without these conscious intentions, our practices can become dry and we can become silently separated from the intentions that move us to practice.

'Focus' and 'Attention'

Throughout the text, the terms 'focus' and 'attention' also appear frequently. As used here, these terms are interchangeable and have the same general meaning. They are used to describe our attempts to bring meditative skills to bear in the moment. Sometimes they will mean very intensive laser-like concentration, and sometimes they will mean a softer and more general understanding and approach to the situation being explored. The terms will be self-explanatory depending on the context being used.

Formal Meditation

The phrase 'formal meditation' is frequently used throughout these guides. In general, formal meditation is when the *yogi* brings the entire mental focus to whatever mental or physical object arises in consciousness by using either *sati* or *samatha* for extended periods of time in one of a variety of postures. Buddhist practices prescribe four postures:

- Sitting
- Standing
- Walking
- Lying down

For the purpose of these guides, 'formal meditation' means either sitting or walking meditation based on the techniques described in the *Satipaṭṭhāna Sutta* (MN 10).

Using the Appendices

The following appendices apply to this guide, *A Householder's Vinaya*, and *The Saṅgha Nonresidential Retreat Guide*:

Appendix 1: Glossary
Appendix 2: Table of Quotations and Aphorisms
Appendix 3: Table of Abbreviations
Appendix 4: Table of Lists, Chants and Reflections
Appendix 5: Bibliography and Suggested Reading
                and Listening List
Appendix 6: Retreat Centers and Monasteries

The Glossary is intended to be more than a quick glance at the meaning of a word or to the context of a phrase. You will find a rich vein of information with links to commentaries and original texts, along with a few definitions and comments I have provided.

The appendices offer the reader the opportunity to consult a variety or resources and study the necessary fundamentals of this meditation practice. Using them provides the best way to utilize *The Home Retreat Guide*.

TIP:

Using the appendices can open doors to scriptural study and, for many, can be a key to a better understanding of what meditation does and is about.

CHAPTER 1

Daily Life, Home Practice, and Home Retreat

Home Practice and Daily Life

JUST LIKE OUR LIVES WHILE ON RETREAT, our everyday lives mold our mental attitudes and provide opportunities for insight to be realized and to be strengthened or weakened depending on our intention and follow-through. For a householding *yogi* who aspires to deeper meditative wisdom, home practice with the use of home retreat must be seen as a vital part of a spiritual life.

With home practice, we can practice meditative continuity during everyday life. Home life can be a time to give greater attention to the development of various types of skillful means [Pāli: *upāya*], as well as investigate, develop and master them. It can be a time to learn new techniques and a time to explore new ways of applying and testing meditative wisdom in very complex real-life situations.

With home practice, daily life activities are not seen as just segments of time when we try to hold our practice together amidst a busy life. We don't see our everyday life as a holding pattern between retreats. Done in the context of home practice, and with the support of home retreat, our activities of daily life offer us opportunities to cultivate a skillfully crafted lifestyle. This will deepen the intuitive understanding of our practice wisdom, which will support the potential of establishing a more intimate life-long everyday integrated practice.

Opportunities of Lay Life

Lay life for a committed *yogi* is exactly the circumstance to explore the wisdom gained on retreat or during formal everyday practice. Lay life offers the householding *yogi* opportunities to practice frequently in constructive ways because that is the nature of the challenge and opportunity for the mind during our everyday lives.

In everyday life we don't have the same environmental conditions for or the intention to observe our inner experiences the way we do on formal retreat. While our thoughts repeat themselves in the same way as on retreat, more often than not, at home we don't pay attention. Rather, we think of other things or just zone out, especially when going from one activity to another. I suggest you use these spaces between activities to bring increased attention and reflection to your life.

A *Householder's Vinaya* and the retreat guides invite, encourage, perhaps cajole us to recondition the mind away from our habits of reactivity and attachment by using our lives as the practice field. Opportunities to practice include performing even mundane, repetitive activities like reaching for door handles, touching our faces or adjusting our glasses. Opportunities to practice walking meditation are available over and over again throughout the day, such as walking to the car or between the rooms in the house.

Developing strong intention to maintain both *sati* and *sampajañña* in formal and everyday life is the purpose of the home retreat. We increase our formal sitting and walking at home, but we also train ourselves out in the world when running our errands, doing our chores, working, being with family. The intention and follow through in maintaining our formal sitting and walking meditation commitments help to create the nuclei of the home retreat; the electrons are what we do throughout the rest of the day. A way to keep it all moving, as just one example, is to do intentional walking meditation while moving about at work, or at the grocery, or while walking to your car. In a similar way you can bring attention to reaching for the dish soap, or lifting a leg to put into a pant leg, or ladling soup into your kid's bowl. Home retreat will succeed or not depending on how many 'in-between moments' you are able to string together with *sati* and *sampajañña* as the filter of the activity.

Yogis can explore and simultaneously learn new facets of skills learned on retreat or in formal practice at home, because they are obliged to apply them in new and complicated circumstances.

Opportunities of Home Retreat

During home retreat, we have the opportunity to stop the unspoken— often untenable—compromise of trying to fit our spiritual practices into our everyday lives. Instead we choose to consciously train ourselves to make our everyday lives just another part of our spiritual lives. Home retreat is one of the most accessible and useful trainings to improve the quality of our spiritual lives.

Home retreat differs in great magnitude from most regular home meditation practice. Many very sincere *yogis* are able to formally meditate just once or twice each day because they focus primarily on managing daily life. Over time, meditation practice becomes a second-tier priority, and habits, preferences and desires increasingly go unobserved, further reconditioning and deepening our blindness to those same habits and patterns and how they affect our lives.

During home retreat, the *yogi* switches those priorities for a pre-scribed amount of time, making the meditation practice the priority and everyday life the practice field. The focus changes from allowing everyday habits and patterns of daily life to overwhelm the intention to pay attention, instead switching the intention to making meditation and reflective living the priority. This switch in focus converts the same daily life conditions into a field of proactive, wholesome effort.

By frequently doing home retreats, *yogis* give themselves unconscious permission to integrate and further advance their use of techniques and wisdom gleaned in home practice, thus creating a continuous platform to deepen practice.

Paying Attention

Inattention undermines our ability to achieve whatever meditative goals we may have. Periods of inattention lead to more periods of inattention. However, continuous attention to meditative goals supports our momentum towards success. Continuous attention leads to longer periods of attention.

The intention to cultivate continuous wholesome [Pāli: *kusala*] attention is the same whether one is on a formal residential retreat or at home. The skill set and much of the emphasis will be different, but the basic teachings and the underlying goals and techniques remain the same. The bedrock of this practice is the cultivation and realization of the Noble Eightfold Path.

Anyone who has been successful at anything in life knows that continuity and perseverance towards the goal, combined with a constellation of additional useful mental factors [Pāli: *cetasika*], support strong focus. When we bring the following mental factors, among others, to any activity, that activity has a greater potential for success:

- Investigation [Pāli: *dhamma-vicaya*].
- Concentration [Pāli: *samādhi*].
- Effort [Pāli: *sammā-vāyāma*].
- Patience [Pāli: *khanti*].

How Home Retreat Differs from Formal Retreat

Despite having core similarities, a home retreat does not look like a formal residential retreat at a retreat center or monastery and should not be regarded in that light. Everyday life is essential to the home retreat. When doing a home retreat, you continue normal activities of daily living, but instead of fitting meditation practice in when it's convenient, the practice becomes the primary focus.

While it's true that a home retreat can be structured to closely resemble a residential retreat, the intention for doing a home retreat is to learn how to integrate the realities of a lay life with the wisdom gleaned from formal practices. One uses everyday responsibilities, choices and distractions as the field for practice.

Template for the Home Retreat

You can use the following template for activities of daily living and necessary human activities to help you before and during the home retreat, as well as to help you create the schedule (*see* Chapter 2). Some of the categories and some of the examples within a category may not apply to you or your schedule and needs. Use the template as a way to investigate and develop a retreat that will work for you:

DOMESTIC CONDITIONS:

1. Discuss your retreat with your family or housemates; explain to them what you are doing and see if they are willing to understand and support you.
2. Be clear about any agreements you make with family or housemates, and make sure they understand what you and they have agreed upon.
3. Once the retreat begins, if agreements don't hold, especially if they are with children, simply notice; watch your inner reactions and try not to redirect those involved. Use the opportunity to observe your reaction carefully and gently rather than the reactions of others.

ACTIVITIES IN GENERAL, INCLUDING WORKING AND MEETING OTHER RESPONSIBILITIES:

1. Make as many short periods of *sati-sampajañña* happen as possible as described in the text.
2. Cultivate micro-moments of mindfulness.

3. Pause:

    a. Stop what you're doing.

    b. Feel what is arising in the body, observe it and see if it remains the same or changes.

    c. Reflect on *sampajañña* and *appamada* [heedfulness].

    d. Watch if the thinking, judging or the controlling deluded mind is present.

    e. See what happens while you are observing.

    f. Notice what happens to any story that was present.

    g. Return to the activity.

4. Restrain the senses according to your personal edge.

5. Slow down physical movements:

    a. Walking meditation as taught in the Mahasi School is done with exaggerated slow movements. (*See* How to Read This Book for walking meditation instructions.)

    b. Be deliberate and precise in bodily actions.

    c. Do things with as much kindness as is available in each moment.

    d. Focus on kindness to animate and inanimate objects alike.

6. Cultivate generous kindness in any personal interaction.

7. Watch for a grumpy and complaining mind, and observe any tendencies you have or have had about behaving with a grumpy mind and not paying attention.

8. If waiting in a line or otherwise not actively using purposeful attention while out and about, center the body and do *mettā* [loving-kindness] practice or *sati*. You can also do a wholesome focused reflection on the following subjects for example:

    a. Uncertainty of the time and manner of death.

    b. Impermanence [Pāli: *annica*]

    c. The noble effort you are making.

9. Pleasant and unpleasant:

    a. As often as possible attend to what pleasures or pleasantness arise in taste or in any activity at any sense door, such as when eating, drinking, brushing your teeth, while at the gym, while hiking, while gardening, etc.

b. Notice whatever pleasant or unpleasant thoughts arise with special attention to your habitual tone and pattern. Observe them as often as possible.

c. Reflect on the consequences of pursuing pleasure, the consequences of *kamma* [Skt. *karma*; cause and effect], and the process of dependent origination [Pāli: *paṭiccasamuppāda*] from a pleasant feeling tone [Pāli: *vedanā*] through to clinging, or an unpleasant feeling tone through to pushing away, or a neutral tone through to confusion and avoidance.

10 Volunteer when appropriate.

SPEECH:

1. Pay very careful attention to speech.
2. As often as possible notice how habitual speech patterns arise.
3. Reboot as often as possible with restraint and *mettā* for yourself and others.
4. Keep a mindful eye on the tone and pattern of inner chatter.
5. Limit speech when doing chores and errands to what is necessary, useful and kind.

ACTIVITIES OF DAILY LIVING, CHORES, ERRANDS, SOCIAL ACTIVITIES:

1. During daily activities, as frequently as possible, cultivate the habit and practice of walking meditation, such as when walking to and from your car, standing and then moving in line at the grocery, walking between rooms at work or at home.
2. Chores:
   a. Shop for groceries and other household necessities as infrequently as possible or as only often as needed:
      i. Bring a list and stick to it.
      ii. No online shopping.
      iii. Limit choices.

b. Keep your residence clean and orderly:

    i. Clean deliberately and slowly and mindfully.

    ii. Set up a cleaning schedule and keep to it. Avoid unscheduled clean ups.

3. Miscellaneous activities: As needed, do regular activities and other activities that arise during scheduled times as much as possible.

4. Social interactions:

    a. Limit nonessential social interactions.

    b. Examine what you believe is essential and nonessential and then question your assumptions about that.

    c. Be particularly sensitive to unnecessary speech and avoid it.

FOOD AND BEVERAGE CONSUMPTION:

1. Simplify, lighten and lessen.
2. Decrease caffeine.
3. Avoid rich and fried foods.
4. Avoid sugar except fruit.
5. Consider taking the Sixth Precept, to eat only between dawn and noon.
6. Consider chanting before a meal.
7. Eat slowly and attentively. Attend to one thing at a time. You can experiment by putting down the utensil between bites. No listening to background music, news or podcasts, and no reading.
8. Watch preferences.

HEALTH AND BODY MAINTENANCE:

1. Waking and sleeping:

    a. Determine the appropriate hours of sleep, for example 9 p.m. to 2 or 3 a.m.

       i. Sleep should be about six hours or less.

      ii. Create structure and balance.

      iii. Make a schedule and keep to it as much as possible.

      iv. If naps become necessary, be very careful to not oversleep. Watch your intention and any aversion to sleepiness or being tired. Watch what you tell yourself. The maximum length of a nap should be 10 to 20 minutes.

    b. Go to bed early, get up early.

2. Exercise:

    a. Do as needed but not more than one hour per day.

    b. Reduce the amount by cutting out what is not necessary.

    c. Use appropriate speech while engaged in exercise if you are in a public setting.

    d. Experiment with bringing mindfulness to repetitive actions such as walking outside or exercising on a machine in the gym.

3. Limit or abstain from sexual activity during retreat. Abstaining is best.

PRACTICE:

1. Report your intended schedule and study focus to a *kalyāṇamitta* [spiritual friend] before, during, and after the retreat.

2. Commit to practicing for however long you decide the retreat is to last and follow through, even if energy is lagging and the mind is complaining.

3. Commit to a specific number of hours for formal practice—both sitting and walking meditation—each day. Tip: If you only have, for example, an hour and a half for formal practice in one chunk each day, and you find sitting for that length of time is too much, alternate sitting, walking, sitting for periods for that time.

4. Incorporate, per above instructions, frequent mini-moments of mindfulness.

5. Cultivate *sampajañña* as often as possible, before, during and after any word or deed.

6. Consider ending each formal meditation with the sharing of merit [Pāli: *puñña*] or *mettā* practice, and explore any resistance.
7. Practice *dāna* [generosity]*:*
    a. Offer a gift or a gesture of kindness to someone each day.
    b. Offer *dāna* to an organization, a resource or a teacher at the end of the retreat.
    c. Take time and actively visualize the benefits of the *dāna*.
8. Attend with a detached observing mind as often as possible to your own inner chatter:
    a. Simply notice with kindness.
    b. Apply mindfulness to what you know about your patterns of thought and the kind of language you use: "Oh, there is that (thought or pattern of thinking) again."

STUDY:

1. Choose a subject and stay on point.
2. Read and study this guide and the suggested reading list in Appendix 5: Bibliography and Suggested and Listening Reading List.
3. Read *A Householder's Vinaya*.

Note: *The Home Retreat Guide* is a bulleted and edited guide. To get the force and meaning of some of the exercises, a reading of *A Householder's Vinaya* is necessary.

ENTERTAINMENT:

1. Screen time:
    a. Limit screen time aside from study and necessary communications in order to meet your work, family, and social responsibilities:
        i. Try to limit screen time to no more than two or three times each day.
        ii. Not using screens at all is better.

    b. Establish a time limit for each use of a screen and for an aggregate for the day.

    c. Use screens at scheduled times.

    d. No recreational streaming, watching videos on YouTube, etc.

2. Using the telephone:

    a. Carefully attend each time you touch the phone for any reason.

    b. Attend to when you feel the intention to use the phone for any reason, including conversation, to check the time, get messages, or get other information. Attend to any resulting action throughout the process and after the action ends.

3. Limit any type of mail to just what is necessary in order to keep up with business and social responsibilities. No new threads.

4. Avoid recreational reading.

5. Avoid recreational television or streaming.

6. Avoid consumption of news using any medium at all.

CHAPTER 2

Preparation for Home Retreat

Foundational Readings

BEFORE BEGINNING THE HOME RETREAT GUIDE

To BEST UNDERSTAND and make use of *The Home Retreat Guide*, I suggest you read the following three texts, which will serve any *yogi* throughout the journey on the Path and are especially useful for doing home retreats:

- Nyanaponika Thera's *The Heart of Buddhist Meditation*, all of Chapter 2, with special attention to the section on *sampajañña*.
- Bhikkhu Bodhi's very short book *The Noble Eightfold Path: The Way to the End of Suffering*.
- Allan Cooper's *A Householder's Vinaya*.
- Note: *The Home Retreat Guide* is a bulleted and edited guide. To get the force and meaning of some of the exercises, a reading of *A Householder's Vinaya* is necessary.

Because it is important, I repeat that before you begin the retreat, even before you set your intended schedule, reread Nyanaponika's commentary on *sampajañña* in *The Heart of Buddhist of Meditation*, even if you have read it before.

PREPARE FOR READINGS AND STUDY DURING THE RETREAT

Before you begin the retreat, make a list of other sources to study — including scriptural sources — during the retreat should you have time. For suggestions on how to use those resources during the retreat, *see* Chapter 3, *Include Reading and Dhamma Study*. However, you can't go wrong by reading only Nyanaponika's *Heart of Buddhist Meditation*, Bhikkhu Bodhi's *The Noble Eightfold Path*, this Guide, and *A Householder's Vinaya*.

SUGGESTIONS FOR PRACTICE:

In deciding what to read among the seemingly endless choices, select a small arc of salient subjects that relate to home practice or home retreat.

- Choose material that supports the practical aspects of the practice, the 'how to.'
- Leave abstract study and intellectual thinking for another time.
- Limit light reading or, better yet, eliminate it altogether.

If you choose to read a particular book or *sutta*, get it and have it available for easy access before the retreat.

- You can access a variety of *suttas* online at www.accesstoinsight.org.
- Appendix 5: Bibliography and Suggested Reading and Listening List may also help you decide what to read.
- Practical podcasts from respected teachers or audio or video recordings of *Dhamma* talks can be very helpful in lieu of being able to hear live *Dhamma* talks. Dharma Seed (www.dharmaseed.org) has a vast selection of recorded *Dhamma* talks. Should this appeal to you, schedule a specific time when you will listen.

Foundational Decisions

There are three important decisions to make about the retreat. These aspects of the retreat are like the white cells in the life blood of the home retreat:

1. The intentional focus of the retreat.
2. The 'in between' practices, how to continue practicing between 'activities.'
3. Reporting to a *kalyāṇamitta* before, during and after the retreat.

An overall focus such as continuity or effort or kindness serves as the fuel to move the intention into maturity. Practicing 'in between' moments of recognized activity can make or break the continuity of the retreat.

Reporting to someone else, the *kalyāṇamitta*, is akin to making a contract with yourself out loud, in public, to someone whose respect has significant meaning for you. Together these parts allow the practice to take root piece by piece and become the way we live on or off retreat.

Consider the intention, practices and reporting carefully. Act on them with respect. Follow through.

Cultivating *Sampajañña*

Applied *sampajañña* during daily activities, coupled with increased formal meditation, gives *yogis* the opportunity to explore, test and then develop a routine to decondition latent tendencies away from habit. Instead, *yogis* move towards a focused and awakened mind. The skill of applying *sampajañña* to many activities throughout our day sets a default habit of pausing before engaging in speech or action, thus creating a field for continuous attention.

Each *yogi* will have their own spheres of blind habit and unique intense preferences. Habits and preferences are often strong and easily seen in relation to food, sleep needs, sexual fantasies or actions, and when and why we partake in entertainment. During home retreat we use habit patterns as the fodder of our focus. When the mind needs to make a choice, we apply *sampajañña* or *sati* whenever possible.

The more a *yogi* practices *sampajañña* by applying sense restraint combined with increased formal sitting periods, the less frequently the mind will turn towards thinking and planning and mindless wandering, not only during formal meditation, but during the activities of daily living as well. This is true not only in time and frequency, but also in making it a priority throughout the day

Cultivating Virtue

Monastics and lay meditators share similar schedules while on formal retreat, despite having very different types of everyday lives when not on retreat. While on formal retreat, both are practicing in the same rarefied environment that funnels all aspects of experience towards the cultivation of the Noble Eightfold Path. A formal residential retreat environment is designed in every way to minimize the clutter of distraction in our daily routines and make room for the cultivation and development of the continuous practice of virtue [Pāli: *sīla*], concentration [Pāli: *samādhi*], and wisdom [Pāli: *paññā*]. In other words, this environment is the most intensive and most structured domain in which to train the mind and heart towards the cultivation of our full potential for wisdom.

How so? The formal retreat environment routine is unencumbered by most of the niggling everyday conflicts and baggage that challenge our everyday virtue and continuity of *sati*. On retreat we restrain ourselves in speech by maintaining Noble Silence. We also choose to limit all unnecessary reading and writing. Almost all of our physical needs are provided thus protecting us from activities that intrude on concentration or challenge our abilities to maintain continuous *sati-sampajañña*.

Formal retreats leave little room for the exercise of our preferences in the big and small choices of everyday life. The structure funnels even the smallest of choices into very narrow parameters which allow us to notice them clearly and to then bring meditative attention into the moment. When we are in a retreat environment, the daily schedule defines for us when to practice walking, sitting and eating meditation. The schedule leaves little time for other activities, such as resting, bathing, doing laundry or cleaning our rooms, and thus there is little room for our preferences to become the default behavior model.

The continuous practice, the silence and the purity of mind that come from many days, weeks or months of formal residential retreat practice allow the mind to become unfettered by any remorse, guilt or shame. These freedoms from unwholesome mental states simultaneously feed a momentum toward greater purity and more precise meditative attention. The triad of retreat practice, environment and virtue permits *yogis* a greater opportunity to investigate and train the mind towards wholesomeness.

As a consequence, lay meditating *yogis* who understand how important virtue is to the progress of meditation will often choose to take vows to follow either the Five or the Eight Precepts [Pāli: *pañca-sīla* or *attha-sīla*, respectively] as active tools of training in everyday practice. The lay *yogi* who takes the Five or Eight Precepts is building a householder's *vinaya*.

Taking the Eight Precepts as a householder is a difficult practice that requires strong resolve, especially if you live with other people who are not practicing the Eight Precepts. Practicing the Sixth (no eating from solar noon till dawn) and the Seventh (not wearing perfume, fancy clothes or adornments; not partaking in entertainments) can cause huge disruptions in the normal flow of everyday life. Practicing with the literal translation of the Eighth Precept (not sitting or sleeping in overly comfortable seats and beds) can also be disruptive. For most *yogis*, I suggest taking the Eight Precepts only on formal residential retreats or on formal home retreat unless you live alone or live with others who are practicing in the same way.

To best understand the core structure of this Precept style of practice, we need to cultivate an attitude that is both specific and general, both disciplined and friendly. For successful home retreat and home practice, we need to do more than simply set our resolve and then look at our calendars and muddle ahead. The development of a householder's *vinaya* must always take its root from applied virtue, as taught in the Noble Eightfold Path: Right Speech, Right Action, and Right Livelihood, which encompass the Precepts. When a *yogi* commits to fulfilling the wholesome intentions of the virtue factors of the Noble Eightfold Path, that exercise by itself turns a *yogi's* mind and heart towards finding ways to cultivate applied *sati-sampajañña* with skillful means.

It is understood from a practice perspective that virtue trains intentions. It is not a situation in which, if you break the rules, you have failed or sinned or are a bad person. Virtue is a training. Training is a process. It takes time and careful attention to perfect any training. It is also helpful to understand that the total uprooting of unwholesome [Pāli: *akusala*] actions and unwholesome mind activity won't happen until deep wisdom has taken root, which might take a lifetime of practice to realize. So give yourself some latitude, exercise patience and learn to enjoy the challenge, while never losing sight of the fact that the perfection of virtue is both the cause and the fruit of all spiritual wisdom.

Understanding that we are in training gives us the room to accept the Five or Eight Precepts as tools, not just rules. Acknowledging that the Precepts are not rules, while at the same time acknowledging that they hold absolute moral authority, may inspire us to strive to perfect this aspect of life by trying again and again when we fail to meet our highest aspirations.

The Precepts are forgiving, yet they remain firm in educating us to what is universal wholesomeness. A *yogi* can use them like a child learning to ride a bicycle. The child often falls and then takes the falling as a method to learn, and then gets up and tries again. There is no rule about falling; if you want to learn to ride, you get back on the bicycle and try again.

This same principle of 'try, try again' applies to home retreat. When we set our intentions for the retreat, when we make our schedule, when we live our lives during retreat, we are training ourselves with a forgiving heart in the knowledge that no 'one size fits all' for what we are doing. No 'one size fits all' is also true for each retreat you may do. We are not perfect in our wisdom. Only our intention and our actions steer us towards greater continuity of wholesomeness. Part of this intention is not only the practical necessity to create a retreat structure for ourselves, but also how to hold it, exercise it, and try to perfect it. The Precepts are training goals supported by an attitude of kindness and forgiveness, which is just as important as the unflinching commitment to a determined wholesome outcome.

Decide When to Do the Retreat, the Length of the Retreat, and Participation by Others

When preparing for a home retreat, the first things to determine are:
- When best to do your retreat.
- How long you can commit to the retreat. Much can be accomplished in a week or a ten-day home retreat. However, doing a retreat for a shorter period of time, even just one day, can also be extremely valuable.
- Whether you can find others to do a parallel retreat with you.

Prepare Family and Housemates for the Retreat

Not everyone has the luxury of living alone and having the free time to easily go on a formal residential retreat or even a home retreat. Many if not most of us have domestic partners, children, roommates, or aging parents living with us, not to mention pets, guests, and obligatory social and work responsibilities. Living with others creates functional difficulties in planning for and following through with a home retreat. Yet, these very life factors, if addressed with skill and follow-through, will provide the opportunities for wisdom and wholesome habit to become second nature. In fact, in many ways this Guide is written for you.

Munindraji was a lay teacher from India most often associated in the West with being Joseph Goldstein's and Dipa Ma's teacher. His impact on how *Theravāda* Buddhism is understood in the West cannot be overstated. In the book *Living This Life Fully: Stories and Teachings of Munindra*, we are given a most extraordinary example of how to live a home retreat as a layperson. While staying with a senior and very committed *yogi*, he wisely taught her how to make her domestic life a part of her practice. He taught her that while caring for her three children as a single parent, she could use the time performing daily life tasks like washing the dishes, walking to the laundry room, etc. as periods of active meditation. Meditation in motion; meditation as life presents itself.

TALK WITH THOSE WITH WHOM YOU LIVE

"Sure," you might say, "That type of practice is doable at home, but what about the feelings of others when all of a sudden I start acting a bit strange and doing things differently?"

I suggest you talk to your loved ones or roommates before the retreat and get them on board as far as they can be. 'On board' doesn't mean that they will do the retreat with you; it means that they understand what you are doing and why.

SUGGESTIONS FOR PRACTICE:

- Let them know how valuable their understanding and support are to the success of your retreat.
- Tell them how important the retreat is for you.
- Explain in detail what you think will remain the same during the retreat and what will change, including how your behavior will change.

Allowing those with whom you live the opportunity to support you during the retreat could soften any resistance they might have to you taking care of yourself by doing the retreat. Talking with those whom your retreat will affect might open their eyes to how all of us have choices on how we live.

SUGGESTIONS FOR PRACTICE:

Plan for how you will be with them during the retreat:

- Try to avoid surprising them.
- Watch your reactions in each interaction should someone do or not do what they said they would. It doesn't matter. They are with you as far as they can be.

The rest is your responsibility to make your inner experience a field for *sati-sampajañña*. Your housemates might step up to offer to help you in your retreat; they might not. In either case, offer them as much ease and grace as you can with as much *sati-sampajañña* as you can muster.

Plan Meals

Whether you live alone or with others, planning meals before starting your retreat will help support you in sense restraint by limiting this arena of choice each and every time you need to eat. Without planning and setting reasonable expectations, meals have the potential to undermine the continuity of your practice during retreat.

SUGGESTIONS FOR PRACTICE:

- In all respects, limit your choices. Keep it simple.
- Shop for your food before the retreat begins.
- Just cook what is scheduled.
- Eat with careful *sati*.
- Clean up with as much continuous *sati-sampajañña* as possible.
- If possible, cook and freeze food ahead of time.

It is more difficult to maintain *sati* during meals if you live or eat with others such as with family, coworkers or friends. This is especially true if you are a caregiver. As a caregiver, cooking and serving meals may present more challenges and demands from both those who support you and don't understand to those who don't or can't understand and only want conditions to go back to normal. You might face questions like: "How come we're having this again tonight?" "When is your retreat over?" "Why is this night going to be different than other nights?" Should this be the case, it will be helpful to your practice to have some guidelines to discuss with your housemates or family before your retreat begins:

1. Ask for their support with meals; explain why it's important to you and what would be helpful for you on their part.
2. Consider planning menus for the entire retreat and putting them in writing. Your family will know what to expect, and you will not need to make choices every day.
3. Keep meals simple. If there are ways to delegate your responsibility to someone else, do it with expressed gratitude and appreciation for the help.
4. Pay attention to any judgments about or disappointment with yourself or those with whom you are engaging; pay attention to any sense of success as well.
5. Speak with as much kindness and patience as you can offer.

Working During Retreat

Work is challenging and could be more difficult than being at home during the retreat. Those of us who work may not be able to take time off, which adds another layer of complications and planning.

TIP:

Unless you work in a very special place and with very special people, the fact that you are doing a home retreat may not mean anything to your boss or your workmates. Telling them you are on retreat might, in fact, make you appear strange and suspect and could affect their ability to see you skillfully in the future. Plan to do your work as you normally would.

Prepare a Schedule

Even a person with a busy schedule can do a home retreat; it's a matter of making the retreat the way you live your life. In preparing a daily schedule, make the retreat your priority! Within the schedule, make sitting your priority!

FACTORS TO CONSIDER

Once you've decided the length and dates of your home retreat, create your daily schedule. In creating the schedule, consider the following:

- Prioritize an emphasis on continuous *sati-sampajañña* in all activities by introducing a heightened focus of the simplicity of sense restraint.
- Schedule as much formal meditation as your daily responsibilities permit.
- Bring a focused intensity to your meditative goals by practicing wise reflection through applied *sampajañña*.
- Take into account any necessary appointments and chores.
- If possible, start your retreat on a day when you can give more hours to formal practice than you expect to be able to do for the rest of the retreat.

TASKS FOR CREATING THE SCHEDULE

- Decide how many hours of sitting, walking and formal study you will do each day.
- Set a formal sitting, walking, study schedule.
- Plan when you'll do your activities of daily living:

~ Plan for work-related activities, like commuting, electronic and face-to-face communications, work projects, etc.

~ Plan for fulfilling family and community commitments and responsibilities such as meals, chores, errands, exercise, sleep, etc.

~ If you decide to allow yourself entertainment, decide when, what kind and for how long. Note: It is best to avoid entertainment. Instead, just sit and study.

FACTOR IN YOUR SITUATION AND YOUR SKILL SET

To create a balanced schedule, carefully assess your situation and your skills. The goal is to limit distractions and situations that create choice or situations that cultivate the opiated buzz of distraction as much as possible:

- Stay aware of which activities create choice and encourage preferences, and which will support a successful continuity of practice and investigation during your home retreat.
- Do activities that are important in your life. For example, if exercise is important to balance your energy or to sustain good health, get your exercise.
- Don't exclude all pleasant, nurturing daily activities such as a short hike or a few minutes in the garden. Be careful to pay attention and not do the activity or extend how long you do it mindlessly.
- Try to create a schedule that is doable and balanced and kindly towards both your goal and towards this unique type of practice.

SAMPLE SCHEDULES

Here are two schedules as examples. One is for someone like myself: a retired, experienced *yogi*. The second is for a *yogi* who is working and living with family and does not have a lot of retreat experience.

Profile: Retired *yogi*

- Awaken between 2 and 4 a.m.
- Tea from 2:15 to 2:30 a.m.
- Formal meditation
  ~ Sit: 2:30 to 3:20 a.m.
  ~ Walk: 3:20 to 4:10 a.m.
  ~ Sit: 4:10 to 5:00 a.m.
- Breakfast: 5:00 to 5:30 a.m.
- Check emails and other business on the Internet: 5:30 to 6:15 a.m.
- Chores: 6:15 to 8:00 a.m.
  ~ Clean house
  ~ Start laundry
  ~ Prep for lunch
  ~ Other activities of daily living
- Sit: 8:00 to 9:00 a.m.
- Exercise, hike, run errands: 9:00 to 11:30 a.m.
- Lunch and clean up followed by a period of rest or meditation: 11:30 a.m. to 1:30 p.m.
- Sit: 1:30 to 2:30 p.m.
- Garden or other work: 2:30 to 4:00 p.m.
- Sit: 4:00 to 5:00 p.m.
- Snack: 5:00 to 5:45 p.m.
- Study or listen to *Dhamma* talk: 5:45 to 7:00 p.m.
- Sit and walk: 7:00 p.m. to whenever the body requires rest or sleep
- Rest

Profile: Employed *yogi*

- Awaken 5 a.m.
- Tea or coffee from 5:15 to 5:30 a.m.
- Formal sitting meditation: 5:30 to 6:15 a.m.
- Breakfast alone or with family: 6:15 to 6:45 a.m.
- Work (including commute both ways) and other activities of daily living: 6:45 a.m. to 5:15 p.m.

- Pre-dinner household chores: 5:15 to 6:00 p.m.
- Dinner and post-dinner chores: 6:00 p.m. to 6:45 p.m.
- Formal meditation:
  ~ Sit: 6:45 to 7:30 p.m.
  ~ Walk: 7:30 p.m. to 8:15 p.m.
- Study or listen to *Dhamma* talk: 8:15 to 9:15 p.m.
- Sit: 9:15 p.m. to whenever the body requires rest or sleep
- Rest

ONCE YOU'VE ESTABLISHED A SCHEDULE

- Put it in writing.
- Post it or put it where you will see it.
- Read it frequently.
- Commit to following it.

TIP:

By doing these things, you strengthen the mental factor of intention and you make yourself accountable for a greater willingness to follow through. This is critical because Right Intention, which is one factor of the Noble Eightfold Path, is necessary for the success of a home retreat.

After reviewing and committing to the schedule, share it with a retreat friend or someone you respect in practice. All too often in practice we fall prey to thinking we know best while forgetting how often we confuse what is best with what is easy or pleasant. Allowing new notions and new perspectives to be tested can open our eyes and can also open the horizon to new skills and new perspectives:

- Send your schedule to this person in an email.
- Include:
  ~ How many days you intend to be on home retreat.
  ~ How many sits each day you intend to do.

~ How long you intend to sit each time.

~ Any particular formal study focus you might want to pursue.

• Solicit this *kalyāṇamitta*'s advice.

• Consider all new ideas and points of view your *kalyāṇamitta* offers, and see if and how what is being offered might serve you. An example of an offering from your *kalyāṇamitta* would be: "If you have the time and the energy to sit more than the scheduled period, you can mindfully stand, do 15 to 30 minutes of walking meditation, and then sit for whatever extra time you have to commit."

Once you have scheduled your activities for each day and taken into account what you need to accomplish while you are on retreat, make sure you keep appointments and perform chores that are necessary:

• Jettison any activities that can be postponed, such as:

~ An art or writing project you're working on.

~ Morning coffee with friends at the coffee house.

~ Reading or watching the news.

~ Going online to get email or be on Facebook more than scheduled.

• Notice if there are days, like on the weekend, when you can adjust your schedule for more sitting.

• Always keep an eye on how you might refine your understanding of *sampajañña* when examining all those appointments, tasks and activities of daily life.

• Always keep in mind that you are on a retreat, and, as with all retreats, you will be assisted by exercising sense restraint, having a healthy disregard for thoughts arising from doubt and maintaining continuity of practice.

Take another careful look at your list of activities of daily living and the schedule you made. Especially look at those activities that define you as a human being. To name just a few examples: All humans must eat. We must sleep. We must attend to our bodies with cleaning, toileting, addressing sexual impulses, maintaining health and strength. And we must attend to our surroundings in regards to safety and interaction with other humans and other species. These are the types of hard-wired necessities that our entire lives are built upon. A householder's activities are a construction of these basic human needs. Genetically we are hardwired to do certain things. How these activities manifest will be different depending on the society, history, context and the character of the individual.

The roots of these types of activities are the most difficult to watch or understand with our rational minds. It takes special meditative effort to break through the veils or armor of these basic habits. It is helpful and important to pay attention to them while on retreat, because they will affect your choices and behaviors. Pay particular attention to hunger, tiredness, restlessness or anxiety or fear. What do they feel like in the body and the mind? How do they affect your thoughts, speech and behaviors? Are they mixed with pleasantness or unpleasantness? The more intimate and familiar we are with these basic human experiences, the stronger the probability we will not succumb to them and then react out of habit rooted in desire, aversion, or ignorance. Hunger or sleepiness might arise, but instead of grabbing an apple, having a cup of tea or taking a nap, we continue with our commitment to the schedule.

Create Strong Intention

Your home retreat schedule is your choice. Whichever way you choose to make your schedule, your ability to maintain it will affect whether you strengthen patterns of continuous attention or not. You may choose to sit one hour each day for the first few days and increase the time gradually, or if your schedule and energy can handle it, you could start with ten hours of sitting and walking a day right off the bat.

Each of us is different, and each time we do a home retreat we will discover different conditions that will allow us to explore and develop new perspectives and skills, and tools to face new situations. Each retreat shares and builds on prior retreats to improve the quality and follow-through of your intention and commitment.

It doesn't matter if you've scheduled a light or a very heavy schedule. It does matter whether or not you've honored your intention and commitment with skillful means that will provide you with the most reward.

Schedule Retreats With and Report to Other *Yogis*

When possible, scheduling parallel retreats with other *yogis* will support your retreat. Sharing a period of time and being partnered with another *yogi* while practicing in your own home will increase the focus, commitment and energy of the practice.

If possible, schedule video or phone connections with the other retreatants to further support your retreat by making yourself accountable to them. Accountability to self and others is an important part of the learning curve. The more successful you are in maintaining the retreat schedule, the greater the likelihood of increased access to deeper wisdom.

CHAPTER 3

Practice During Home Retreat

Activities of Daily Life

DURING THE RETREAT, the *yogi* continues with the activities of daily life while bringing the reflective qualities of *sati-sampajañña* and sense restraint to as many activities as possible. Examples of activities of daily life include:

- Jobs
- Childcare
- Shopping
- Cooking
- Cleaning
- Gardening
- Exercising
- Appointments
- Appropriate socializing

This includes bringing the reflective qualities of *sampajañña* and sense restraint to the spaces between activities. How often between activities does the mind flow to planning or wandering, for instance, and neglect the walking, touching, hearing, seeing, etc. that is occurring during those in-between moments? The home retreat is an opportunity to find out how, how often and when the mind tends in this direction and to do something about deconditioning habits in favor of a field of continuous awareness.

Although we do more formal practice than usual during a home retreat, the retreat's primary focus is to bring greater meditative intention and attention to our activities of everyday living. The ambiguities and variables of everyday life create the perfect testing ground in real time. Here we are able to explore and test our understanding and compassion for self and others, and to learn new patterns that assist us in the development of the skills necessary for navigating a life based in virtue, concentration and wisdom.

When creating a life in which meditation can help with balance, it is useful to apply mindfulness in extreme situations as well as those that are considered normal or not intense. Exercising at the gym, getting sick or injured, and dying are great places to learn and apply meditation. Exercising at the gym is more accessible and less risky than the other two. While at the gym, testing how your mind works when lifting a heavy weight or doing another rep or challenging your limits are all good examples of activities that other everyday activities and formal meditation don't provide.

Moving the Mind Toward Wholesomeness

When we combine Right Intention and Right Effort, we create a wholesome mental environment that allows us to experiment with fresh tools. This mental environment actually obliges the mind to move towards wholesomeness.

When we have a wholesome mental environment, we have more opportunity to pause and reflect using *sampajañña* before engaging in any speech or other action. A mind unhindered by unwholesome mental qualities like doubt and distraction is able to focus. Using this environment of mind conditions a continuity of intention towards further and deeper wholesomeness. With strong wholesome intention, the mind and heart naturally begin to develop more types of skillful action, which further support a heart and mind unfettered by unwholesomeness. A continuous loop is created.

Combining these practices and applying them with a self-friendly diligence, we begin to break down the unwholesome habits of mind that frequently arise if not noticed during our normal activities. A home retreat becomes a laboratory to test new ways to cultivate and strengthen our wholesome intentions through our everyday speech and actions. When our speech and actions begin to spontaneously reflect virtue, compassion and harmlessness, we can rest assured that the link between intention and action is becoming increasingly based in wisdom.

Meals and Relationship to Food

A few guidelines for meals during the retreat:
- Keep it simple and try to stay focused.
- Try to eat meals at the same time each day.
- Practice gratitude for the food you are about to eat by reflection, chanting, or both.
- Do not snack unless medically necessary.
- Consider taking the Sixth Precept, meaning that you do not eat at inappropriate times, basically from noon until dawn the next day. Having hunger as an object of unpleasant sensation that comes and goes, is not debilitating, is not dangerous and is clear and can be useful as an exercise to hone your faith, effort, mindfulness, concentration and wisdom.
- Try not to admonish or criticize yourself or others for breaking agreements you've made with family or housemates. Adapt and move on.

Above we discussed how certain things we do are basic to our survival and are therefore hard-wired. When motivations are hard-wired, they are more difficult to work with, but they can also be easier to notice.

Food and the socialization that surround eating are both basic to our survival and therefore obvious and valuable places to watch ourselves.

Of course, when one lives alone, eating can be a fairly simple process. When you are alone you can choose what, how and when you eat. In addition, you have the choice to try to maintain silence by not reading or listening to or watching something, while giving your focus to the *sati* of eating. However, if you have certain forms of aversion or greed surrounding food, a meal eaten alone can still be a very complex situation. On retreat, set your intention to be as mindful as possible throughout the entire process of meal preparation, eating, and clean-up.

Working

There are many ways you can subtly and silently make room for practice during the work day while on a retreat. It is important to try to create a field of practice and to remember your commitment to the home retreat as often as possible, and, at the same time, sustaining an attitude of integrity toward your work. Remember that while at work, you are fitting in your home retreat with work.

SUGGESTIONS FOR PRACTICE:

- As often as possible, commit to five minutes of practice every hour.
- Make your commute and walking to and from your workstation at the beginning and end of the work day opportunities to start and end the work day mindfully.
- Use any time you leave your work situation to practice mindful movement. Notice the intention to leave, standing, turning, mental changes, etc.
- During a break, walk mindfully to the refrigerator or water cooler or bathroom; use any time you walk somewhere as an opportunity for walking meditation.

- Rather than taking an elevator, if you can take a flight of stairs and practice walking meditation.
- Stop working, turn your chair away from your desk if possible, put down any tools you use, and sit or stand quietly with mindfulness for a few moments.
- Make your lunch an exercise in eating meditation.

Communication

In every way possible, on home retreat we give special emphasis to all forms of communication and to any situation presenting choices or opportunities for proliferation of mind [Pāli: *papañca*] to arise. We need to watch not just our participation in these activities, but observe how, when and why we choose to or by habit engage in them.

Communications in this case include any of the following, among others:

- Speaking
- Reading
- Writing
- Exposing yourself to visual and volitional auditory impressions, such as:
  - ~ Televisions
  - ~ Computers
  - ~ Email
  - ~ Smartphones
  - ~ News
  - ~ Radio
  - ~ Music
  - ~ Wandering glances

Pay Attention to Social Contact

Minimize unnecessary social contact when doing your chores and errands and at work. The following tips will help you focus your attention towards the many ways your unique experience either will or will not be supported by your choice of actions while on home retreat:

- Combine activities if possible. If I need to go to the grocery store and the hardware store during a home retreat, I try to visit both in one trip. I make sure I pay attention to any social contact by, for example, trying to cultivate a silent loving attitude towards the person in front of me in line.
- Limit social interaction. When I go to the gym, which in my case is frequently, I make sure that my interactions with friends at the gym have a point, have kindness at their root, and that they serve a purpose. I try to limit chatter, useless speech. I must also pay attention to any inclination to please the other person with my humor or cleverness.

Making Choices and Observing Preferences

This part of the practice starts by becoming aware of preferences as they present themselves. The sooner we become aware of our preferences, and the more familiar we are with how our minds behave in the face of our likes and dislikes, the sooner we become skilled in being able to pause before speaking or acting. This pause offers us an increasing potential for wisdom to become the greater part of our process. The more we investigate preferences, the more we will see how they arise and how they affect our lives. At the same time, we strengthen our use of investigation, effort and concentration, which are all necessary mental factors [Pāli: *cetasika*] on the gradual path to enlightenment. The less we allow preferences to move us from pleasantness to liking and wanting or to not liking and not wanting, the greater the potential for wisdom to arise.

HINT:

As soon as you notice a pattern occurring in thought, speech or action, regardless which one, immediately bring your investigative focus to whether there is a feeling tone of pleasant, unpleasant or neutral that arises with the pattern in either the body, the mind or both. Ask yourself:

- Does this pattern comfort me?
- If so, how?
- If so, why? (meditatively, not psychologically)
- Does this object or experience create further sequences of pleasant, unpleasant, or neutral feelings in the body or the mind or both?

Preferences will arise during almost all activities, from the most mundane, such as using the left leg to start walking, all the way to your favorite ice cream. They will also arise in more important situations, such as deciding whether to purchase a new car, change jobs, get married, stay married, plan or hope for the kids, stay put or move to a retirement home, and on and on.

SUGGESTIONS FOR PRACTICE:

For activities that present a need for exercising choice and preference:

- Bring heightened attention to the choices and watch your preferences while they arise.
- Whatever the situation, with as little judgment as possible, bring heightened investigative examination using *sati* or *sampajañña* to your choices and preferences.
- Notice the preferences with as little identification as possible.
- Notice the difference between being in the story and observing the story as merely a process of thinking.
- Avoid making big life decisions while on any kind of retreat. Wait until after the retreat.

Focus on Continuity and Follow-Through

We need to cultivate and sustain continuity and follow through to skill-fully accomplish any activity. This is true for everyday activities, during retreat practice or during home practice. If you are like me, checking-in becomes critical to maintain the kind of wholesome intention and continuity that inspired us to choose to do a home retreat in the first place.

On home retreat I do everything I can to support the continuity of my intention to pay attention. By chipping away at my automatic behaviors, I am supporting my intention and purpose for the retreat:

- I constantly check in with myself to see what my energy and intention might be doing, and then I do what I can to balance myself mentally and physically.
- I apply as many of my retreat-learned meditative tools as I can as often as I can throughout the day.
- I try to slow down; I watch the beginning, middle, and end of movements or thoughts when appropriate.
- I silently ask myself over and over again, "Is this speech useful, kind, and timely, and if so, how?"
- I am scrupulously careful to watch if the practice is beginning to take a back seat to my preferred routines and habits.

Focus on Finishing Tasks

Focus on getting tasks done. I try to finish tasks once I start. Less unfin-ished business allows for fewer opportunities to choose, plan or distract myself, and fewer opportunities for laziness to arise.

Micro-Moments Make a Whole

All too often during our everyday lives, the momentum of getting things done creates an illusion of constancy — the illusion of a forest rather than many individual trees. Home retreat supports us to look at the trees in order to better appreciate and understand the forest.

A tool that supports our study of the forest is to notice micro-moments of direct and clear *sati* when they arise. For many of us these moments happen spontaneously. They also happen frequently. Every day there will be moments when we experience a sight, sound, smell, taste, sensation or even a thought in an almost neuro-chemical way, a moment when a sight is just seeing, a sound is just sound, etc. We see, hear, taste, smell or feel something simply as it is or simply notice a thought being a thought. We sense only a touch or a color or form with little or no concept or attachment in the moment.

Fortunately and unfortunately, these moments are brief, which allows us to move on with our task and our day. Yet ignoring these moments and not supporting them with a few added moments of reflection can cause them to lose some of their power and value.

I suggest two exercises to help notice these moments:

1. When a micro-moment of pure *sati* arises:
   ~ Bring your focus to it.
   ~ See what happens with this added focus on it.
   ~ See if you can notice the quality of the *sati*.
   ~ Notice what happens next. Are you simply noting, "Watching or observing," or does it quickly become, "*I* am watching and observing"? If the latter, notice the posture of "I am watching," and try not to evaluate or judge.
   ~ Just carry on and try to remember what just watching was like.
2. Cultivate these types of micro-moments of *sati* on a fairly regular basis throughout the day. The more frequently we support the arising and noticing of micro-moments of *sati*, the more we strengthen a variety of mental factors. This in turn enables us to access *sati* more readily and in ever more basic ways, both spontaneously and when doing formal practice.

QUICK TIPS:

1. Take an activity that you do mindlessly over and over again throughout the day. Bring a moment of quick *sati* or reflective *sampajañña* to that activity. For example, your experience with using keys:

   a. Notice the intention to pick up the keys and investigate conceptually by asking yourself: "Am I going someplace for wholesome reasons?" "Is this trip necessary?"

   b. Pay attention to reaching for, then touching, then holding the keys.

   c. Investigate your nonconceptual experience: Are they cold, sharp, heavy, light?

   d. Pay attention to reaching toward, then touching, then using pressure to open, pass through and close the door.

   e. Focus on anything else arising at the same time, such as the urge to urinate or defecate, the intention to do so, the process of getting to the bathroom, the process of evacuating or urinating. Notice also what the mind is doing, paying attention to cleaning and going on to the next activity.

2. Wake up to the automatic behaviors that surround your use of screen time. This could be the most challenging as well as the most rewarding investigation. This is especially true regarding a smart phone. Bring attention to every urge to touch your phone. Either observe the urge until it changes or the decision to act on the urge. If you decide to act on it, observe:

   a. Reaching for the phone.

   b. The activity of using the phone.

   c. The value of the activity.

   d. Putting it away.

The more often we string moments of *sati-sampajañña* together or simply add these types of moments to our day, the more effectively we decondition our patterns as well as our blindness to those patterns. I often look at this type of practice like a string of pearls. Our lives are the string and the pearls are moments of wisdom. The more pearls we string together, the more valuable and beautiful the necklace becomes.

Lead with Strength

Start the day by making it special with whatever it takes to create focused heartfelt intention, with whatever moves you. This might include:

- Chanting.
- Making an offering of *dāna* to a teacher or an organization.
- Reading a favorite inspirational quote.

After several days, many *yogis* experience a slump when effort lags and doubt prevails. Consider a day of determination or a few focused sits to revitalize your momentum and commitment. Each person will have their own ways of strengthening intentions. The key is to experiment and find your own technique, and then do it.

Cultivate Wise Flexibility

While it's important to have a schedule, it is best to hold the schedule with a light hand. You don't have to adhere to the schedule in a rigid way. As a matter of fact, right here, at the place where your expectations and your druthers meet the unexpected, having a light and flexible attitude becomes the all-important mental skill to examine and develop.

For example, I have found from experience that it is best for me to sit five or six times each day for 45 to 75 minutes each time. I try to schedule my sits so that there are two early in the morning, one mid-morning, one mid-afternoon, and a couple near the end of the day. However, there has never been a day that my intended schedule fit perfectly with my projected notion of what the day or the retreat would look like.

This training is to be applied in all activities, not just during the sittings and not just during the activities of daily living. By maintaining your focus and commitment you strengthen your intention. The form of the retreat is not as important as your intention to make *vipassanā* or *samatha* coupled with *sampajañña* your focus for this specific period of time.

A lighter formal sitting retreat means more attention to *sampajañña*; a heavier retreat means more emphasis on *sati*. For example, you may discover that two hours of formal practice is all you can manage, but you are still making home retreat your priority. Other times you may find you have the time and conditions to do a more formal style retreat at home, and you can sit and walk five to ten hours a day with infrequent interruptions.

Bring Friendly Determination to Practice

Whether you choose to sit and walk for one, two, four or eight sessions of formal practice a day, and whether the sessions are 15, 60 or 120 minutes long, remember that it's the quality of kindly determination [Pāli: *adhitthāna*] and your follow through that will infuse your retreat with a continuity of intention. The same applies to whether or not you can apply skillful restraint and renunciation to your schedule. We use restraint for the purpose of exploring, of strengthening determination, and as a vehicle to discover what generosity and compassion are. As much as possible, it will help to remove 'shoulds' from your intentions and supplant them with kindness and investigation.

And just like on a formal residential retreat, on home retreat we need balanced effort to avoid either over-efforting or laziness. We also need to balance our spiritual faculties [Pāli: *indriya*] and the needs of our bodies. We need to prioritize our intentions towards general and specific types of attention and make sure they are coupled with friendly determination.

Without a determined effort geared towards continuous attention imbued and saturated with friendliness for self and others, we will burn out. Continuous attention is supported on home retreat by emphasizing *sampajañña* in all activities of daily living, coupled with increased formal *vipassanā* practice and, once again, with a firm determination and a friendly gentleness.

CAUTION:

If you begin to see that you are trying to squeeze in formal sitting sessions or careful attention towards *sampajañña* during the day, and you notice that your continuous attention during activities of daily living is becoming sporadic, your practice during the home retreat is weakening. Allowing yourself to zombie walk through the retreat is a training in unskillful habits. Letting things slide is a slippery slope heading down towards reinforcing blindness to your own intentions. Watch your intentions and their quality. Remember: It is your retreat, and a valuable component of home retreat is discovering what works best for you within your unique circumstances. This will not occur if you are not doing your absolute best.

View Change and the Unexpected as Practice Opportunities

In our daily lives, we all frequently experience unexpected events. The unexpected will happen during home retreat as well. It is important to not use unexpected circumstances to dilute the quality of the retreat with excuses, denial, or laziness. Whatever the circumstances, be prepared for surprises to arise.

Different techniques to address reactions to the unexpected will serve different retreatants in different ways. On home retreat, unexpected events demand flexibility in working with the schedule and with attitude. When they do arise, it's fine to amend your daily schedule. Make the needed changes with conscious intention, and change the remainder of the day to refocus towards the practice. Make flexibility and continuity your priority. Integrate everything into the practice; it's the point of the retreat.

Changes or unexpected events that arise on home retreat are, in fact, the very heart of this type of practice. Our everyday lives are by their nature in constant flux; the added unpredictability of big surprises is just another, more intense level at which we can notice something new. It may be helpful to keep in mind that there are no interruptions on retreat. Everything that happens, everything that is noticed, is an opportunity to observe with an intention towards appropriate attention.

You don't need to put the retreat on hold until the unforeseen event is taken care of. Switching gears while keeping an eye open to noticing how the mind is switching the gears allows for flow throughout the retreat. Switching gears over and over teaches us more subtle tools that assist in the development of investigation and effort in practice and in everyday life. We are learning both. In the end, they become the same thing.

SUGGESTIONS FOR PRACTICE:

As the gears shift, ask yourself:

- Is there resistance?
- Does planning arise immediately?
- Is the mind able to simply be present and respond?
- Recognize that all events, all mind objects, in fact everything, is part of your home retreat.
- Be part of the flow of whatever is arising whether it is pleasant or unpleasant. Assuming a posture of settling back with attention to what is happening will help you cultivate patience and equanimity.

Different techniques will serve different retreatants in different ways. For example, when my day is interrupted by unforeseen circumstances that force changes to my schedule (*e.g.*, car trouble, a surprise doctor or dentist appointment, an unscheduled business-related email, etc.), I typically respond by replacing my usual hour-long sits with a number of sits throughout the day that are one to ten minutes long whenever the opportunity allows. This permits me to continue the momentum of my practice and even deepens my intention, and it helps me develop new tools while still attending to the situation at hand.

Another good technique to practice and develop when sudden changes arise is to cultivate the *pāramī* [spiritual perfection] of patience. Always check to see if the quality of friendliness is present in the mind and heart. The first step toward real patience is to notice whether a mental tone of friendliness, acceptance or kindness is present when unpleasantness arises. If not, it isn't real patience. In the face of the unexpected, when real patience is present, flexibility of mind and heart will be noticed and accessible. Forgiveness and compassionate humor are useful tools in this process.

SUGGESTIONS FOR PRACTICE:

- Check to see if there is friendliness, acceptance or kindness is present.
- If they are not present, simply notice, pause and see if you can allow them to arise.
- You may find other techniques or strategies or ways to change your schedule that work better for you. The important thing is to stay aware, experiment, and stay committed.

REMEMBER:

Being flexible equals kindness toward yourself and others. This is a major part of the training. Without flexibility and without paying special attention to kindness for self and others, the practice becomes a chore. Remind yourself that you are doing this for the benefit of yourself and for all sentient beings everywhere.

Comparing Mind

Not surprisingly, your mind will behave differently while doing a home retreat than it does while doing a formal retreat, especially when doing formal meditation. Try not to start your retreat in a way that results in blocking yourself from skillful use of your time by having unrealistic expectations. Try and try again not to judge or compare your formal meditations to the best you've ever done or your home retreat experience to what you've experienced in past formal retreats. Try to make no comparisons at all.

Home retreat is a different practice than a formal residential retreat. The conditions are different, and, though many of the tools we use are similar or the same, we use the skills that we are exercising and developing in different ways and under different conditions. On a formal retreat we are provided an environment in which the retreat center or the monastery supports a very intense level of sense restraint, and we are further encouraged as individuals to take sense restraint to ever more subtle levels. On home retreat we also practice sense restraint, but on a much more active and wide-ranging level. After all, the practice of home retreat is in the world, and as a consequence, the continuity of concentration will be different than on formal retreat.

Hindrances and *Yogi* Mind

On home retreat, we examine investigation and effort on a different level with varying degrees of intensity than on a formal retreat. We apply much more reflection, more *samapajañña*, and, as a consequence, during formal meditation our minds will often be more active with various kinds of thinking.

Most people who do home retreat will experience fairly intense mental chatter, which will lead to the arising of the hindrances [Pāli: *nīvaraṇani*] and *yogi* mind in very big ways. *Yogi* mind is a tsunami of hindrances that overwhelm the mind, a common occurrence along the meditation path. These are some of the strongest reasons to practice home retreat. To liberate the mind from sensual desire, ill will and ignorance, we must examine these states of mind in all aspects of life and not just on the cushion. The open-handedness of equanimity [Pāli: *upekkhā*] permits the mind to mature and change.

The tools and skills we bring to bear when the mind is scattered or uncooperative while meditating during home retreat are the same as those we use on a formal meditation retreat. We bring the intention and skills we have to aim our minds to the object and try and try again to maintain and sustain the placing of *sati* onto the object under investigation [Pāli: *vitakka-vicāra*]. What is different on home retreat is how much and how often we consciously add a posture of interested non-involved reflective investigation and *sampajañña*. The more frequently we combine *sati* with *sampajañña*, the more we train our minds towards hitting the bull's eye that is the target of the Buddha's teaching.

Slow Down

Slowing down during the home retreat is more important than it might appear to be on the surface. Aside from your formal sitting and walking practice and your focus on *sampajañña*, slowing down can be the single most useful technique in developing the continuity of your attention in any situation.

Slowing down allows us time to reflect and gives us time to generate *sati-sampajañña* toward the sense object or activity at hand. It is fuel for the cultivation of intention, effort, *sampajañña* and patience. It takes strong restraint and renunciation to slow down, which allows us to exercise greater intention, energy and investigation.

SUGGESTIONS FOR PRACTICE:

As much as possible during normal everyday activities, make physical actions deliberate and couple these actions with *sati-sampajañña.*

Try to notice physical actions throughout a sequence in which they appear:

- Start with noticing the intention to move.
- Then notice the beginning of the actual movement.
- Watch for when the sequence ends.

Pay particular attention to how often your body moves unconsciously such as:

- Your fingers touching your face.
- Wiggling your foot.
- Scratching an itch.
- Adjusting your glasses or your posture while sitting or standing.

HINT:

When you miss the beginning of a movement, start at the point at which you notice it, and pay particular attention to the end of the movement. For instance, when you put something down, if you've missed being attentive to the beginning of that movement, start to observe it at that point and then pay particular attention to the moment of completion of the movement. Attending to the end of a movement or the end of your awareness of a sense object heightens attention, giving rise to a greater probability of capturing the beginning of your next physical action or your next awareness of a mind object. Everything is more clearly known by slowing down as much as possible.

Cultivate Right Speech

The noble factor of Right Speech can become another edge to the practice. *Sampajañña* will serve you as you explore Right Speech.

SPEAKING • SUGGESTIONS FOR PRACTICE:

- Pause and reflect before you speak.
- Examine whether speaking serves a purpose.
- If you find a purpose:
  - ~ Notice what that purpose is and examine your intention through the four categories of *sampajañña*.
  - ~ If speaking serves only for self-reference and inflates feelings of well-being, see if there are alternatives to speaking.
  - ~ If there are no alternatives, ask yourself how you might choose to consciously affect what you are saying.
- Check whether what you are about to say is suitable to the situation.
- Ask yourself if the motivation for speaking is pure, unwholesome or a mix of both.
- If attention is strong, see if you can identify the intention to speak, the feeling tone when speaking and the results of speaking for yourself and others.

HINT:

If silence will make someone uncomfortable or cause confusion, it is Right Speech to offer your best and even chat for a short time. On the other hand, if silence is acceptable, try to use it.

LISTENING • SUGGESTIONS FOR PRACTICE:

Ask yourself:

- What are your physical and mental postures while listening?
- Is there judgment, compassion or wanting to say your piece and get the discussion over with?
- Bring your attention to how you listen and try to add kindness and patience if you hear yourself being unskillful.

- Just notice and try to listen more carefully.
- Recognize that the person to whom you are speaking is trying the best they can.

Investigate Sleep

Explore how much you sleep and when you sleep. Even on a short formal retreat it is not uncommon to discover that we need only six hours of sleep each night; on longer retreats, it may be only four hours or less. The decreased need for sleep can also occur on home retreat, although usually to a lesser degree.

While on home retreat, I try to reduce the amount I sleep by very small amounts each night until I find a healthy balance. There is no right amount for everyone. It depends in part on how active and social your day is and what your body needs. If you are working, for instance, you might not be able to reduce the number of hours you sleep by very much.

On residential retreats, *yogis* often find themselves naturally waking up earlier and earlier. This can happen on home retreat as well. Waking early can provide support for the mental factors of intention and effort. Incremental development of wholesome patterns deepens one's balance in all activities. Going to bed early and waking early can be very helpful to support formal practice in an everyday practice. This is especially true during home retreat.

When we get up early, we have an hour or two of focus before the rest of the world awakens. This is important for those who have partners, children, pets, jobs, volunteer work or other chores they must attend to early in the day during the retreat. Making a solid start to your day and being certain to carry out your formal practice each day are among the most important tools that support a home retreat. Choosing to get up early also obliges you to go to bed earlier. Even casual investigation will reveal that most evening and nighttime activities tend towards leisure, which are almost always preference-reinforcing activities. You might want to keep early birds and worms in mind.

Napping is another practice edge where we can explore how much sleep we need. It can be difficult to sleep more than four hours at a stretch while on retreat, which often translates to slumps during the day. A well-considered short nap can be skillful.

CAUTION:

Be careful: Naps are an edge of practice that can cut both ways. They can be of service in balancing your energy, and they can be opportunities for unseen laziness and distraction to arise. Careful attention to thoughts and bodily sensations will help to inform you whether or not a nap is necessary. Another marker to observe if your motivation for the desire to nap is laziness or balance is how long you nap. Usually a nap of 5-15 minutes is all that the mind needs to help balance a drop in energy due to lack of sleep.

Use Chanting, Reflection and Determinations

Regularly scheduled chanting and formal reflections are valuable tools to inspire faith [Pāli: *saddhā*], set intention and galvanize effort. Respecting what we do establishes wholesome intention, which, when coupled with wise reflection, matures commitment and deepens practice.

Chanting offers an opportunity to utilize reflection, which otherwise is often underemphasized and therefore underutilized in Western-style *vipassanā* practice. Chanting is also a mirror on the mind's engagement and clarity. When chanting notice whether you are chanting the words and phrases by rote or if you have a reflective and respectful attention. Watching carefully offers a way to assess the qualities of investigation, effort and faith, and to notice if the hindrances are present.

Suggestions for chants and reflections (*see* Appendix 4: Table of Lists, Chants and Reflections):

- Paying homage to the Buddha.
- Taking refuge in the Buddha, *Dhamma*, *Saṅgha*

- Taking the Precepts.
- Sharing merit.
- Doing *mettā* practice or practicing any of the other three *Brahma-vihāras* [the Four Divine Abodes].
- Asking and offering forgiveness [Pāli: *khama*].
- Chanting or reflecting on the *pāramīs*.

SUGGESTIONS FOR PRACTICE:

- Consider a formal forgiveness practice for yourself and others as a preliminary practice before every formal meditation session. For an example of how to do formal forgiveness practice, *see* Appendix 4, Table of Lists, Chants and Reflections.
- Chant in your native tongue or in Pāli or in English (if it's not your native tongue) depending on how you think you will reap the best benefit; translate chants and see which works better for you.
- Apply a silent loving chuckle into the mind stream when you reflect on failures. Remind yourself that you are starting again fresh.
- Use mealtimes as an excellent opportunity to develop a chanting practice.

Determinations [Pāli: *adhiṭṭhāna*] as a tool are seldom taught to lay *yogis*. They are done by silently repeating your wholesome intention three times before a sit or at the beginning of the day.

SUGGESTIONS FOR PRACTICE:

- Choose the determinations carefully and make sure that the determination is appropriate for the circumstance.
- A few examples:
  - ~ "During this sit, may my mindfulness remain unbroken for five (or ten, etc.) minutes."
  - ~ "May this practice lead to deeper wisdom."

> ~ "May this practice lead to greater harmlessness in self and others."

- Use determinations appropriate to the time, your skill, and the conditions.
- Choose your phrases with care and repeat them the same way each time.
  - ~ Allow yourself to forget them until the next formal opportunity to use them again.
  - ~ Let them heat up on their own.

CAUTION:

Making unreasonable determinations will weaken your practice and create striving, judging and anxiety in the practice. Be careful. A determination such as, "May enlightenment arise in this sit," is not useful despite its wholesome sounding intention.

Cultivate Patience and *Mettā*

Home retreat obliges us to be in contact with others. A helpful exercise during home retreat is to steer the mind and heart towards *mettā* and patience while navigating chores and errands. Going to the grocery store, waiting in a line at the Post Office, or exercising on a treadmill at the gym are chances to cultivate wholesome states of mind.

SUGGESTIONS FOR PRACTICE:

When interacting with others:
- Experiment with doing silent reflection or chanting.
- Offer *mettā* to the clerk checking out your groceries or to the person in front of you fumbling with their credit card.
- Use this time as often as possible to cultivate loving attention for self and others. Make this mental state your heart's posture as often as possible.

Experiment with Balance

Meditation practice deepens and enlightenment has the potential to arise when balance of the five spiritual faculties [Pāli: *indriya-samatta*] is achieved. The fulcrum of both wisdom and compassion is the balance in one's own mind.

SUGGESTIONS FOR PRACTICE:

- Keep an eye on balancing your energy and your mental posture.
- Check in with yourself and ask if you are striving or becoming lazy.
- Try to notice if any mental or physical pattern is beginning to become predominant. Example: Laziness seems to arise with frequent thoughts about how difficult this is or how you might not sit the next scheduled sit.
    - ~ If a pattern like that has manifested, try to bring careful, nonjudgmental *sati-sampajañña* to the situation and apply whatever your wisdom calls you to do.
    - ~ Assess the results.
    - ~ Bring attention and investigation.
    - ~ Bring up appropriate amounts of energy or effort.
    - ~ Make a determination to sit.

Include Reading and *Dhamma* Study

Reread, at least once during the retreat:

- *The Home Retreat Guide.*
- *A Householder's Vinaya.*
- Nyanaponika's commentary on *sampajañña* in *The Heart of Buddhist Meditation*, even if you have read it before. The four categories of *sampajañña* are practical pointers.

SUGGESTIONS FOR PRACTICE:

- Reflect on all three readings.
- Apply your understanding of the four categories of *sampajañña* to your intentions for home retreat and to any changes that come up throughout the retreat.
- Ask yourself: How can I apply these lessons in my daily life during this retreat?
- When you read this Guide, make sure you understand the material in the Appendices, especially the Glossary:
  ~ Don't just gloss over them. Read them deeply and make them objects of study and reflection.
  ~ Go to the source material to support your intention and effort. You will get a better perspective on how and why this training can support you on your path to liberation.

Should you have time beyond the study of this guide, *A Householder's Vinaya* and Nyanaponika's commentary, make time each day for some formal study related to the practice, including scriptural study. For discussion of how to prepare for study before the retreat, *see* Chapter 2, *Foundational Readings*.

SUGGESTIONS FOR PRACTICE:

- Read only during a prescribed time in the day unless your job or other circumstances oblige you to change the time.
- Read only from the material you chose before the retreat.
- Read a little bit and reflect on what you've read before reading more.
- Don't just jump around to new ideas and new areas of study. This only encourages choice and following preferences.
- Avoid starting to read after the arising of a thought like: "Oh, maybe I could read a bit right now. I've got a few minutes be-

fore my appointment," or after you hear your internal voice say, "I need a break, and reading the *Dhamma* is more wholesome than some other activity."

~ This type of reading is more about distraction and less about practice.

~ Giving in to this type of thought or action conditions the mind more towards blind preference than towards the material to be read.

~ When these types of thoughts arise:

– Sit for a couple of minutes.

– Watch the boredom or restlessness, no matter how subtle.

– See what happens to the thoughts and any accompanying sensations. Do they increase, decrease, stay the same?

– Simply observe and be present for whatever arises.

– If patient observation is not appropriate in the situation, do a few moments of *mettā* practice.

• After finishing, carry on with your schedule.

If you choose to listen to podcasts or video or audio recordings of *Dhamma* talks or other material:

• Make as much effort as possible to listen or watch with your full attention from beginning to end.

• Listen only at scheduled times.

• Caution: Do not listen while driving or doing other activities.

TIP:

No matter what you're doing—reading or exercising, checking email or offering yourself some entertainment—staying on topic gives the mind a chance to have a mental anchor like the breath does in the body physically, which gives perspective when preferences or boredom arise.

Use Daily and End-of-Retreat Reviews

DAILY REVIEW

Late in the day before your last sit, review how the day went. You may find a five to ten-minute period of journaling or reflection about an incident during the day can bring greater clarity and stimulate effort the next day.

SUGGESTIONS FOR PRACTICE:

- Do the review with as much kindness and curiosity as possible.
- Choose one incident — skillful or unskillful — to review, or conduct an overview of the type of mental factors that were most predominant throughout the day.
- Examine the quality of each of the following:
  ~ The intention that preceded the incident.
  ~ The quality of thought, speech or action that accompanied the incident or the mental factor being examined.
  ~ The consequences both for the short and long term of the incident.
- Notice if judgment accompanies the assessment of the incident or if there's space to simply observe.
  ~ In either case, notice the judgment or the space.
- Continue your review with kindness.
- With active, nonjudgmental analysis, look at what might be done should something similar arise in the future. Ask yourself:
  ~ How can I improve or tweak the practice tomorrow to support my stated goals?
  ~ How can I use this retreat time to train in increased friendliness when applying investigation and discipline?

RETREAT REVIEW

At the end of the home retreat, make an appointment with a *kalyāṇamitta* to review what you've done, what you've not done and what you've learned during the retreat.

SUGGESTIONS FOR PRACTICE:

- Be meticulously honest with yourself and the person with whom you are speaking.
- Report to them:
  - ~ What your intentions were at the beginning of the retreat.
  - ~ What you did and didn't do.
  - ~ What you learned.
  - ~ What you want to improve during your next home retreat.

CHAPTER 4

Seeing the Results of
Home Retreat Practice

I've DESCRIBED IN Chapters 2 and 3 some of the techniques I have found useful when planning and practicing a home retreat. Many of these instructions will apply to you, but some won't. After experimenting with them, you'll discover those that are useful to you, those that are not and some that will come from your own wisdom as the retreat unfolds. You'll also likely notice that what is useful on one home retreat may not be as useful on another.

CAUTION:

In assessing the techniques you used and plan to use, be careful not to confuse easy and pleasant with wise and skillful practice. Remind yourself of this over and over again. All too easily and all too frequently we forget and just try to do what is easy, rather than what might be useful.

By training ourselves using home retreats, we gain immeasurable benefits both in the short and the long haul. For example, we strengthen the indeterminate mental factors such as intention, effort, concentration, etc., making them more easily accessible. According to the *Abhidhamma Piṭaka*, the indeterminate mental factors are states of mind that by themselves have no intrinsic qualities of wholesomeness or unwholesomeness. These indeterminate mental factors accompany all thought, speech and action and can be used for wholesome or unwholesome ends. Wholesome mental factors can be strengthened when we consciously evoke them. Unwholesome mental factors can be weakened when we don't use them, or when we choose wholesome mental factors in their place. During home retreat, we strengthen the indeterminate mental factors to become second nature, link them with wholesomeness and learn how to apply them both during formal practice and in our everyday activities.

By training the mind to couple wholesomeness with these indeterminate mental factors, we bring greater wholesome results into all our daily activities. Continuity of wholesomeness in all activities is the linchpin, and balance is the grease. Home practice and home retreat are the active forces at play.

We actualize our paths towards spiritual freedom when we meet all experience, no matter what that experience might be, with a wholesome and accepting hand and an open heart coupled with *sati-sampajañña*. A day full of interruptions and resistance is as valuable as a day when we meet whatever arises with wise attention. Both deserve our full and equal attention. Friendliness towards self and others, adapting to the unexpected and investigation with no fixed agenda are all tools that will support the momentum, maturity, and integration of our practice.

The Saṅgha Nonresidential Retreat Guide

PART IV: THE SAṄGHA NONRESIDENTIAL RETREAT GUIDE
TABLE OF CONTENTS

The Saṅgha
Nonresidential Retreat Guide

Why a *Saṅgha* Home Retreat Guide?

LAY LIFE GIVES US THE OPPORTUNITY to put the Buddha's teachings into context in real time while experiencing all of life's ups and downs, successes and failures, gains and losses. This is the practice field that will mold lay life into a whole rather than one in which we continue to believe that meditation practice and everyday life are separate.

As lay people on a residential meditation retreat at a retreat center or monastery, we take the Five or Eight Precepts, restrain our senses, apply ourselves to the practice and cultivation of continuous mindfulness [Pāḷi: *sati*], all of which are hallmarks of an extremely skillful baseline for clear comprehension [Pāḷi: *sampajañña*]. However, everyday life can be — must be — where our meditation practice meets the road. A *saṅgha* nonresidential home retreat presents the perfect confluence of conditions to bring together our personal home practices, our everyday life practices and our community practice.

> *Clear comprehension is most famously [and frequently] invoked*
> *by the Buddha in tandem with mindfulness practice in the*
> *Satipaṭṭhāna Sutta: . . . "[H]e lives contemplating mental objects*
> *in mental objects, ardent, clearly comprehending and mindful,*
> *having overcome, in this world, covetousness and grief."*
> — Wikipedia definition of *sampajañña*

Because the residential retreat environment is designed to support and condition continuous *sati*, the environment itself simultaneously establishes an extremely high level of *sampajañña* so that very little teaching or attention to its practice is necessary. However, upon leaving the retreat center or monastery, the *yogi* is confronted with a radically different set of circumstances.

For most householders, the expectation that we can practice *sati* at home continuously is unrealistic unless we are highly enlightened. Lay life does not naturally support the practice of formal *sati* the way a retreat does. At best, some of us are able to do formal *sati* meditation an hour or two each day; others of us let our sitting practices fall away till the next time we can go on a formal retreat.

A mind devoid of clear comprehension is like a pot with holes;
it cannot retain in memory what has been learned, thought over
or meditated.
                              – Santideva, quoted in Nyanaponika Thera,
                                         The Heart of Buddhist Meditation

Because *sampajañña* is not overtly emphasized or taught on retreat, this critically important tool in our meditative practice may not be known or available to the lay *yogi* at home. Living our daily lives as householders is precisely when we can — and must — study, practice and cultivate *sampajañña* if our spiritual wisdom is to develop and deepen. When we utilize *sampajañña* at home, we have the opportunity to practice with and test the insights and skills we gleaned on retreat.

It is the daily little negligence in thoughts, words, and deeds
going on for many years of our lives . . . that is chiefly responsible
for the untidiness and confusion we have in our minds. This neg-
ligence creates the trouble and allows it to continue. Thus the old
Buddhist teachers have said: "Negligence produces a lot of dirt.

As in a house, so in the mind, only a very little dirt collects
in a day or two, but if it goes on for many years, it will grow
into a vast heap of refuse."
 — Nyanaponika Thera, *The Power of Mindfulness*

After a retreat, when we're back home, all too often we lose our ability to contextualize our retreat realizations in everyday life because *sati* is the tool we are taught, but it is not the only tool we can use. As a consequence, our retreat insights lose their power in a normal everyday life with its tendency to overwhelm the senses. When our senses are overwhelmed, the normal tendency is to revert to our previous patterns of understanding and behaving. Unfortunately, what we learned on retreat, which might otherwise be available to us, seems to get lost and remain hidden and unobserved.

After a retreat a householder may try to create an environment that mimics the environment of the retreat in order to be inspired to sustain meditative momentum. However, the householder will almost always be unsuccessful, and as a consequence their practice can suffer under the weight of added guilt or shame or self-judgment. If we are not already practicing *sampajañña*, this is precisely when this practice can become our most important meditative tool.

Enlightened wisdom becomes second nature only if the practice of meditation is not just about formal sitting practice, but also a way of being in all activities. We must learn how to incline the mind towards meditative attention from the time we get up in the morning until the moment when we fall asleep at night. The *combination* of both *sati* and *sampajañña* are the practices the Buddha offers us to achieve this promise.

Like practicing *sati* on retreat, practicing *sampajañña* at home begins to teach us how to make this practice both the background and the foreground of our daily experiences. The application of *sampajañña* in a leading role in our everyday practice deepens our wisdom and primes our intentions for liberation with focus and wholesomeness

[Pāḷi: *kusala*]. It also supports our *sati* and wisdom through our growing understanding of the true nature of reality, so that the next time we go on retreat we can begin the retreat with a practice field that has been supported instead of one that has been forgotten and lost.

The Home Retreat Guide and *A Householder's Vinaya* provide sets of instructions and practices that directly address how to combine *sati* and *sampajañña* outside of a formal retreat. We can individually develop our practices through the cultivation of the instructions and practices in *A Householder's Vinaya* and *The Home Retreat Guide*. This guide is another tool we can use to support community practice in the form of a *sangha* retreat.

Who Can Use This *Sangha* Retreat Guide

Throughout the world there are now many lay *sanghas*, which, like churches, mosques and synagogues, serve a community of like-minded folks and brings them together to support, share and model aspects of their practices. Relying on *A Householder's Vinaya* and *The Home Retreat Guide*, lay *sanghas* have the tools to offer this new way to practice. A lay *sangha* can be the nucleus for the teaching of *sampajañña*, which, on a variety of levels, will automatically deepen the wholesomeness of the community and the meditation practice of each individual who actively engages in its practice.

With this guide, lay *sanghas* now have the opportunity to exponentially raise the level of support they offer their congregations by offering nonresidential *sangha* retreats. They can offer a higher octane, more focused experience, and at the same time offer appropriately tailored *satipatthāna* meditation techniques to the lay *yogi*.

A Householder's Vinaya and *The Home Retreat Guide*

> *Vinaya is thus, in its essence, the Buddhist lifestyle [meditation coupled with virtue]: the way serious Buddhist practitioners*

arrange, organize, and structure their lives in order to support
Dhamma study, practice, realization, and service. This covers all
physical and verbal actions. It involves all forms of relationships:
interpersonal, social, economic, political, ecological, as well as
with one's own body.

– Badiner & Hill, p. 303

A Householder's Vinaya and *The Home Retreat Guide*, like the
monastic *Vinaya* and full-on formal residential retreat, were created
for the express purpose of inviting the householding *yogi* to train the
heart and mind not only during formal practice, but also during all daily
activities, including working, doing household chores, attending to childcare, exercising, etc.; in other words, during the 'whole catastrophe.'
A Householder's Vinaya takes a lot of its inspiration from the *Vinaya
Piṭaka*, which contains the *Pātimokkha*, the monastic rules of conduct.
When monastics practice according to their *Vinaya* with integrity, all
of their waking attention is directed towards the cultivation of *sīla,
samādhi, paññā* [virtue, concentration, wisdom, respectively].

The Home Retreat Guide, which can be found at householdersvinaya.
com, provides the meditator practical instructions on why and how to
plan and do home retreats. A home retreat is very much like a *saṅgha*
retreat but without the *saṅgha*. We do it alone or in parallel with others
doing the same thing in their own homes, often across the country or in
other places around the world. Having the time and the willingness and
following the instructions allow sincere *yogis* to schedule more frequent
and more intensive style practice into their everyday lives.

A Householder's Vinaya and *The Home Retreat Guide* are designed
to offer lay people the opportunity to live and practice with a quality of
attention similar to that of the monastics when they are not on retreat.
They recognize that many householders have similar intentions for their
lives as monastics. However, they do not try to make the householder's
life into an ongoing formal retreat as if the they had gone to a retreat
center or monastery.

Without trying to turn householders into something they're not, *A Householder's Vinaya* and *The Home Retreat Guide* offer practices to give householders the tools to transform lay life from practice between retreats to a seamless lifetime of practice. They embrace the conditions of a householder's situation and use those conditions to alchemize what is normal and difficult into what is normal and freeing. Another such tool is this guide, *The Saṅgha Nonresidential Home Retreat Guide*.

How Does a *Saṅgha* Home Retreat Work?

A *saṅgha* home retreat is a nonresidential retreat that draws its inspiration from the *Vinaya Piṭaka* and uses *A Householder's Vinaya* and *The Home Retreat Guide* as instruction manuals. A *saṅgha* retreat uses the personal relationships of *saṅgha* members and the *saṅgha* facility itself as two out-of-the-ordinary tiles in the mosaic of this mural. This style of retreat offers lay *yogis* the opportunity to dramatically 'up' their practices during select and limited periods of time while still navigating daily life.

Depending on the personal conditions of the *yogis*, the retreat may look quite intense with lots of formal sitting meditation, meetings with other retreatants and mentors; or it may look much less structured. Each person tailors the retreat to suit their own unique circumstances. For example, a retiree's retreat may look very different from the retreat of an employed single parent. There is room and there are tools for everyone who sees themselves wanting to be part of the retreat. It isn't about what we do; it's about how we do it.

The overall purpose of the retreat can be likened to the *yogi* saying, "Yes, I can bring more *sati-sampajañña* and *pañña* into my everyday life. I don't have to relegate my practice to just the cushion, or a *Dhamma* talk at the *saṅgha's* center, or while on a residential retreat. I can bring many more moments of awakening into my life should I choose to adjust my attitude, intention and focus towards what I'm doing right now."

Prerequisites for Participation

Before the retreat begins, each participant should have read the following:

- *The Saṅgha Nonresidential Home Retreat Guide.*
- *The Home Retreat Guide.*
- Nyanaponika Thera's commentary on *sampajañña* in *The Heart of Buddhist Meditation.*

Although not required, it is highly suggested that participants read:

- *The Noble Eightfold Path: The Way to the End of Suffering* by Bhikkhu Bodhi.
- *A Householder's Vinaya* by Allan Cooper.

Participants are also required to listen to the following *vipassanā* meditation instructions given by Joseph Goldstein:

- https://www.dharmaseed.org/talks/audio_player/96/36191.html
- https://www.dharmaseed.org/talks/audio_player/96/36192.html
- https://www.dharmaseed.org/talks/audio_player/96/36190.html

Preparation for the Retreat

Yogis:

Read and listen to the required material in the section *above* on prerequisites.

- Create a schedule:
  - ~ Use *The Home Retreat Guide* to create a personal schedule.
  - ~ Coordinate your schedule with the *saṅgha* schedule for *Dhamma* talks, group meetings and mentor interviews.
- Have a pre-retreat interview with one of the *saṅgha* mentors to discuss your schedule, focuses, and goals.
- Schedule interviews during the *retreat* with one of the mentors.

KALYĀṆAMITTA SAṄGHA COORDINATION:

- For first time mentors: schedule a time for them view a video blog or participate in a scheduled instruction session with a trained *saṅgha* retreat mentor.
- Schedule interviews for before and during the retreat:
  ~ Identify mentors for interviews.
  ~ Arrange times with *yogis*.
- Schedule *kalyāṇamitta* [spiritual friend] support group meetings to meet during the retreat.
  ~ Set a maximum of 5 *yogis* per group.
- Schedule meditation periods at the *saṅgha's* center during the week:
  ~ Schedule times for formal meditation periods on a drop-in basis.
  ~ Schedule required group meetings with the *yogis* during the week.
  ~ Arrange for group leaders.
  ~ Determine if any meditation periods during the week are required for the *yogis*.
- Plan *Dhamma* talks:
  ~ Schedule the talks.
  ~ Arrange for speakers to give them.
- Plan the weekends:
  ~ Arrange for leaders and instructors for the weekend retreats.
  ~ Schedule the weekend, including:
    – Formal meditation periods
    – *Dhamma* talks
    – Talks for encouragement
    – Instructions

THE SAṄGHA AS A COLLECTIVE:

- Invite local and other speakers to give *Dhamma* talks before, during and after the retreat to explain:

~ What a *saṅgha* home retreat is.

~ How to best use it.

~ How a *saṅgha* home retreat can be of service to one's practice.

• Make handouts announcing and explaining the *saṅgha* home retreat available so that the entire community is aware of the event.

~ If the *saṅgha* has a website, use it to announce the event and explain how the retreat works and when it will be.

~ Make frequent announcements at group sittings and events months in advance.

~ Make a *saṅgha* contact for the retreat available.

WHEN SHOULD THE RETREAT BEGIN AND END?

• Retreats can last anywhere from a weekend to 10 days.

• Begin and end the retreat on a weekend to permit a variety of scheduling choices and more types of exercises than a weekend alone or a week-long retreat without weekends.

Retreat Structure

In general, a *saṅgha* retreat should follow the structure for individual home retreats provided by *The Home Retreat Guide*, which can be found at www.householdersvinaya.com.

SUPPORT GROUP MEETINGS DURING THE RETREAT

Kalyāṇamitta support group meetings are valuable. It is important for the *yogis* to express themselves in the group and have the chance to engage in a give and take with the group and receive group support. Group meetings are about practice only; they are not about world affairs, current events or likes and dislikes.

Group meetings are monitored by mentors. Each group should have a maximum of 5 *yogis*.

The meetings provide the opportunity to share questions, doubts, missteps in practice, advice for others, etc. These meetings can be likened to a lay version of monastics reciting their *Pātimokkha*, the rules for ordained monastics: one monastic recites the rules after which the members of the *saṅgha* share any transgressions of the rules and receive advice if appropriate. This practice helps to build a community by having *yogis* share experiences and language and enabling the *yogis* to take risks. It also assists *yogis* in ways that are way outside the usual norm in their lives.

INDIVIDUAL INTERVIEWS DURING THE RETREAT

At least two individual meetings with a mentor are required for each *yogi* during the week. I strongly encourage face to face individual meetings with mentors.

Retreat Schedule

- Each *saṅgha* will have different needs and conditions. The template *below* is an example of a schedule. Each *saṅgha* should adjust the schedule according to their conditions and needs.
- Amending the schedule and incorporating new ideas will be an integral part of the development of the *saṅgha* home retreat.
- The filter that inhibits clear understanding will always be the limit of our ability to see the true nature of the Buddha's teachings and whether we have the willingness to do what might be difficult. Committing to and maintaining a retreat schedule allows us to examine all the habits we might have to shine on this or that sit, this or that meeting. The schedule in and of itself offers us teachings.

FIRST WEEKEND

Friday: 6:00 - 8:15 p.m.
- 6:00 - 6:45 p.m.: *Dhamma* talk with a few instructions given by a mentor.
- 6:45 - 7:30 p.m.: Meditation.
- 7:30 - 8:15 p.m.: Taking the Precepts and instructions.

Saturday: 7:30 a.m. - 8:30 p.m.
- 7:30 - 11:30 a.m: Morning meditation with alternating sitting and walking periods.
- 11:30 a.m. - 12:45 p.m.: Lunch.
- 12:45 - 5:30 p.m.: Afternoon meditation with alternating sitting and walking periods.
- 5:30 - 6:30 p.m.: Break.
- 6:30 - 8:30 p.m.: Evening meditation with alternating sitting and walking periods.

Sunday: 7:30 a.m. - 3:30 p.m.
- 7:30 - 11:30 a.m.: Morning meditation alternating sitting and walking periods.
- 11:30 a.m. - 12:45 p.m.: Lunch.
- 12:45 - 3:30 p.m.: Afternoon meditation with alternating sitting and walking periods.

WEEKDAYS, MONDAY THROUGH FRIDAY

- 7 - 9 a.m., 1 - 5 p.m., 6 - 8 p.m.: Open sitting periods with regular bells.
  ~ Drop-ins invited.
  ~ Staffed by trained *saṅgha kalyāṇamitta*.
- 6 - 8 p.m., Wednesday night:
  ~ 6:00 - 6:45 p.m.: Meditation
  ~ 6:45 - 7:45 p.m.: Interviews
  ~ 7:45 - 8:00 p.m.: Offering merit

- Interviews:
  ~ Minimum of 2 during the week.
  ~ Additional interviews on request.

SECOND WEEKEND:

- *Friday*:   6:00 - 8:15 p.m.
  ~ 6:00 - 6:45 p.m.: *Dhamma* talk with a few instructions
    given by a mentor.
  ~ 6:45 - 7:30 p.m.: Meditation.
  ~ 7:30 - 8:15 p.m.: Instructions.

- *Saturday*: 7:30 a.m. - 8:30 p.m.
  ~ 7:30 - 11:30 a.m: Morning meditation with alternating sitting
    and walking periods.
  ~ 11:30 a.m. - 12:45 p.m.: Lunch.
  ~ 12:45 - 5:30 p.m.: Afternoon meditation with alternating sit-
    ting and walking periods.
  ~ 5:30 - 6:30 p.m.: Break.
  ~ 6:30 - 8:30 p.m.: Evening meditation with alternating sitting
    and walking periods.

- *Sunday*: 7:30 a.m. - 3:30 p.m.
  ~ 7:30 - 11:30 a.m.: Morning meditation alternating
    sitting and walking periods.
  ~ 11:30 a.m. - 12:45 p.m.: Lunch.
  ~ 12:45 - 3:00 p.m.: Afternoon meditation with
    alternating sitting and walking periods.
  ~ 3:00 - 3:30 p.m.: Closing ceremony.

During the Retreat

YOGIS

- Attend the first weekend of the retreat.
- Attend scheduled interviews.
- Attend scheduled *kalyāṇamitta* support group meetings.
- Attend regular sitting and walking periods at the *saṅgha* during the week, at which instruction will be available.
- Attend the scheduled retreat meeting on Wednesday evening for a sit and discussion.
- Attend the second weekend of the retreat.

After the Retreat

YOGIS:

- Attend the scheduled post-retreat interview.
- If desired, continue voluntary participation with the group through continued check-ins with retreat participants.
- Do solo home retreats.

PART FIVE

Appendixes

APPENDICES

Glossary

SOURCES OF DEFINITIONS:

- Access to Insight (www.accesstoinsight.org)
- Nyanatiloka, *Buddhist Dictionary*: Manual of Buddhist Terms and Doctrines:
  https://books.google.com/books?printsec=frontcover&vid=
    ISBN9552400198#v=onepage&q=nibbana&f=false
- Dhammadana.org
- Wikipedia
- Allan Cooper

NOTE:

This glossary, which is also available at householdersvinaya.com (https:// householdersvinaya.com/glossary/), is a quick reference to commonly used Pāli words, English words and frequently used phrases in *A HOUSEHOLDER'S VINAYA, THE HOME RETREAT GUIDE,* and *THE SAṄGHA NONRESIDENTIAL RETREAT GUIDE,* and in general usage in *Theravāda* Buddhism.

Abhidhamma Piṭaka
   1. English, literally: Basket of Higher Doctrine.
   2. Last of the three *pitakas* [baskets] constituting the Pāli Canon, the scriptures of *Theravāda* Buddhism. First two are the *Vinaya Piṭaka* and the *Sutta Piṭaka.*

3. Detailed scholastic analysis and summary of the Buddha's
teachings set out in the *Sutta Piṭaka*. The *suttas* [discourses]
are reworked into a schematized system of general principles
that often is called the "Buddhist Psychology" in English. The
generally dispersed teachings and principles of the *suttas* are
organized into a coherent methodology of Buddhist doctrine.

Adiṭṭhāna

1. English: determination; resolution.
2. Commitment to training into a certain kind of conduct
or to moral principles.
3. One of four foundations of an *arahant's* mentality.
4. One of the ten *pāramīs*: Perfection of resolution.

Akusala

Unwholesome. *See Kusala/Akusala.*

Anāgāmi

Non-returner. *See Nibbāna.*

Anattā

1. English: non-self; not-self.
2. One of the three characteristics of existence [Pāli: *ti-lakkhaṇa*].
3. Refers to the Buddhist doctrine that there is no unchanging,
permanent self, soul or essence in living beings.

Annicā

1. English: impermanence.
2. One of the three characteristics of existence [Pāli: *ti-lakkhaṇa*].
3. Refers to the Buddhist doctrine that all of conditioned existence,
without exception, is "transient, evanescent, inconstant." All
temporal things, whether material or mental, are compounded
objects in a continuous change of condition, subject to decline
and destruction.

Appamāda

1. Quite significant in the Pāli Canon; the essence of the meaning
cannot be captured with one English word: Heedfulness,
diligence, conscientiousness, concern all capture some aspects.

2. Taking great care concerning what should be adopted and what should be avoided.

Arahant/Arahantship [Skt: *arahat*]

1. A fully enlightened being; the state of being fully enlightened.
2. Person who has eliminated all the unwholesome roots that underlie all mental defilements, and who, upon death, will not be reborn in any world, since the bonds that bind a person to being reborn have been finally dissolved.
3. In the Pāli Canon, '*Tathāgata*' sometimes used as a synonym for *arahant*, although *Tathāgata* usually refers to the Buddha alone.
4. One who has gained insight into the true nature of existence and has achieved *nibbāna*.

Ariya

Enlightened being. *See Nibbāna.*

Ariyo aṭṭhaṅgiko maggo

The Noble Eightfold Path. *See* Noble Eightfold Path.

Attha sīla

The Eight Precepts. *See Sīla.*

Avijjā

1. English: ignorance.
2. Refers to ignorance or misconceptions about the nature of metaphysical reality, in particular about the doctrines of impermanence and non-self with regard to reality.
3. The root cause of *dukkha* [suffering, pain, unsatisfactoriness].
4. Mentioned within the Buddhist teachings as ignorance or misunderstanding in various contexts:
   a. Four Noble Truths.
   b. The first link in the twelve links of dependent origination [Pāli: *paṭiccasamuppāda*].
   c. One of the ten fetters in the *Theravāda* tradition.

Bhāvanā

1. Mental or meditative development; progression, development of concentration

2. Training in developing concentration.

3. When used on its own signifies contemplation and spiritual cultivation generally.

4. Normally appears in conjunction with another word forming a compound phrase such as *citta-bhāvanā* [development or cultivation of the heart and mind] or *mettā-bhāvanā* [development and cultivation of lovingkindness].

Bhikkhu

A fully ordained *Theravāda* Buddhist monk.

Bhikkhunī

A fully ordained *Theravāda* Buddhist nun.

Bojjhaṅgā

The Seven Factors of Enlightenment:

1. Mindfulness [Pāli: *sati*]

2. Investigation [Pāli: *dhamma-vicaya*]

3. Effort [Pāli: *viriya*]

4. Joy [Pāli: *pīti*]

5. Calm [Pāli: *passaddhi*]

6. Concentration [Pāli: *samādhi*]

7. Equanimity [Pāli: *upekkhā*]

Brahma-vihāras

1. English: Divine Abodes:

a. *Mettā* [lovingkindness]

b. *Karunā* [compassion]

c. *Muditā* [empathetic joy]

d. *Upekkhā* [equanimity]

2. Sublime states of concentration and mental qualities that can be developed in everyday life.

3. Four suitable concentration objects for the cultivation of *jhāna*. *See* http://www.vipassana.com/meditation/four_sublime_states.php.

Bright faith: *See* Faith.

Cattārimāni sammappadhāna

Four Right Exertions; *see* Effort.

Cetasika: See Mental Factors.

Citta

English: mind, consciousness, state of consciousness.

Clear comprehension: *See Sati-sampajañña.*

Concentration: *See Samādhi.*

Dāna

1. Gift, offering, generosity.
2. In Hinduism, Buddhism, Jainism and Sikhism, the practice of cultivating generosity. It can take the form of giving to an individual in distress or need or philanthropic public projects that empower and help many.
3. The practice of giving, taking place through the development of states of mind such as generosity and disinterestedness.
4. The first of the 10 perfections [Pāli: *pāramī*].

Defilements: *See Kilesas.*

Dependent origination [Pāli: *paṭiccasamuppāda*]

1. Synonymous with 'dependent arising' or 'dependent co-arising.'
2. A key doctrine of Buddhist philosophy that all *dhammas* [phenomena] arise in dependence upon other *dhammas*: "If this exists, that exists; if this ceases to exist, that also ceases to exist."
3. Expressed in 12 links, a linear list of elements, each arising in dependence on the preceding link.
4. Traditionally interpreted as describing the conditional arising of rebirth in *saṃsāra* and the resultant *dukkha* [suffering, pain, unsatisfactoriness]. Alternative *Theravāda* interpretation is that the list describes the arising of mental formations and the resultant notions of 'I' and 'mine,' which are the source of *duḥkha*.
5. Reversal of the causal chain is explained as leading to the annihilation of mental formations and rebirth.

Determination: *See Adiṭṭhāna*.

Dhamma [Skt: *Dharma*]

1. A key concept with multiple meanings in Indian religions such as Hinduism, Buddhism, Jainism, Sikhism and others. No single-word translation in Western languages.
2. In Buddhism, "cosmic law and order." Also, the teachings of the Buddha and the fourth foundation of mindfulness.
3. In Buddhist philosophy also the term for "phenomena."
4. In Hinduism, *dharma* signifies behaviors considered to be in accord with *Ṛta*, the order that makes life and universe possible, and includes duties, rights, laws, conduct, virtues and "right way of living."
5. In Jainism, *dharma* refers to the teachings of *tirthankara* (Jina) and the body of doctrine pertaining to the purification and moral transformation of human beings.
6. In Sikhism, *dharm* means the path of righteousness and proper religious practice.

Dhamma-vicaya

1. English: investigation.
2. Investigation of all phenomena.
3. One of the Four Roads to Power, Four Predominants of Truth.
4. Second of the Seven Factors of Enlightenment [Pāli: *bojjhaṅgā*].

Diverse *saṅgha*

A *saṅgha* that doesn't look as if you are looking in a mirror; consists of practitioners of any age, race, ethnicity, class, gender, sexual orientation, physical ability, etc.

Divine Abidings or Abodes: *See Brahma-vihāras*.

Doubt: *See Vicikicchā*.

Dukkha

1. English: commonly translated as "suffering," "pain," "unsatisfactoriness" "dissatisfaction" or "stress."
2. Refers to an important Buddhist concept: the fundamental

unsatisfactoriness and painfulness of mundane life.

3. The first of the Four Noble Truths.

4. One of the three characteristics of existence [Pāli: *ti-lakkhana*].

Dusty life

"Household life is crowded, a realm of dust, while going forth is the open air." *Pabbaja Sutta*: The Going Forth (Sn 3.1).

Effort [Pāli: *vāyāma*], Right Effort [Pāli: *sammā-vāyāma*], Four Right Efforts [Pāli: *cattārimāni sammappadhāna*]

1. Integral part of the Buddhist path to Enlightenment.

2. Sixth factor of the Noble Eightfold Path; first concentration factor.

3. Four Right Exertions encourage relinquishing harmful mental qualities and nurturing beneficial mental qualities:

   a. Restraint [Pāli: *samvara padhāna*] of the senses.

   b. Abandonment [Pāli: *pahāna padhāna*] of defilements.

   c. Cultivation [Pāli: *bhāvanā padhāna*] of Enlightenment Factors.

   d. Preservation [Pāli: *anurakkhana padhāna*] of concentration.

4. Built on the insightful recognition of the arising and non-arising of various mental qualities over time and of our ability to mindfully intervene in these ephemeral qualities.

5. In contemporary usage, commonly used interchangeably with 'energy' [Pāli: *vīrya*].

See Magga-vibhanga Sutta: An Analysis of the Path (SN 45.8).

Eightfold Path: *See* Noble Eightfold Path.

Exertion, Right Exertion: *See* Effort.

Faith [Pāli: *saddhā*]

1. In early Buddhism, focused on the Triple Gem:

   a. The Buddha

   b. His teaching [Pāli: *Dhamma*; Skt: *Dharma*]

   c. Community of spiritually developed followers or monastic community seeking enlightenment [Pāli: *Saṅgha*].

2. In more contemporary understanding: To have verified confidence not only in meditation and ability to undertake the

meditation, but in the teacher and the teachings of the Buddha.

3. Belief in the law of *kamma* [Skt: *karma*].

4. Confidence in *Dhamma*.

5. One of the Five Spiritual Faculties. *See Indriya*.

6. Verified faith:

    a. Unshakable faith based in intuitive understanding.

    b. According to the Path of Purification [Pāli: *Visuddhimagga*]:
Begins to take root after purification of view [Pāli:
ditthi-visuddhi], and becomes unshakeable at First Path
Enlightenment, *Sotāpanna* [once-returner; *see Nibbāna*].

7. Bright faith: Excited immature faith not significantly based
in experiential wisdom; easily swayed.

Feelings: *See Vedanā*.

Five Hindrances: *See Nīvaraṇa*.

Five and Eight Precepts [Pāli: *pañca sīla* and *attha sīla*]: *See Sīla*.

Five Spiritual Faculties: *See Indriya*.

Four Foundations of Mindfulness:

1. Mindfulness of body [Pāli: *kāya*].

2. Mindfulness of feeling affects or tones [Pāli: *vedanā*].

3. Mindfulness of mind or consciousness [Pāli: *citta*].

4. Mindfulness of five groups of *dhammās* ("specifically intended
to invest the mind with a soteriological orientation"– Gyori):

    a. Five hindrances. *See Nīvaraṇa*.

    b. Six sense bases [Pāli: āyatana].

    c. Aggregates [Pāli: *khanda*].

    d. Seven factors of enlightenment. *See Bojjhaṅgā*.

    e. Noble Eightfold Path. *See* Noble Eightfold Path.

Four requisites

1. Four requirements of everyday living, offered by lay people
to *Theravāda* Buddhist monastics:

    a. Nutrition (food, beverages, etc.).

    b. Shelter, housing (monastery, hut).

    c. Clothing (robes).

    d. Medicine (medicaments, remedies, first aid,

hygienic products, etc.).

2. For *Theravāda* Buddhist monastics, limitation of needs to a minimum; contentment with whatever is offered and given; renunciation of everything superfluous; avoidance of anything that could induce pleasure, comfort or distraction.

See https://www.usamyanmar.net/Buddha/Article/The%20four%20 requisite%202.pdf

Four Sublime States: *See Brahma-vihāras.*

Going for refuge: *See* Taking Refuge.

Happiness

1. State of mind that is stable and filled with wisdom and compassion.

2. Relative happiness: Less stable, fleeting.

Heavenly Abidings: *See Brahma-vihāras.*

Hindrances: *See Nīvaraṇa.*

Hiri: See Moral dread and fear of wrongdoing.

Home practice

1. Whatever practice a meditator has at home to try to improve themselves with attention to virtue, concentration and wisdom.

2. Can be very focused or loose.

3. Crucial to knowing how to hold a meditative life: If we hold our spiritual life as our core, we can consider our life as being a home practice.

4. *A Householder's Vinaya.*

Home retreat

Retreat practiced in one's home, not in a residential retreat center or a monastery.

See *The Home Retreat Guide.*

Householder

A Buddhist who is not a monastic; one who lives a 'dusty life.'

Householder's *Vinaya*

1. Code of practice and trainings for the householder.

2. Trainings and practices for the householder rooted in the development of *dāna, sīla, bhāvanā* [generosity, virtue, mental development], and of wisdom [Pāli: *paññā*].

Householding *yogi: See Yogi.*

Ignorance: *See Avijjā.*

Indriya

1. Spiritual faculties; also known as Five Spiritual Faculties [Pāli: *indriya-samatta*].

2. Balancing of mental factors, allowing the mind to engage intuitively with reality as well as being necessary for the maturing of meditative wisdom:

   a. Faith [Pāli: *sadha*]

   b. Energy or effort [Pāli: *vāyāma*]

   c. Mindfulness [Pāli: *sati*]

   d. Concentration [Pāli: *samādhi*]

   e. Wisdom [Pāli: *pañña*]

3. Equilibrium, balance, or harmony of the faculties.

4. More important to practice of *vipassanā* than definition seems to imply. Balance of mind and heart opens us to enlightenment. Practice of meditation is a constant process of refining our intuitive abilities through understanding the Three Characteristics [Pāli: *ti-lakkhaṇa*]; only when spiritual faculties are balanced can this occur.

   See *Indriya-vibhanga Sutta*: Analysis of the Mental Faculties (SN 48.10).

Indriya-saṃvara

1. English: restraint of the senses.

2. A multi-tiered meditative practice encompassing a conscious effort to restrain speech and actions in the outer or relative world and to bring *sati* to any sense object at the moment of its arising in consciousness.

3. Not indulging in habit of taking that which is pleasant in a mental process that leads to clinging or that which is unpleasant in a mental process that leads to aversion; training the mind to stay with what is.

4. Practice within the practice of clear comprehension [Pāli:

sati-sampajañña]; circumstances define what skills to apply.

5. Applied sense restraint: Gradual path supported by continuous determination imbued with a caring patience.

See:

1. *Attantapa Sutta*: Discourse on Self-Mortification (AN 4.198)

2. *Aparihani Sutta*: No Falling Away (AN 4.37)

3. *Samaññaphala Sutta*: The Fruits of the Contemplative Life (DN 2:64).

4. *Mahatanhasankhaya Sutta*: The Greater Craving-Destruction Discourse (MN 38).

Investigation: *See Dhamma-vicaya.*

Jhāna

1. A state of mental absorption.

2. A state of strong concentration focused on a single physical sensation or mental notion.

Kalyāṇamitta

1. In common English usage: spiritual friend.

2. Buddhist concept of spiritual friendship within community life, applicable to monastic and householder relationships. One involved in relationship is known as a "good friend," "virtuous friend," "noble friend," "admirable friend."

3. Admirable friendship.

4. Original meaning was someone who could give good instructions in the *Dhamma*.

5. A teacher or knower of the way.

Kamma [Skt: *Karma*]

1. Cause and effect.

2. Impersonal, natural law operating in accordance with our actions.

3. A law in of itself with no lawgiver. Operates in its own field without the intervention of an external, independent, ruling agent.

See: https://www.budsas.org/ebud/whatbudbeliev/87.htm

Kāmacchanda

1. English: sensual desire.

2. The first of the five hindrances. *See Nīvaraṇa.*

Karunā

English: compassion. *See Brahma-vihāras.*

Khama

1. English: forgiveness.

2. Forgiveness with an open heart.

3. Practice and training in forgiveness.

Khanika samādhi

1. English: momentary concentration.

2. Skill of being able to train the mind to be present to any object that arises and passes in and out of consciousness.

3. Necessary skill for realization of *nibbāna.*

Khanti

1. English: patience, forbearance, tolerance, acceptance, endurance.

2. One of the Ten Perfections [Pāli: *pāramīs*].

3. More than forbearance. State of mind that allows forgiveness and empathy to arise; state of equipoise in the face of either pleasant or unpleasant.

4. Mentioned immediately after energy in list of *pāramīs*. because patience is perfected by energy: "The energetic man, by arousing his energy, overcomes the suffering imposed by beings and formations." Acariya Dhammapala, *The Treatise on the Pāramīs.*

Kilesas

1. Most commonly in English: defilements.

2. Contemporary translators use a variety of English words including: afflictions, defilements, destructive emotions, disturbing emotions, negative emotions.

3. Mental states that cloud the mind and manifest in unwholesome actions.

4. Includes states of mind such as anxiety, fear, anger, jealousy, desire, depression, etc.

5. An *arahant* is free of all *kilesas*.

Kusala/Akusala

  Kusala:

  1. English: wholesome.
  2. That which is good, free from fault.
  3. Proper, convenient, skillful.
  4. Good action, benevolent deed, meritorious action.
  5. Any positive action by means of thought, speech and body; naturally begets some benefit to one performing it.
  6. Skillful means: In early Buddhist texts, skillfulness that enables one to abstain from committing actions that retard or obstruct spiritual development and to limit oneself to doing only actions that help to bring about spiritual development. Next and more important step is deliberate cultivation of positive qualities that are opposite to negative ones.
  7. Binding agent for all spiritual growth; meditative wisdom cannot be realized without being rooted in it.
  8. "And what is the wholesome? Abstention from the destruction of life is wholesome; abstention from taking what is not given is wholesome; abstention from sexual misconduct is wholesome; abstention from false speech is wholesome; abstention from divisive speech is wholesome; abstention from harsh speech is wholesome; abstention from idle chatter is wholesome. . . . [A]nd what is the root of the wholesome? Non-greed is a root of the wholesome; non-hatred is a root of the wholesome; non-delusion is a root of the wholesome." *Sammādiṭṭhi Sutta*: The Discourse on Right View (MN 9).

  Akusala:

  Unwholesome; opposite of *kusala*.

Mahābhūta

  Four primary elements:
  • Earth [Pāli: *pruṭhavī-dhātu*]
  • Fire [Pāli: *teja-dhātu*]
  • Water (or liquid) [Pāli: *āpa-dhātu*]

- Air (or wind) [Pāli: *vāyu-dhātu*]

Meditative wisdom

Intuitive insights into Three Characteristics, leading to freedom
from unwholesome patterns of mind, speech and action:

1. Impermanence [Pāli: *annica*]
2. Suffering or unsatisfactoriness [Pāli: *dukkha*]
3. Non-self [Pāli: *anattā*]

Mental development: *See Bhāvanā.*

Mental factors [Pāli: *cetasika*]

1. Identified in *Abhidhamma* (Buddhist psychology) as aspects of
   the mind that apprehend the quality of an object and that have
   the ability to color the mind.
2. Within the *Abhidhamma* categorized as formations concurrent
   with mind.
3. Alternate translations include mental states, mental events and
   concomitants of consciousness.

Merit: *See Puñña.*

Mettā

1. English: lovingkindness, kindliness, friendliness.
2. Benevolence, friendliness, amity, good will, active interest in others.
3. First of the four sublime states. *See Brahma-vihāras.*
   Note: Is the balance of all four.
4. One of ten *pāramīs* [perfections] of *Theravāda* school of
   Buddhism.
5. Object of concentration practice for the cultivation of *jhāna*.

Mindfulness: *See Vipassanā.*

Moral dread and fear of wrongdoing

1. Pāli: *Hiri* and *ottappa* respectively; English synonyms:
   Conscience and concern; moral shame and moral dread.
2. Twin emotions, known as the "guardians of the world,"
   associated with all skillful actions.
3. *Hiri*: an inner conscience that restrains us from doing deeds that
   would jeopardize our own self-respect. *Ottappa*: A healthy fear
   of committing unskillful deeds that might bring about harm to

ourselves or others.

4. Associated with all karmically wholesome consciousness.

5. "To be ashamed of what one ought to be ashamed of, to be ashamed of performing evil and unwholesome things: this is called moral shame. To be in dread of what one ought to be in dread of, to be in dread of performing evil and unwholesome things: this is called moral dread." Pug, 79, 80.

Morality: *See Sīla.*

Muditā

1. English: empathetic or sympathetic joy.

2. Third of the sublime abidings. *See Brahma-vihāras.*

Nekkhamma

1. English: renunciation.

2. First practice associated with Right Intention in Noble Eightfold Path.

3. Third in *Theravāda* list of ten perfections [Pāli: *pāramī*].

4. Involves non-attachment and limiting choices.

5. Everyday practice that can simplify a person's life by eliminating habitual reliance on habit and preference.

See Salayatana-vibhanga Sutta: An Analysis of the Six Sense-media (MN 137:10-15).

Nibbāna [Skt: *Nirvana*]

1. English: enlightenment.

2. Probably the subtlest and most difficult Pāli term to understand; inconceivable by definition or concept.

3. Reality bearing neither object nor consciousness; physical and mental phenomena no longer appear.

4. Being who experiences *nibbāna* becomes an *ariya* [enlightened one], no longer inclined to commit strongly negative actions such as killing or stealing, and will never take birth within lower worlds.

5. Can be experienced a large number of times and last from the fraction of a second up to many hours, according to the intensity of concentration being developed.

6. Four levels, as defined in *Theravāda* Buddhism:

    a. Stream enterer [Pāli: *sotāpanna*]

    b. Once returner [Pāli: *sakadāgāmi*]

    c. Non returner [Pāli: *anāgāmi*]

    d. Fully enlightened [Pāli: *arahant*]

7. *Parinibbāna*: Experience of an *arahant* at death, who will never more take birth in any realm.

Nīvaraṇa

1. English: hindrance.

2. Any unwholesome mental state that clouds the mind and hinders concentration.

3. Specifically, five qualities that are obstacles to the mind and blind mental vision:

    a. Sensual desire [Pāli: *kāmacchanda*]

    b. Ill will [Pāli: *vyāpāda*]

    c. Sloth and torpor [Pāli: *thīna-middha*]

    d. Restlessness and worry [Pāli: *uddhacca-kukkucca*]

    e. Subjective, skeptical doubt [Pāli: *vicikicchā*]

4. In common usage, mental states preventing the *yogi* from concentrating the mind on a continuous basis; because they are so common to the mind stream, they are especially rich objects to bring *sati-sampajañña* to.

5. One of five groups of *dhammas* referred to in the Fourth Foundation of Mindfulness.

See Nīvaraṇa Sutta: Hindrances (AN 9.64).

Noble Eightfold Path [Pāli: *Ariyo aṭṭhaṅgiko maggo*]

1. Early summary by the Buddha of the path of practices leading to liberation from *saṃsāra* [painful cycle of death and rebirth]; a principal teaching of *Theravāda* Buddhism leading to *arahantship*.

2. Fourth Noble Truth, consisting of eight practices:

    a. Right View [Pāli: *sammā-ditthi*]

    b. Right Intention or Resolve [Pāli; *sammā-sankappa*]

    c. Right Speech [Pāli: *sammā-vaca*]

    d. Right Action or Conduct [Pāli: *sammā-kammanta*]

    e. Right Livelihood [Pāli: *sammā-ājīva*]

    f. Right Effort [Pāli: *sammā-vāyāma*]

    g. Right Mindfulness [Pāli: *sammā-sati*]

    h. Right Concentration [Pāli: *sammā-samādhi*]

4. Also summarized as consisting of three categories:

    a. Sīla [morality]

    b. Samādhi [meditation]

    c. Paññā [wisdom]

5. Core teachings of Buddhist philosophy and 'how to' foundation for all Buddhist meditative practices.

Noble Silence

1. Refraining from speaking or participating in any type of communication unless absolutely necessary.

2. Protection from inner or outer distraction, and tool to support meditation.

3. In the Pāli Canon, internal state synonymous with *jhāna*.

Ottapa: See Moral dread and fear of wrongdoing.

Pāli

1. Middle Indo-Aryan language native to Indian subcontinent; widely studied because it is the language of the Pāli Canon [Pāli: *tipiṭaka*].

2. Sacred language of some religious texts of Hinduism and all texts of *Theravāda* Buddhism.

3. Pāli Canon: Traditional term for the Buddhist scriptures in English in *Theravāda* Buddhism; earliest archaeological evidence comes from Pyu city-states inscriptions found in Burma dated to mid 5th to mid 6th century CE.

Pañca Sīla

Five Precepts. *See Sīla.*

Paññā

1. English: wisdom.

2. Wholesome wisdom.

3. Discernment; intelligence; common sense; ingenuity;

understanding, knowledge.

4. Insight into the true nature of reality, primarily the *ti-lakkhaṇa* [Three Characteristics] of existence:

    a. *Anicca* [impermanence]

    b. *Dukkha* [dissatisfaction or suffering]

    c. *Anattā* [non-self]

5. One of ten perfections [Pāli: *pāramīs*] in *Theravāda* Buddhism.

6. First grouping of factors of Noble Eightfold Path, consisting of Right View and Right Intention.

7. Intuitive knowledge bringing about four stages of Enlightenment and realization of *Nibbānna*, consisting of penetration of *ti-lakkhaṇa*.

Papañca

1. English: proliferation.

2. Complication; objectification.

3. Mental proliferation: tendency of the mind to proliferate issues.

4. Conceptualization of the world through use of ever-expanding language and concepts.

Pāramī

1. English: perfection.

2. In *Theravāda* tradition, ten qualities leading to Buddhahood; spiritual trainings to develop ten qualities developed by the Buddha in lifetimes before his birth into the lifetime in which he achieved Buddhahood:

    a. Generosity, giving, liberality [Pāli: *dāna*]

    b. Virtue, ethical or moral conduct [Pāli: *sīla*]

    c. Renunciation [Pāli: *nekkhamma*]

    d. Wisdom [Pāli: *paññā*]

    e. Energy [Pāli: *viriya*]

    f. Patience, forbearance [Pāli: *khanti*]

    g. Truthfulness [Pāli: *sacca*]

    h. Resolve, resolution, determination [Pāli: *adhiṭṭhāna*]

    i. Kindness [Pāli: *mettā*]

   j. Equanimity [Pāli: *upekkhā*]

3. In *Mahayana* tradition, six qualities known as *pāramitās*:

   a. *Dāna*: generosity, giving of oneself.

   b. *Śīla*: virtue, morality, discipline, proper conduct.

   c. *Kṣānti*: patience, tolerance, forbearance, acceptance, endurance.

   d. *Vīrya*: energy, diligence, vigor, effort.

   e. *Dhyāna*: one-pointed concentration, contemplation.

   f. *Prajñā*: wisdom, insight.

See https://www.insightmeditationcenter.org/books-articles/articles/
theparamis/ (Insight Meditation Society).

Parinibbāna: *See Nibbāna*.

Path of Purification: *See Visuddhimagga*.

Patience: *See Khanti*.

Pātimokkha

1. Rules to which Buddhist monastics agree to adhere when they are ordained: 227 for monks [Pāli: *bhikkhus*]; 311 for nuns [Pāli: *bhikkhunīs*].

2. *Note*: Despite the Buddha's statement to his attendant Ananda while dying that monastics could discard the "minor rules," (*see Maha-Paranibbāna Sutta*: The Great Discourse on Total Unbinding (DN 16)), no rules were ever discarded because monastics at the First Buddhist Council after the Buddha's death thought it wiser to leave the *Pātimokkha* alone rather than risk schism resulting from debate of what was and what was not a minor rule.

Paying homage

1. Expressing respect for and appreciation of the Buddha.

2. Formally in English in *Theravāda* tradition: "I pay homage to the Blessed One, the Perfected One, the Fully Self-Enlightened One."

See Appendix 4: Table of Lists, Chants and Reflections.

Piṭaka

1. English, literally: basket.

2. One of three parts of the Pāli Canon.

See also:

1. *Abhidhamma Piṭaka*

2. *Sutta Piṭaka*

3. *Vinaya Piṭaka*

Preceptor

1. Spiritual teacher.

2. Specifically in context of Buddhist monastics: *Bhikkhu* or *bhikkhunī* with authority to confer full monastic ordination.

Puñña

1. English: merit.

2. Considered fundamental to Buddhist ethics; brings good and agreeable results, determines the quality of the next life and contributes to growth towards enlightenment.

3. Beneficial and protective force that accumulates as a result of good deeds, acts or thoughts.

4. Cultural overlay fundamental to the relationship between lay and monastic communities and the living and dead, especially in Southeast Asia.

5. *Puñña-dhārā* [sharing merit]: To offer merit earned by one's actions to another; to silently or out loud offer phrases such as, "I share whatever merit I have with all beings everywhere so they too, like myself, may attain happiness, peacefulness and complete freedom from suffering."

See

1. https://en.wikipedia.org/wiki/Merit_(Buddhism).

2. Thanissaro Bhikkhu, *Merit: A Study Guide*.

3. Access to Insight, *Muditā: The Buddha's Teaching on Unselfish Joy*.

Rebirth

Buddhist teaching that actions lead to rebirths into new existence after deaths in endless cycles called *saṃsāra*. *See Saṃsāra*.

Renunciation: *See Nekkhamma*.

Requisites: *See* Four requisites.

Restraint of the senses: *See Indriya-saṃvara*.

Right Action [Pāli: *sammā-kammanta*]

Fourth factor of the Noble Eightfold Path; second of the morality factors.

Right Concentration: *See Samādhi*.

Right Conduct: *See* Right Action.

Right Effort or Exertion: *See* Effort.

Right Intention [Pāli; *sammā-sankappa*]

Second factor of Noble Eightfold Path; second of wisdom factors.

Right Livelihood [Pāli: *sammā-ājīva*]

Fifth factor of Noble Eightfold Path; third of morality factors.

Right Mindfulness: *See* Mindfulness.

Right Resolve: *See* Right Intention.

Right Speech [Pāli: *sammā-vaca*]

Third factor of Noble Eightfold Path; first of morality factors.
See

1. *Maha-cattarisaka Sutta*: The Great Forty (MN 117:3).

2. *Ambalaṭṭhikārāhulovāda Sutta*: Advice to Rāhula at Ambalaṭṭhikā (MN 61:4).

3. *Samaññaphala Sutta*: The Fruits of the Contemplative Life (DN 2:5).

4. *Magga-vibhanga Sutta*: An Analysis of the Path (SN 45.8).

5. *Vaca Sutta*: A Statement (AN 5.198)

6. *Cunda Kammaraputta Sutta*: To Cunda the Silversmith (AN 10.176).

Right View [Pāli: *sammā-ditthi*]

First factor of Noble Eightfold Path; first of wisdom factors.

Saddhā: See Faith.

Sakadāgāmi

Once returner. *See Nibbāna*.

Samādhi

1. English: concentration.

2. Calm, serenity.

3. Clarity of mind caused by sharp concentration that is the

fruit of sustained training.

4. Practice of centering the mind in a single sensation or preoccupation, usually to the point of *jhāna*. See also *Khanika samādhi*; *Jhāna*.

5. Mental state of being firmly fixed; fixing of the mind on a single object.

6. *Sammā-samādhi*: Right Concentration. Eighth factor of Noble Eightfold Path and third factor of concentration factors.

See also Samatha.

Samatha

1. English: tranquillity.

2. Concentration, serenity; synonym of *samādhi*.

3. One pointedness of mind and non-distractedness.

4. Quality of mind developed in tandem with *vipassanā* by calming the mind and its 'formations' or 'fabrications' by practicing single-pointed meditation, most commonly through mindfulness of breathing, producing *khanika samādhi* [momentary concentration], or by itself leading to *jhāna* [absorption].

5. Concentration meditation; attending to a single object of meditation without interruption.

6. Common to many Buddhist traditions.

Samatha-vipassanā

1. Tranquility and insight, identical with concentration [Pāli: *samādhi*] and wisdom [Pāli: *paññā*].

2. Two branches of mental development [Pāli: *bhāvanā*].

Sammā-samādhi: See Samādhi.

Sampajañña

1. English: clear comprehension.

2. Contemplation of all physical and mental phenomena in order to know them both impersonally and with the intention to incline

the mind towards wholesomeness.

3. While the *suttas* do not elaborate on what the Buddha meant by *sampajañña*, Pāli commentaries analyze it in terms of four contexts for developing comprehension:

   a. Purpose [Pāli: *sātthaka*]: refraining from activities irrelevant to the Path.

   b. Suitability [Pāli: *sappāya*]: pursuing activities in a dignified and careful manner.

   c. Domain [Pāli: *gocara*]: maintaining sensory restraint consistent with mindfulness.

   d. Non-delusion [Pāli: *asammoha*]: seeing the true nature of reality, three characteristics of existence (*see Ti-lakkhaṇa*).

See *Satipaṭṭhāna Sutta*: The Four Foundations of Mindfulness (MN10:3).

Saṃsāra

1. Painful cycle of rebirth and death; beginningless cycle of repeated birth, mundane existence and death.

2. Considered to be *dukkha* [unsatisfactory and painful] perpetuated by desire and *avijjā* [ignorance] and resulting *kamma* [cause and effect].

Saṃvega

1. English: spiritual urgency.

2. Sense of shock, anxiety and spiritual urgency to reach liberation and escape the suffering of *saṃsāra*.

Saṅgha

1. Monastic community of Buddhism, who follow canonical texts called the *Vinaya Piṭaka*.

2. Commonly used to mean anyone who identifies with and practices Buddhist meditation.

3. *Ariya saṅgha*: Community of enlightened ones.

Sāsana

1. Dispensation. A range of English translations: teaching, practice, doctrine.

2. Buddha *sāsana*: The teaching of the Buddha; used by Buddhists

to refer to their religion.

3. May refer to dispensation of a particular buddha; we are living in the *sāsana* of the Sakyamuni Buddha.

Sati

1. English: mindfulness; attention; remembering. Often used interchangeably with *"vipassanā"* and "insight meditation."

2. One of Five Spiritual Faculties, Five Spiritual Powers; first of Seven Factors of Enlightenment.

3. Seventh factor of Noble Eightfold Path.

4. In its widest sense, a mental factor inseparably associated with all karmically wholesome and karma-produced lofty consciousness.

5. For present purposes, it is helpful to translate *vipassanā* to mean *sati-sampajañña*, and to keep in mind that *sati* and *sampajañña* have different and distinct meanings.

Satipaṭṭhāna: See Four Foundations of Mindfulness.

Sati-sampajañña

1. English: mindfulness and clear comprehension, respectively.

2. Two Pāli terms combined to mean one thing:

a. *Sati* is the function of the mind that can bring meditative focus on any conscious object and get to know it without self-referencing or preference. Without *sampajañña*, *sati* is simply a function of the mind without understanding.

b. *Sampajañña* is the wholesome attempt to understand what an object or action is, what it can do, and what to do in order to incline the mind towards wholesomeness. *Sampajañña* without *sati* is speculation.

3. When combined into *sati-sampajañña*, they become mental functions that can decondition and reorient the mind towards freedom from unwholesome patterns of mind, speech and action.

See

1. *Satipaṭṭhāna Sutta*: The Four Foundations of Mindfulness (MN 10:3).

2. Nyanaponika Thera, *The Heart of Buddhist Meditation*.

Seven Factors of Awakening: *See Bojjhaṅgā.*
Sīla
   1. English: morality or right conduct.
   2. Virtue, conduct, good behavior, attitude.
   3. Mode of mind and volition manifested in speech or bodily actions [Pāli: *kamma*].
   4. One foundation of entire Buddhist practice.
   5. Second of three divisions of Noble Eightfold Path, consisting of Right Speech, Right Action, and Right Livelihood. *See Sīlakhandha.*
   6. Without training in *sīla*, progress on Path in lasting or meaningful ways is impossible.
   7. *Pañca sīla* [Five Precepts]: Five rules of training that are the most important system of morality for Buddhist laity and constitute basic code of ethics undertaken by lay followers of Buddhism:
      1) Abstaining from killing living beings.
      2) Abstaining from stealing.
      3) Abstaining from sexual misconduct.
      4) Abstaining from lying.
      5) Abstaining from the use of intoxicants.
   8. *Aṭṭha sīla* [Eight Precepts]: Eight rules of training generally observed by lay devotees on observance days and festivals, consisting of the Five Precepts with a change to the third: abstaining from *all* sexual conduct, and:
      6) Abstaining from eating at inappropriate times.
      7) Abstaining from the use of cosmetics and adornments, dancing or other entertainment.
      8) Abstaining from overly comfortable seating and sleeping accommodations.
   See Five and Eight Precepts in Appendix 4: Table of Lists, Chants and Reflections.
Sīlakhandha

Three factors of Noble Eightfold Path constituting division of moral discipline:

1. Right Speech [Pāli: *sammā-vaca*]
2. Right Action [Pāli: *sammā-kammanta*]
3. Right Livelihood [Pāli: *sammā-ājīva*]

Skillful Means: *See Upāya.*

Sotāpanna

Stream enterer. *See Nibbāna.*

Spiritual Faculties: *See Indriya-samatta.*

Spiritual Friend: *See Kalyāṇamitta.*

Spiritual Urgency: *See Saṃvega.*

Story

In the context of this practice, any thought or emotion in which the mind gets consumed in the content and forgets or is unable to see the process as just thinking or having an emotion.

Striving: *See* Effort.

Sublime Abidings: *See Brahma-vihāras.*

Sutta

English: discourse.

See Sutta Piṭaka.

Sutta Piṭaka

1. English, literally: Basket of Discourses.
2. First of the three *pitakas* [baskets] constituting the Pāli Canon, the scriptures of *Theravāda* Buddhism. The other two are the *Vinaya Piṭaka* and the *Abhidhamma Piṭaka.*
3. Collection of the discourses given by the Buddha and senior disciples to the monastic community and lay people and poetry and sayings of the Buddha, consisting of the following *nikāyas* [volumes]:
   a. *Digha Nikāya* [Long Discourses]
   b. *Majjhima Nikāya* [Middle Length Discourses]
   c. *Samyutta Nikāya* [Collected Discourses]

    d. *Anguttara Nikāya* [Numbered Discourses]

    e. *Khuddaka Nikāya* [Minor Collection]

Taking the Precepts

    Commitment to undertaking moral trainings underpinning the practice.

    See Sīla; *see also* Appendix 4: Table of Lists, Chants and Reflections.

Taking Refuge

    1. Expressing commitment to and refuge in the Three Jewels: Buddha, *Dhamma* and *Saṅgha*.

    2. In English in the *Theravāda* tradition: "I take refuge in the Buddha. I take refuge in the *Dhamma*. I take refuge in the *Saṅgha*."

Ten thousand cuts

    1. Chinese: *Lingchi*: "The slow process," "the lingering death," "slow slicing," "death by a thousand cuts": Form of torture and execution used in China from roughly 900 CE until banned in 1905.

    2. "Death by a thousand cuts": In psychology, the way a major negative change that happens slowly in many unnoticed increments is not perceived as objectionable. A process by which a major change can be accepted as normal and acceptable if it happens slowly through small, often unnoticeable, increments of change.

The Path of Purification: *See Visuddhimagga*.

Theravāda

    1. English: School of the Elders.

    2. Oldest extant form of Buddhist practice.

    3. Most commonly found in Myanmar, Thailand, Sri Lanka, Cambodia, and Laos.

    4. Western *vipassanā* finds most of its roots in this school.

Thīna-middha

    1. English: sloth and torpor.

2. Third of the five hindrances. *See Nīvaraṇa.*

Three Characteristics: *See Ti-lakkhaṇa.*

Ti-lakkhaṇa

1. Three marks, characteristics, or signata of all existence:

   a. Impermanence [Pāli: *anicca*]

   b. Unsatisfactoriness or suffering [Pāli: *dukkha*]

   c. Non-self [Pāli: *anattā*]

2. Central themes in Buddhist Four Noble Truths and Noble Eightfold Path that humans are subject to delusion about them, resulting in suffering or dissatisfaction; removal of delusion results in the end of suffering or dissatisfaction.

See Maggavagga: The Path (Dhp XX, 277, 278, 279).

Tipiṭaka

1. Traditional term for Buddhist scriptures.

2. Version canonical to *Theravāda* Buddhism is generally referred to in English as the Pāli Canon. *See* Pāli Canon.

3. *Tripiṭaka*: In *Mahayana* Buddhism, is authoritative and includes various derivative literature and commentaries composed much later.

Uddhacca-kukkucca

1. English: restlessness and worry.

2. Fourth of the five hindrances. *See Nīvaraṇa.*

Upāya

1. English: skillful means.

2. Skills necessary to think, speak and act with wholesomeness.

3. Way, means, expedient, stratagem.

Upekkhā

1. English: equanimity.

2. Third of the *Brahma-vihāras*. *See Brahma-vihāras.*

3. Last of the *pāramī* [Ten Perfections]. *See Pāramī.*

Vedanā

1. English: feeling tone; sensation. Not to be confused with emotions.

2. Refers to pleasant, unpleasant and neutral sensations that occur

when our internal sense organs come into contact with external sense objects and the associated consciousness.

Vedic religion

1. Ancient religion of Aryan peoples who entered northwestern India from Persia c. 2000–1200 BCE.

2. Precursor of Hinduism; beliefs and practices are contained in the *Vedas*.

3. Predominant religion of India at the time of the Buddha.

Verified faith: *See* Faith.

Vicikicchā

1. English: doubt.

2. Fifth of the five hindrances [Pāli: *nīvaraṇa*].

3. State of mind like a cancer that has a canker, easily seen with thoughts like, "I can't do this." "This practice is wrong." "This isn't the right time."

4. Mostly the enticing thinking and concomitant sensation that leads the mind and heart from the object and task at hand.

Vinaya

1. English, literally: leading out; education; discipline.

2. Code of conduct.

3. Livelihood.

See also Vinaya Piṭaka.

Vinaya Piṭaka

1. English, literally: Basket of the Discipline.

2. Second 'basket' of the Pāli Canon, containing rules (*see Pātimokkha*) and conventions, as well as origin stories for the rules and discourses and commentary.

3. Canonical texts setting forth the regulatory framework for the *sangha* or monastic community of Buddhism.

Vipassanā

1. English: insight.

2. Insight into the true nature of reality defined as three characteristics of all conditioned or fabricated phenomena (*see Ti-lakkhaṇa*).

3. Seeing things as they really are.

4. Attending to objects of consciousness with bare attention.

5. Often used interchangeably with "*sati*" and "insight" to describe the meditation practice of bringing unfiltered attention to experience at any of the six sense doors.

6. One of India's most ancient techniques of meditation rediscovered by Gotama Buddha more than 2500 years ago and taught by him as a universal remedy for universal ills.

7. Non-sectarian technique aiming for the total eradication of mental impurities and resulting highest happiness of full liberation.

See https://www.dhamma.org/en/about/vipassana.

Virtue: *See Sīla*.

Visuddhimagga [The Path of Purification]

1. "Great treatise" on *Theravāda* Buddhist doctrine, compiled by Buddhaghosa in approximately the 5th century CE in Sri Lanka.

2. Manual that condenses and systematizes 5th century understanding and interpretation of the Buddhist Path as maintained by the elders of the Mahavihara Monastery in Anuradhapura, Sri Lanka.

3. Considered most important *Theravāda* text outside of the *tipiṭaka*, the canon of scriptures.

Vitakka-vicāra

1. Interpreted by *Theravāda* Buddhist commentarial tradition as initial and sustained application of attention to a meditational object, culminating in the stilling of the mind.

2. In the Pāli Canon, can refer to the normal process of discursive thought suppressed by concentration in the second *jhāna*.

3. First two mental factors of concentration.

Vyāpāda

1. English: ill will.

2. Second of the five hindrances. *See Nīvaraṇa*.

Wholesome/Unwholesome: *See Kusala.*

Wisdom: *See Pañña.*

Yoga, Seva, Samādhi

  Hindi. In this context:

  1. *Yoga*: Practice

  2. *Seva*: Service or work

  3. *Samādhi*: Meditation

Yogi

  1. *Theravāda* school: One who trains in the development of
     concentration or *satipaṭṭhāna* meditation.

  2. Synonym for meditator.

  3. Householding *yogi*: One who is not a monastic, lives a lay life
     and seeks to train the mind towards enlightenment.

Yogi mind

  A contemporary term for a specific mental state arising
  during retreat, in which the mind can manifest any of
  the following:

  • Obsession

  • Mood swings

  • Refusal to cooperate

  • Frequent arising of the hindrances

  • Being under a cloud of intense confusion.

  • Acting on and believing the mind stream.

Table of Quotations and Aphorisms

From Acknowledgments

The greatest gift is the act of giving itself. Traditionally, three kinds of giving are spoken of. There is beggarly giving, which is when we give with only one hand, still holding onto what we give. In this kind of giving we give the least of what we have and afterward wonder whether we should have given at all.

Another kind of giving is called "friendly" giving, in which we give open handedly. We take what we have and share it, because it seems appropriate. It's a clear giving.

Then there's the type of giving that's called "kingly" giving. That's when we give the best of what we have, even if none remains for ourself. We give the best we have instinctively with graciousness. We think of ourselves only as temporary caretakers of whatever has been provided, as owning nothing. There is no giving; there is just the spaciousness which allows objects to remain in the flow.

– Levine, *A Gradual Awakening*

Meditate, bhikkhus [meditators], do not delay or else you will regret it later. This is our instruction to you.

– *Dvedhavitakka Sutta*: Two Sorts of Thinking (MN 19:27)

From A Householder's *Vinaya*

Rouse yourself! Sit up!
Resolutely train yourself to attain peace.
Do not let the king of death, seeing you are careless,
lead you astray and dominate you.

– *Utthana Sutta*: On Vigilance (Sn 2.10)

No other thing do I know, O monks [meditators], that brings so much harm as a mind that is untamed, unguarded, unprotected and uncontrolled. Such a mind, indeed, brings much harm.

No other thing do I know, O monks [meditators], that brings so much benefit as a mind that is tamed, guarded, protected and controlled. Such a mind indeed, brings great benefit.

– *Ekadhamma Suttas*: A Single Thing (AN 1.21-40)

(selected excerpts)

Giving is good, dear sir!
Even when one has little, giving is good.
An offering given from what little one has
is worth a thousand times its value.

– *Saddhu Sutta*: Good (SN 1:33)

Do no evil. Engage in what is skillful and purify your mind. This is the teaching of the Buddhas.

– *Buddhavagga*: The Buddha (Dhp XIV, 183)

Mind precedes all mental states. Mind is their chief; they are all mind-wrought. If with an impure mind a person speaks or acts, suffering follows him like the wheel that follows the foot of the ox.

Mind precedes all mental states. Mind is their chief; they are all mind-wrought. If with a pure mind a person speaks or acts, happiness follows him like his never-departing shadow.

– *Yamakavagga*: Pairs (Dhp I 1-2)

There ain't no free lunch.

– Anonymous

If it's easy, it's cheap.

– U Pandita

Meditation doesn't guarantee enlightenment, it just increases
its probability.

– Anonymous

Enlightenment is always an accident. Meditation just makes those
who practice accident prone.

– Anonymous

When, bhikkhus [meditators], a carpenter or a carpenter's
apprentice sees the impressions of his fingers and his thumb on the
handle of his adze, he does not know: 'I have worn away so much
of the adze handle today, so much yesterday, so much earlier'; but
when it has worn away, he knows that it has worn away. So too,
when a bhikkhu [meditator] is intent on development, even though
he does not know: 'I have worn away so much of the taints today,
so much yesterday, so much earlier,' yet when they are worn away,
he knows that they are worn away.
   – *Bhāvanānuyutta:* Committed to Development (AN 7.71)

If, on the other hand, one habitually yields to all whims, or allows
oneself too easily to be deflected from one's purpose, then such
qualities as energy, endurance, concentration, loyalty, etc., will
gradually be undermined and weakened to such an extent that they
become insufficient for achieving that original purpose, or even for
truly appreciating it any longer. In that way, it often happens that,
unheeded by the person concerned, his ideals, religious convictions,
and even his ordinary purposes and ambitions, are turned into
empty shells which he still carries along with him, solely through
habit.
– Nyaniponika Thera, *The Heart of Buddhist Meditation*, p. 48.

Vinaya is thus, in its essence, the Buddhist lifestyle [meditation
coupled with sīla]: the way serious Buddhist practitioners arrange,
organize, and structure their lives in order to support Dhamma

*study, practice, realization, and service. This covers all physical
and verbal actions. It involves all forms of relationships:
interpersonal, social, economic, political, ecological, as well as
with one's own body.*

– Badiner & Hill, p. 303

*It is very important to keep trying to maintain the intention to
remain aware all the time, whether awareness is actually
continuous or not. This points to the essential quality of Right
Effort: persistence. It's not a forceful effort but rather an inner
determination to sustain the tiny bit of energy you need in each
moment to know you are aware and to keep that going.*

– U Tejaniya

*Continuous effort—not strength or intelligence—is the key to
unlocking our potential.*

– Winston S. Churchill

*Milarepa and his student came to a bridge. . . . When the student
had crossed the bridge, Milarepa called him back. "Come back
once more, I have a very special teaching to give you. If I do not
give you this advice, to whom shall I give it?". . .*

*He cautioned him not to waste the advice, but to put it in the
deepest recesses of his heart. Then Milarepa turned his back on the
student, lifted up his robe, and showed him his bare bottom. The
student saw that Milarepa's bottom was all calloused, just
like hardened leather.*

*Milarepa said, "For practice there is nothing greater than
meditation — provided you know what to meditate on and how to
meditate on it. I, who have gained knowledge and understanding
of many different meditation methods, meditated until my bottom
became as hard as leather. You need to do the same. This is your
last teaching."*

– Geshe Ngawang Dhargyey

*When we meditate at home and in daily life, the challenges and
benefits of practice become much more real than when we are on a
meditation retreat. It takes a real practice to deal with real situations and real unwholesome reactions.*

– U Tejaniya

*After reflecting again and again, actions by deed, word and
thought should be done. ... Before doing such actions by deed,
word and thought, while doing and after doing them, one should
reflect thus: "Does this action lead to the harm [or benefit] of
myself, to the harm [or benefit] of others, to the harm [or benefit]
of both?" After reflecting again and again one should purify one's
actions by deed word and thought. Thus, O Rāhula, should you
train yourself.*

– *Ambalaṭṭhikārāhulovāda Sutta*:
Advice to Rāhula at Ambalaṭṭhikā (MN 61)

*I should add the Ven. Nyanaponika himself did not regard
"bare attention" (sati) as capturing the complete significance of
satipaṭṭhāna, but as representing only one phase, the initial phase,
in the meditative development of Right Mindfulness. He held that
in the proper practice of Right Mindfulness, sati has to be
integrated with sampajañña, clear comprehension, and it is only
when these two work together that Right Mindfulness can fulfill
its intended purpose.*

– Correspondence between Alan Wallace and the
Venerable Bhikkhu Bodhi, Winter 2006.

*It is the daily little negligence in thoughts, words, and deeds
going on for many years of our lives . . . that is chiefly responsible
for the untidiness and confusion we have in our minds. This
negligence creates the trouble and allows it to continue. Thus the
old Buddhist teachers have said: "Negligence produces a lot of*

*dirt. As in a house, so in the mind, only a very little dirt collects in
a day or two, but if it goes on for many years, it will grow into a
vast heap of refuse."*

– Nyanaponika Thera, *The Power of Mindfulness*, p. 106

*When I was a boy of fourteen, my father was so ignorant I could
hardly stand to have the old man around. But when I got to be
twenty-one, I was astonished at how much he had learned in
seven years.*

– Attributed to Mark Twain

*Just as the ocean has a gradual shelf, a gradual slope, a gradual
inclination, with a sudden drop off only after a long stretch, in the
same way this Doctrine and Discipline has a gradual training, a
gradual performance, a gradual progression, with the penetration
to nibbāna only after a long stretch.*

– *Uposatha Sutta*: Uposatha (Ud 5.5)

*In Buddhism, patience [Pāli: khanti] is one of the "perfections"
[Pāli: pāramīs] that a bodhisatta [Skt: bodhisattva] trains in and
practices to realize perfect enlightenment. The Buddhist concept
of patience is distinct from the English definition of the word. In
Buddhism, patience refers to not returning harm, rather than
merely enduring a difficult situation. It is the ability to control
one's emotions even when being criticized or attacked. In verse
184 of the Dhammapada it is said that 'enduring patience is the
highest austerity.'*

- Acharya Buddharakkhita

*Let's say another person is talking and you have heard it all before.
If you remain interested in your reactions and not interested in
what the other person is saying—their stories and complaints—
then you will have something interesting to do while the person*

*drones on. No matter what the situation, in this way you'll always
learn a lot as you listen.*

– U Tejaniya

*Rūpa is not matter as in the metaphysical substance of materialism.
Instead it means both materiality and sensibility—signifying, for
example, a tactile object both insofar as that object is made of
matter and that the object can be tactically sensed [that which can
be cognized through the 5 material sense doors; seeing, hearing,
smelling, tasting, and physical sensations]. In fact rūpa is more
essentially defined by its amenability to being sensed than its being
matter: just like everything else it is defined in terms of its function;
what it does [in the mind], not what it is. As matter, rūpa is traditionally analysed in two ways: as four primary elements [Pāli:
mahābhūta: Earth, Wind, Water, Fire]; and, as ten or twenty-four
secondary or derived elements.*

– Lusthaus, p. 183.

*The Dhamma I [the Buddha] have attained is profound, hard to s
ee and hard to understand, peaceful and sublime, unattainable
by mere reasoning, subtle, to be experienced by the wise. But this
generation delights in attachment, takes delight in attachment,
rejoices in attachment. It is hard for such a generation to see this
truth, namely specific conditionality, dependent origination.*

*And it is hard to see this truth, namely, the stilling of all
formations, the relinquishing of all acquisitions, the destruction
of craving, dispassion, Nibbāna. If I were to teach the Dhamma,
others would not understand me.*

– *Ariyapariyesana Sutta*: The Noble Search (MN 26:19)

*We live in illusion and the appearance of things. There is a reality.
We are that reality. When you understand this, you see that you are
nothing, and being nothing, you are everything. That is all.*

– Kalu Rinpoche

No self, no problem.

> – Anonymous

And what is right speech? Abstaining from lying, from divisive speech, from abusive speech, and from idle chatter: This is called right speech.

> – *Magga-vibhanga Sutta*: An Analysis of the Path (SN 45.8)

Speak only the speech that neither torments self nor does harm to others. That speech is truly well spoken.

> *Subhasita Sutta*: Well-Spoken (Sn 3.3)

Monks, a statement endowed with five factors is well-spoken, not ill-spoken. It is blameless and unfaulted by knowledgeable people. Which five?

> *It is spoken at the right time. It is spoken in truth. It is spoken affectionately.*

> *It is spoken beneficially. It is spoken with a mind of goodwill.*

> – *Vaca Sutta*: A Statement (AN 5.198)

There is no companionship with a fool;
> *It is better to go alone.*
Travel alone, at ease, doing no evil
> *Like the elephant Matanga in the forest.*

> – *Nagavagga*: Elephants (Dhp XXIII 330)

"No, Ananda," the Buddha told him, "having good friends isn't half of the Holy Life. Having good friends is the whole of the Holy Life."

> – *Upaddha Sutta*: Half (of the Holy Life) (SN 45.2)

Think of your home as a retreat center. Begin by altering the way you see your home. When you begin to view your home in the same way that you view a meditation center, your practice will become

*smoother. Keep checking your attitudes and views, your thinking
and your background ideas.*

– U Tejaniya

*[W]hen walking, a bhikkhu [meditator] understands: "I am
walking;" when standing, he understands; "I am standing;"
when sitting, he understands: "I am sitting;" when lying down, he
understands; "I am lying down;" or he understands accordingly
however his body is disposed.*

*[A] bhikkhu [meditator] is one who acts in full awareness
when going forward and returning; who acts in full awareness
when looking ahead and looking away; who acts in full
awareness when flexing and extending his limbs; . . . [who acts
in full awareness dressing and wearing clothes]; . . . who acts acts
in full awareness when eating, drinking, consuming food, and
tasting; who acts in full awareness when defecating and urinating;
who acts in full awareness when walking, standing, sitting, falling
asleep, waking up, talking, and keeping silent . . . .not clinging to
anything in this world. That is how a bhikkhu [meditator] abides
contemplating body in body.*

– *Satipaṭṭhāna Sutta*:
The Four Foundations of Mindfulness (MN 10:3, 8-9)

*The Great Way is not difficult, for those who have no preferences.
Let go of longing and aversion, and it reveals itself.
Make the smallest distinction, however, and you are as far from it
as heaven is from earth.
If you want to realize the truth, then hold no opinions for or
against anything.
Like and dislike is the disease of the mind.
When the deep meaning [of the Way] is not understood the
intrinsic peace of mind is disturbed.*

As vast as infinite space, it is perfect and lacks nothing.
Indeed, it is due to your grasping and repelling that you do not see
things as they are.

– Third Zen Patriarch

If by renouncing a lesser happiness one may realize a greater
happiness, let the wise man renounce the lesser, having regard for
the greater.

– *Pakinnakavagga*: Miscellaneous (Dhp XXI 290)

Believe in Allah, but always tie your camel to a fencepost.

– Sunan al-Tirmidhī 2517

Pleasant practice is not always good practice.

– Allan Cooper

With regard to external factors, I don't envision any other single
factor like admirable friendship as doing so much for a monk in
training, who has not attained the heart's goal but remains intent
on the unsurpassed safety from bondage. A monk who is a friend
with admirable people abandons what is unskillful and develops
what is skillful.

– Iti. 1.17

I have not failed. I've just found 10,000 ways that won't work.

- Thomas Edison

Buddhism is simple but doing it doesn't make me a simpleton.

– Munindraji

Buddhist practice is simple but not easy.

–U Pandita

If . . . one habitually yields to all whims, or allows oneself too easily to be deflected from one's purpose, then such qualities as energy, endurance, concentration, loyalty, etc., will gradually be undermined and weakened to such an extent that they become insufficient for achieving that original purpose, or even for truly appreciating it any longer. In that way, it often happens that, unheeded by the person concerned, his/her ideals, religious convictions, and even his/her ordinary purpose and ambitions, are turned into empty shells which he/she still carries along with him/her, solely through habit.

> – Nyanaponika Thera, *The Heart of Buddhist Meditation*,
> pp. 52-53.

Additional Quotes From The *Sangha* Nonresidential Retreat Guide

Clear comprehension is most famously [and frequently] invoked by the Buddha in tandem with mindfulness practice in the Satipaṭṭhāna Sutta: . . . [H]e lives contemplating mental objects in mental objects, ardent, clearly comprehending and mindful, having overcome, in this world, covetousness and grief.

> – Wikipedia

A mind devoid of clear comprehension [sampajañña] is like a pot with holes; it cannot retain in memory what has been learned, thought over or meditated.

> – Santideva, quoted in Nyanaponika Thera,
> *The Heart of Buddhist Meditation*

Other Favorite Quotes

Buddhist teachings are not a religion, they are a science of the mind.
— His Holiness the Dalai Lama

In Buddhism, the essential meaning of the word "study" is the unceasing, dedicated observation and investigation of whatever arises in the mind, be it pleasant or unpleasant. Only those familiar with the observation of mind can really understand Dhamma.
— Buddhadasa Bhikkhu, *Heartwood of the Bodhi Tree*

The Buddha compares his teaching to the rainfall that descends without discrimination on the earth. That this rain causes some seeds to grow into flowers and some into great trees implies no differentiation in the rain, but rather is due to the capacities of the seeds that it nurtures. Thus, the teaching of the Buddha is of a single flavor, but benefits beings in a variety of ways according to their capacity.
— Donald S. Lopez, Jr., *Buddhism in Practice.*

These four things, O monks, are conducive to the growth of wisdom.
What four?
Association with superior persons, hearing the good Dhamma, proper attention and practice in accordance with the Dhamma. These four things are conducive to the growth of wisdom. These four things are also a great help to a human being.
— *Seyyāsutta*: Lying Postures (AN 4.246)

The speed and distance that you travel on the path is determined by the level of your courage to go in the opposite direction from what you have been doing since beginningless time.
— Chamtrul Rinpoche

Weblinks to the teachers quoted or mentioned in
A Householder's Vinaya

JOSEPH GOLDSTEIN:
https://en.wikipedia.org/wiki/Joseph_Goldstein_(writer)

MAHASI SAYADAW:
https://en.wikipedia.org/wiki/Mahasi_Sayadaw

SAYADAW U PANDITA:
https://en.wikipedia.org/wiki/U_Pandita Nyanaponika

NYANAPONIKA THERA:
https://en.wikipedia.org/wiki/Nyanaponika_Thera

BHIKKHU BODHI:
https://en.wikipedia.org/wiki/Bhikkhu_Bodhi

MUNINDRAJI:
https://en.wikipedia.org/wiki/Anagarika_Munindra

U VIVEKANANDA:
http://www.panditarama-lumbini.info/teaching.html

Table of Abbreviations

AN: *Aṅguttara Nikāya*
Dhp: *Dhammapada*
DN: *Digha Nikāya*
Iti: *Itivuttaka*
KN: *Khuddaka Nikāya*
MN: *Majjhima Nikāya*
Pug: *Puggala-paññatti*
Skt: Sanskrit
SN: *Saṃyutta Nikāya*
Sn: *Sutta Nipāta*
Ud: Udana

Table of Lists, Chants, and Reflections

Lists

FOUR NOBLE TRUTHS AND NOBLE EIGHTFOLD PATH:

Note: This is not a literal translation. *See* Appendix 1, Glossary.

1. All life knows suffering. Nobody gets what they want out of life.
2. The cause of suffering is ignorance and clinging. Wanting is the problem.
3. There is a way to end suffering. By learning not to want it.
4. This is the way to end suffering: The Eightfold Path.
   a. Right Understanding: Learning the nature of reality and the truth about life.
   b. Right Aspiration: Making the commitment to living in such a way that our suffering can end.
   c. Right Effort: Just Do It. No Excuses.
   d. Right Speech: Speaking the truth in a helpful and compassionate way.
   e. Right Conduct: Living a life consistent with what are wholesome values.
   f. Right Livelihood: Earning a living in a way that doesn't harm self or others.

g. Right Mindfulness: Recognizing the value of the moment; living where we are.

h. Right Concentration: Expanding our consciousness through meditation.

– Dan Bammes

FOUR FOUNDATIONS OF MINDFULNESS

1. Body
2. Feelings
3. Mind
4. *Dhammas*
   a. Five Hindrances
   b. Six Sense Bases
   c. Five Aggregates
   d. Seven Factors of Enlightenment
   e. Four Noble Truths and the Eightfold Noble Path

FIVE HINDRANCES

1. Sensual desire
2. Aversion
3. Sloth and torpor
4. Restlessness and worry
5. Skeptical doubt

SIX SENSE DOORS

1. Eye – seeing
2. Ear – hearing
3. Nose – smelling
4. Tongue – tasting
5. Body – sensing
6. Mind – thinking

FIVE AGGREGATES

1. Materiality
2. Feelings
3. Perceptions
4. Mental formations
5. Consciousness

SEVEN FACTORS OF ENLIGHTENMENT

1. Mindfulness
2. Investigation
3. Energy
4. Rapture/Joy
5. Tranquility
6. Concentration
7. Equanimity

FOUR KINDS OF CLEAR COMPREHENSION

1. Clear Comprehension of Purpose
2. Clear Comprehension of Suitability
3. Clear Comprehension of Domain of Meditation
4. Clear Comprehension of Reality

– Nyanaponika Thera,
The Heart of Buddhist Meditation, pp. 45-56

FIVE CONTROLLING FACULTIES

1. Faith
2. Energy or Effort
3. Mindfulness
4. Concentration
5. Wisdom

TEN PĀRAMĪS

1. Generosity
2. Morality
3. Renunciation
4. Wisdom
5. Energy
6. Patience
7. Truthfulness
8. Resolution
9. Loving-kindness
10. Equanimity

ACTIVITIES OF DAILY LIFE

- Eating
- Sleeping
- Maintaining health
- Socializing; maintaining family relationships
- Working
- Sheltering
- Making a livelihood
- Maintenance
- Being creative
- Having sex
- Exercising
- Having a spiritual practice
  ~ Formal
  ~ Engaged
- Engaging in entertainment
  ~ Daily
  ~ Special
- Studying
  ~ Thinking; daydreaming; planning

Chants:

PAYING HOMAGE TO THE BUDDHA, THE DHAMMA AND THE *SAṄGHA*

Namō tassa bhagavatō arahatō sammā-sambuddhassa (3x)
Translation:
Homage to Him, the Blessed One, the Perfected One, the Fully
Self-Enlightened One.

TAKING REFUGE

Ti-Sarana—The Three Refuges
Buddham saranam gacchāmi.
Dhammam saranam gacchāmi.
Saṅgham saranam gacchāmi.
Dutiyampi Buddham . . .
Tatiyampi Buddham . . .

Translation:
I go to the Buddha as my refuge.
I go to the *Dhamma*—The Teachings, as my refuge.
I go to the *Saṅgha*—The Community, as my refuge.
For the second time I go to the Buddha as my refuge . . .
For the third time I go to the Buddha as my Refuge . . .

TAKING THE FIVE *(PAÑCA-SILA)* OR EIGHT *(ATTHA-SILA)* PRECEPTS

1. *Pānātipātā veramṇī sikkhāpadam samādiyāmi.*
2. *Adinnādnā veramṇī sikkhāpadam samādiyāmi.*
3a. Celibate, monastic or *yogi* on retreat: *Abrahmacariyā veramṇī sikkhāpadaṁ samādiyāmi.*
3b. Householder: *Kāmesu micchācārā veramṇī sikkhāpadaṁ samādiyāmi.*
4. *Musāvādā veramṇī sikkhāpadam samādiyāmi.*

5. *Surā Mēraya majja pamādatthānā veramṇī sikkhāpadam samādiyāmi.*

6. *Vikāla bhojanā veramṇī sikkāpadaṁ samādiyāmi.*

7. *Nacca gīta vādita visūkadassana mālāgandha vilepana dhārana maṇḍana vibūsanaṭṭhānā veramaṇī samādiyāmi.*

8. *Uccāsayana mahāsayanā veramṇī sikkhāpadaṁ samādiyāmi.*

Translation:

1. I undertake the training to abstain from destroying [*or* harming] living beings.

2. I undertake the training to abstain from taking things not [*add:* freely] given.

3a. *Celibate, monastic or yogi on retreat*: I undertake the training to refrain from sexual intercourse [*or* all sexual activity].

3b. *Householder:* I undertake the training to abstain from sexual misconduct.

4. I undertake the training to abstain from false [*or* wrong] speech.

5. I undertake the training to abstain from liquor [*or* all mind-altering drugs or activities] causing intoxication and heedlessness.

6. I undertake the training to refrain from taking food at improper times [*or* after solar noon till dawn the next day].

7. I undertake the training to refrain from dancing, singing, music, shows; from the use of garlands, perfumes, cosmetics, adornments and ornaments.

8. I undertake the training to refrain from using high and luxurious seats [*add:* or beds].

FOOD/MEAL CHANT:

I take this food not to beautify the body nor for sensual pleasure but to enable me to practice the Buddha *sāsana*, so that existing disease may be cured and new disease not arise and so that I may be comfortable in the four bodily positions.

I vow to eat this food with appropriate mindfulness and gratitude.

Reflections

HOUSEHOLDER'S REFLECTION

I am of the nature to decay. I have not gotten beyond decay.
I am of the nature to be diseased. I have not gotten beyond disease.
I am of the nature to die. I have not gotten beyond death.
All that is mine, precious and pleasing, will change and vanish.
We are all the owners of our *kamma*, born of our *kamma*, related
through our *kamma*, abide supported by our *kamma* and live
dependent on our *kamma*. Whatever we do, for good or for evil,
to that we will fall heir.
  – *Upajjhatthana Sutta*: Subjects for Contemplation (AN 5.57)

SHARING MERIT:

I share whatever merit I have with all beings everywhere so they too,
like myself, may attain happiness, peacefulness and complete freedom
from suffering.

MEAL BLESSING

All living things are struggling for life. May we all have enough food to
eat today.

This food I intend to eat is from the whole universe—the earth, the
sky, and much hard work. May I live in a way that makes me worthy to
receive it. May I transform unskillful states of mind while I partake of
this food. May I take this food with the wholesome intention to prevent
illness and to remove feelings of hunger and provide sufficient strength
in order to liberate this mind from all greed/hatred and delusion.

Sweet, sour, salty, bitter, spicy, and bland.

Many hands.

A USEFUL FORGIVENESS TRAINING TOOL

To those whom I may have caused harm, knowingly or unknowingly, through my thoughts, word, and or actions, I ask your forgiveness.

To those who may have caused me harm, knowingly or unknowingly, through their thoughts, words and or actions, I offer my forgiveness as best I am able.

For any harm I may have caused myself, knowingly or unknowingly, through my thoughts, words, and or actions, I offer my forgiveness as best I am able.

May I be mindful of my thoughts, words, and actions so that I may not be the cause of further pain and suffering in this world.

May the merit of these efforts help to ease the pain and suffering in this world.

– P. Moffitt *et al.*

Bibliography and Suggested Reading and Listening List

Bibliography

-----, *Encyclopedia of Buddhism*, https://encyclopediaofbuddhism.org/wiki/Vinaya (last checked March 16, 2020).

-----, *Pāḷi English Glossary*, https://en.dhammadana.org/glossary.htm (last checked March 16, 2020).

Acariya Dhammapala, *A Treatise on the* Pāramīs: *From the Commentary to the Cariyapitaka*, translated from the *Pāḷi* by Bhikkhu Bodhi (Buddhist Publication Society 1998).

Access to Insight: *A Glossary of Pāḷi and Buddhist Terms*. https://www.accesstoinsight.org/glossary.html (last checked March 16, 2020).

Acharya Buddharakkhita. *Dhammapada, 184* (Buddhist Publication Society) https://www.accesstoinsight.org/tipitaka/kn/dhp/dhp.14.budd.html last checked March 16, 2020.

Badiner, Allan Hunt (Ed.), Hill, Julia Butterfly (Foreword), *Mindfulness in the Marketplace: Compassionate Responses to Consumerism* (Parallax Press, 2002).

Bhikkhu Bodhi, *The Noble Eightfold Path: The Way to the End of Suffering*, The Wheel Publication No. 308/311 (Buddhist Publication Society, 1984, 2d edition (revised) 1994); Pariyatti Publishing 2020). https://www.accesstoinsight.org/lib/authors/bodhi/waytoend.html; http://www.buddhanet.net/pdf_file/noble8path6.pdf (last checked March 16, 2020).

Bhikkhu Bodhi & Allan Wallace, *The Nature of Mindfulness and Its Role in Buddhist Meditation*, Correspondence between Alan Wallace and the Venerable Bhikkhu Bodhi, Winter 2006, p.4, http://shamatha.org/sites/default/files/Bhikkhu_Bodhi_Correspondence.pdf (last checked March 16, 2020).

Geshe Ngawang Dhargyey, *The Life of Gampopa*, https://studybuddhism.com/en/tibetan-buddhism/spiritual-teachers/gampopa/the-life-of-gampopa (last checked March 16, 2020).

Lusthaus, Dan, *Buddhist Phenomenology: A Philosophical Investigation of Yogācāra Buddhism and the Ch'eng Wei-shih Lun* (Routledge 2002).

Knaster, Mirka, *Living This Life Fully: Stories and Teachings of Munindra* (Shambhala 2010).

Levine, Steven, *A Gradual Awakening* (Anchor 1989).

Nyanaponika Thera, *The Four Sublime States: Contemplations on Love, Compassion, Sympathetic Joy and Equanimity* https://www.accesstoinsight.org/lib/authors/nyanaponika/wheel006.html (last checked March 16, 2020).

_____, *The Heart of Buddhist Meditation: The Buddha's Way of Mindfulness* (Samuel Weiser, Inc. 1962, 1988).

_____, *The Power of Mindfulness* (Routledge 1971, 2008).

Nyanatiloka Thera, *Buddhist Dictionary: Manual of Buddhist Terms and Doctrines* (Nyanatiloka [Taiwan] 1998, orig. pub. 1952) (electronic editions: https://www.budsas.org/ebud/bud-dict/dic_idx.htm, https://www.dhammatalks.net/Buddhist.Dictionary/dic1-titel.htm, https://www.academia.edu/4482851/Buddhist_Dictionary_by_Venerable_Nyanatiloka, https://urbandharma.org/pdf/palidict.pdf (all last checked March 16, 2020).

Powell, Colin, *All Colin Powell Quotes About Giving*, https://www.inspiringquotes.us/author/7158-colin-powell/about-giving (last checked March 16, 2020).

Soma Thera, *The Way of Mindfulness: The Satipatthana Sutta and Its Commentary*, The Factors of Enlightenment, https://www. accesstoinsight.org/lib/authors/soma/wayof.html#factors (last checked March 16, 2020).

Thanissaro Bhikkhu (Geoffrey DeGraff), *The Buddhist Monastic Code: The Pātimokkha Rules Translated & Explained* (3d ed. 2013), https://www.accesstoinsight.org/lib/authors/thanissaro/bmc1.pdf (last checked March 16, 2020).

Tuffley, David, *The Four Sublime States: Contemplations on Love, Compassion, Sympathetic Joy and Equanimity* (Altiora Publications 2014).

Twain, Mark, https://quoteinvestigator.com/2010/10/10/twain-father/ (last checked March 16, 2020).

Suggested readings:

SUTTAS

Access to Insight (www.accesstoinsight.org) and SuttaCentral (www.suttacentral.net) are good resources for finding *suttas* on-line.

Instructions to the laity:

1. *Kalama Sutta*: To the *Kalamas* (AN 3.65).
2. *Sigalovada Sutta*: The Buddha's Advice to *Sigala* (DN 31).
3. *Vyagghapajja Sutta*: Conditions of Welfare (AN 8.54).
4. *Anathapindikovada Sutta*: Instructions to Anathapindika (MN 143).

Other useful suttas for lay practitioners:

1. *Satipaṭṭhāna Sutta*: The Four Foundations of Mindfulness (MN 10).
2. The *Ambalaṭṭhikārāhulovāda Sutta*: Advice to Rāhula at Ambalaṭṭhikā (MN 61).
3. *Anapanasati Sutta*: Mindfulness of Breathing (MN 118).
4. *Anatta-lakkhana Sutta*: The Discourse on the Not-self Characteristic (SN 22.59) (also known as *Pañcavaggi Sutta*: Five Brethren).

5. *Dhammacakkappavattana Sutta*: Setting the Wheel of Dhamma in Motion (SN 56.11).

NIKĀYAS (SUTTA COLLECTIONS)

1. Walsh, Maurice, translator, *The Long Discourses of the Buddha, A Translation of the Dīngha Nikāya*, (Wisdom Publications 2d ed. 1995).
2. Bhikkhu Ñanamoli, Bhikkhu Bodhi, translators, *The Middle Length Discourses of the Buddha, A Translation of the Majjhima Nikāya*, (Wisdom Publications 1995).
3. Bhikkhu Bodhi, translator, *The Connected Discourses of the Buddha, A Translation of the Saṃyutta Nikāya* (Wisdom Publications 2d ed. 2003).
4. Bhikkhu Bodhi, translator, *The Numerical Discourses of the Buddha, A Complete Translation of the Aṅguttara Nikāya* (Wisdom Publications 2012).

Suggested reading and listening list for home practice and retreat

READING

----------, *Everyman's Ethics: Four Discourses of the Buddha*, adapted from the translations of Narada Thera (Buddhist Publication Society 1959, 1966, 1979, 1985; BPS Online Edition 2006): https://www.bps.lk/olib/wh/wh014_Narada_Everymans-Ethics--Four-Discourses-of-Buddha.pdf (last checked March 16, 2020).

Acariya Dhammapala (author), Bhikkhu Bodhi (translator), *A Treatise on the Pāramīs: From the Commentary to the Cariyapitaka* (Buddhist Publication Society 1978). https://www.dhammatalks.net/Books/Acariya_Dhammapala_A_Treatise_on_the_Paramis.htm (last checked May 3, 2020)

Bhadantacariya Buddhaghosa (author), Bhikkhu Ñanamoli (translator), *The Path of Purification: Visuddhimagga* (Buddhist Publication Society 1975, 1991, 2010). https://www.accesstoinsight.org/lib/authors/nanamoli/PathofPurification2011.pdf (last checked March 16, 2020).

Bhikkhu Anālayo, *Satipaṭṭāna: The Direct Path To Realization* (Windhorse Publishing 2004).

Bhikkhu Bodhi, *The Noble Eightfold Path: The Way to the End of Suffering* (BPS Pariyatti Editions 1994).

Bhikkhu Bodhi, General Editor, *A Comprehensive Manual of Abhidhamma: The Abhidhammattha Sangaha* (Pariyatti Publishing 1999).

Goldstein, Joseph, *The Experience of Insight: A Simple & Direct Guide to Buddhist Meditation* (Shambhala 1987).

Goldstein, Joseph, *Insight Meditation, The Practice of Freedom* (Shambhala 1976).

Goldstein, Joseph, *Mindfulness: A Practical Guide to Awakening* (Sounds True Publishing 2013).

Kornfeld, Jack, *A Path With Heart* (Bantam 1993).

Mahasi Sayadaw, Vipassanā Mettā Foundation Translation Committee (translator), *Manual of Insight* (Wisdom Publications 2016).

Nyanaponika Thera, *The Heart of Buddhist Meditation: The Buddha's Way of Mindfulness* (Samuel Weiser, Inc. 1962).

Nyanatiloka Thera, *Buddhist Dictionary: Manual of Buddhist Terms and Doctrines* (Frewin & Co., Ltd. 1972).

U Pandita, Wheeler, Kate (editor), *In This Very Life: Liberation Teachings of the Buddha* (Wisdom Publications 2012).

LISTENING:

Joseph Goldstein

Meditation instructions:

https://www.dharmaseed.org/talks/audio_player/96/36191.html

https://www.dharmaseed.org/talks/audio_player/96/36192.html

https://www.dharmaseed.org/talks/audio_player/96/36190.html

Walking meditation instruction:

https://www.dharmaseed.org/talks/audio_player/96/1293.html

(walking instructions begin at 28:34)

U Vivekananda

Residential retreat instructions including sitting, walking
and daily practices:

https://www.dharmaseed.org/talks/audio_player/186/23326.html

Dharma Seed

www.dharmaseed.org has a vast selection of recorded *Dhamma*
talks given by a wide variety of teachers.

Retreat Centers and Monasteries

IN THE MAHASI SAYADAW SCHOOL of *Theravāda* Buddhism, there are many excellent monasteries and retreat centers in Myanmar, Sri Lanka, Malaysia, and Europe, as well as here in the United States. For brevity's sake the list *below* mentions just a few that Allan has practiced at or visited, so he is familiar with and can vouch for them. He can also vouch for the listed monasteries and retreat centers outside of the Mahasi school. In the future, as referrals can be verified, they will be added:

UNITED STATES:

1. *Insight Meditation Society* (IMS), Barre, MA. An excellent retreat center for those just developing a long-term practice and those who consider themselves as having an intermediate to advanced practice. Located in a rural area of central Massachusetts and an ideal place to practice. Offers mostly nine-day to three-month residential retreats throughout the year. Teachers mostly rely on *Theravāda* teachings rooted in the *Path of Purification*, but not always; each teacher may have their own understanding and emphasis. *Dhamma* talks offered daily and interviews required two or three times each week. Can be expensive: Retreats offered on a sliding scale, and *yogis* can

offer *dāna* for the teachers at the end of the retreat; scholarships are available. Excellent accommodations and food. https://www.dharma.org/

2. *Forest Refuge*, Barre, MA. Part of IMS intended for more advanced and self-directed students of meditation; daily schedule is much less structured than at IMS retreats, except during more traditionally structured, guest teacher-led retreats. *Dhamma* talks offered once or twice each week except during retreats. Can be expensive: Retreats are offered on a sliding scale per night, and *yogis* can offer *dāna* for the teachers at the end of the retreat; scholarships are available. Excellent accommodations and food. https://www.dharma.org/

3. *Barre Center for Buddhist Studies*, Barre, MA. Also part of the greater IMS complex, but with a more scholarly approach than IMS or the Forest Refuge. Many courses available, both practice-oriented and intellectually-oriented, throughout the year. Can be expensive: Courses are offered on a sliding scale, and *yogis* can offer *dāna* for the teachers at the end of the retreat; scholarships are available. Excellent accommodations and food. https://www.buddhistinquiry.org/

4. *Southwest Sangha*, San Lorenzo, New Mexico. *Dāna*-based retreat center led by Michael Freeman, whose teachings are based both in *Theravāda* and *Vajrayāna* traditions. Located in high desert, the weather and living conditions are beautiful, intense and rustic. Especially suited for self-directed practice; Michael will offer instructions on request, but best to come with meditation experience. No formal *Dharma* talks offered. Two meals offered daily; evening snack allowed. http://southwestsangha.org/

5. *Tathāgata Meditation Center*, San Jose, CA. Orthodox Mahasi monastery and meditation center offering one-month retreats quarterly and self-retreat opportunities for experienced yogis

who have practiced many month-long retreats at TMC. *Dhamma* talks offered daily. Daily fee $25; *yogis* can offer *dāna* at the end of the retreat; partial retreats available. Two meals offered daily. Spartan accommodations and excellent food.
http://www.tathagata.org/

OUTSIDE THE UNITED STATES:

1. *Panditarama Lumbini International Vipassana Meditation Center*, Lumbini, Nepal (UNESCO World Heritage Site; birthplace of the Buddha). Arguably the best Mahasi-style *Theravāda* meditation center for Westerners in the world. *Lingua franca* is English; Burmese, French, German, Hindi, and Burmese also spoken. Allan's teacher, Sayadaw U Vivekananda, and Sayalay Bhadamanika lead intensive meditation practice nine months each year. Live *Dhamma* talks three times each week and recorded talks the other four. For an Asian style retreat center, accommodations are excellent: Clean water, good food, hot water, mattresses, screens, etc. Mosquito infested and air quality is poor. Takes effort to get there, but practice opportunities are unmatched. *Dāna* based.
http://www.panditarama-lumbini.info/

2. *Panditarama Shwe Taung Gon Meditation Center*, Yangon, Myanmar. Main center in Yangon and Forest Refuge just outside the city offer a variety of practice opportunities. The late U Panditata's home monastery and many of his influences remain: strict and formal practice, open handed, imbued with Burmese culture, and traditionally monastic in orientation. Offerings include: Daily retreat style practice, practice on *Uposatha* days, short and long retreats, temporary and life-long ordination. Daily Dhamma talks in Burmese and English. Frequent practice interviews required. Traditional Burmese Buddhist center with

excellent food and decent accommodations. Many Westerns have practiced and continue to practice here. *Dāna* based. https://www.panditarama.net/

OTHER *THERAVĀDA* SCHOOLS:

Ajahn Chah Thai Forest

1. *Wat Pah Nanachat*, Ubon Rachathani, Thailand. Buddhist monastery in Northeast Thailand in the *Theravāda* Thai Forest Tradition; established by Ven. Ajahn Chah. Uses English for communication and instruction. Offers training as a Buddhist monk to male foreigners (non-Thai), and offers male and female foreigners opportunities to live monastic life as visitors who strictly follow the daily routines of the monastery and join in with all meditation periods, *Dhamma* talks, communal meetings and work activities. Does not offer private meditation teachings, retreats or courses in meditation. *Dāna* based. http://www.watpahnanachat.org/

2. *Amaravati Buddhist Monastery*, Hemel Hempstead, UK. Community of monks and nuns practicing in the Ajahn Chah, Thai Forest *Theravāda* tradition. Lay people are welcome to visit or stay as guests as part of the resident community. Guests follow the daily schedule of monastic routine, working, sharing meals, and meditating with the monastic community. The Retreat Centre is located on the monastery grounds but run separately with its own accommodation facilities, kitchen, and shrine room. Weekend, five-day, ten-day, and thirteen-day retreats are led by monks and nuns trained in the Ajahn Chah tradition, offering the opportunity to listen to daily *Dhamma* teachings. *Dāna* based. https://www.amaravati.org/ Monastic-led retreats also offered at Harnham Buddhist Monastery in Northumberland, UK, another monastery in the Ajahn Chah tradition. https://ratanagiri.org.uk/participate/retreats

3. *Spirit Rock Meditation Center*, Woodacre, CA. Insight
   meditation center founded by, among others, Jack Kornfield,
   who ordained as a monk with Ajahn Chah and was one of the
   founders of IMS. Offers residential retreats of varying lengths,
   up to two months. Retreats are usually led by teams of lay
   teachers from the Spirit Rock teachers collective or other
   well-known visiting teachers, lay and monastic, from the
   broader Buddhist community. Teachers offer daily instructions
   and *Dhamma* talks and regularly scheduled practice meetings
   to provide guidance throughout the retreat. Can be expensive:
   Courses are offered on a sliding scale, and *yogis* can offer
   dāna for the teachers at the end of the retreat; scholarships are
   available. Excellent accommodations and food.
   https://www.spiritrock.org/

Made in United States
North Haven, CT
12 August 2022

22645139R00225